Les K. Wright
Editor

The Bear Book

Readings in the History and Evolution of a Gay Male Subculture

Pre-publication
REVIEWS,
COMMENTARIES,
EVALUATIONS . . .

"*The Bear Book: Readings in the History and Evolution of a Gay Male Subculture* presents the first comprehensive glimpse of a significant but heretofore uncharted aspect of the gay community. Les Wright, as editor of and contributor to this collection of essays, has done a superlative job of bringing together both scholarly and lay treatises to triangulate the essence of what it means to be part of the bear movement.

Every aspect of the global-wide bear phenomenon is explored through this anthology of insightful interviews with pioneers of the movement, including the creation of 'cybearspace,' bear contests, and bear social organizations. Among the scholarly works included in the collection are discussions of the bear as an enduring icon spanning cultures through the ages, analyses of bear imagery represented in the media, and discussions of just what constitutes 'being a bear.'

Dr. Wright, in describing his own research under the auspices of the *Bear History Project*, presents an exhaustive and definitive search for the earliest ruminations of beardom in contemporary gay male culture. This book is essential reading for anyone interested in understanding contemporary male homosexuality in particular, and helpful in studying aspects and expressions of masculinity in general."

Brian J. Kaufman, PhD
Professor of Psychology,
University of Maine
at Farmington

More pre-publication
REVIEWS, COMMENTARIES, EVALUATIONS . . .

"Here, Bears bare all–providing a reader-friendly introduction to a fascinating cultural world and its historical making."

Jonathan Ned Katz
Author, *Gay American History and the Invention of Heterosexuality,*
New York, NY

"Gay male culture is endlessly inventive; there is no place it will not go, no sexual boundary it will not traverse. In the midst of the AIDS epidemic and a popular culture that valorizes the young, hairless, lithe body, 'the bear' emerged as a vibrant alternative and declaration of gay male worth and sexuality. *The Bear Book* is a smart, perceptive, authoritative, and profoundly moving portrait of how and why gay male culture changes and evolves. This is not simply about the aesthetic or sexualization of body type, but about the ability of gay men to imagine and create their own desires and worlds. As sociology it is a revelation; as a work of gay male cultural criticism it is an act of faith and love."

Michael Bronski
Author, *Culture Clash: The Making of Gay Sensibility*,
Cambridge, MA

"Les Wright has assembled a wide array of bear voices, together expressing the range of this fascinating phenomenon of men trying to carve out an alternative to the dominant images of masculinity. What is clear from these highly varied essays is that for all the desire to celebrate what is 'naturally' masculine, bears are remarkably self-conscious about what they are doing. Whether they are challenging the received notions of homosexuality, gay male beauty, or gay sexual practice, these men bring to the discussion a rare mix of romanticism and skepticism, practicality and fantasy, sophistication and innocence, sobriety and silliness. They come to represent all the contradictions affecting contemporary gay life since the advent of AIDS; indeed, the contradictions affecting American life in general.

This book will be required reading for all bears and anyone interested in the bear phenomenon both as a contemporary analysis and as documents for further research. This book takes the bear phenomenon out of the dark cave of ignorance and into the sunlight of cultural analysis so we can taste the pot of honey at the end of the gay rainbow."

David Bergman, PhD
Professor of English,
Towson State University,
Towson, MD

NOTES FOR PROFESSIONAL LIBRARIANS AND LIBRARY USERS

This is an original book title published by Harrington Park Press, an imprint of The Haworth Press, Inc. Unless otherwise noted in specific chapters with attribution, materials in this book have not been previously published elsewhere in any format or language.

CONSERVATION AND PRESERVATION NOTES

All books published by The Haworth Press, Inc. and its imprints are printed on certified ph neutral, acid free book grade paper. This paper meets the minimum requirements of American National Standard for Information Sciences–Permanence of Paper for Printed Material, ANSI Z39.48-1984.

The Bear Book

Readings in the History and Evolution of a Gay Male Subculture

HAWORTH Gay & Lesbian Studies
John P. De Cecco, PhD
Editor in Chief

New, Recent, and Forthcoming Titles:

Homosexuality and Sexuality: Dialogues of the Sexual Revolution, Volume I by Lawrence D. Mass

Homosexuality as Behavior and Identity: Dialogues of the Sexual Revolution, Volume II by Lawrence D. Mass

Sexuality and Eroticism Among Males in Moslem Societies edited by Arno Schmitt and Jehoeda Sofer

Understanding the Male Hustler by Samuel M. Steward

Men Who Beat the Men Who Love Them: Battered Gay Men and Domestic Violence by David Island and Patrick Letellier

The Golden Boy by James Melson

The Second Plague of Europe: AIDS Prevention and Sexual Transmission Among Men in Western Europe by Michael Pollak

Barrack Buddies and Soldier Lovers: Dialogues with Gay Young Men in the U.S. Military by Steven Zeeland

Outing: Shattering the Conspiracy of Silence by Warren Johansson and William A. Percy

The Bisexual Option, Second Edition by Fritz Klein

And the Flag Was Still There: Straight People, Gay People, and Sexuality in the U.S. Military by Lois Shawver

One-Handed Histories: The Eroto-Politics of Gay Male Video Pornography by John R. Burger

Sailors and Sexual Identity: Crossing the Line Between "Straight" and "Gay" in the U.S. Navy by Steven Zeeland

The Gay Male's Odyssey in the Corporate World: From Disempowerment to Empowerment by Gerald V. Miller

Bisexual Politics: Theories, Queries, and Visions edited by Naomi Tucker

Gay and Gray: The Older Homosexual Man, Second Edition by Raymond M. Berger

Reviving the Tribe: Regenerating Gay Men's Sexuality and Culture in the Ongoing Epidemic by Eric Rofes

Gay and Lesbian Mental Health: A Sourcebook for Practitioners edited by Christopher J. Alexander

Against My Better Judgment: An Intimate Memoir of an Eminent Gay Psychologist by Roger Brown

The Masculine Marine: Homoeroticism in the U.S. Marine Corps by Steven Zeeland

Bisexual Characters in Film: From Anaïs to Zee by Wayne M. Bryant

Autopornography: A Life in the Lust Lane by Scott O'Hara

The Bear Book: Readings in the History and Evolution of a Gay Male Subculture edited by Les K. Wright

The Bear Book
Readings in the History and Evolution of a Gay Male Subculture

Les K. Wright
Editor

Harrington Park Press
An Imprint of The Haworth Press, Inc.
New York • London

Published by

Harrington Park Press, an imprint of The Haworth Press, Inc., 10 Alice Street, Binghamton, NY 13904-1580

Cover design by Monica L. Seifert.

Library of Congress Cataloging-in-Publication Data

Wright, Les K.
The bear book : readings in the history and evolution of a gay male subculture / Les K. Wright.
p. cm.
Includes bibliographical references and index.
ISBN 1-56023-890-9 (alk. paper)
1. Gays–Identity. 2. Gay men–Attitudes. 3. Gay men–Psychology. 4. Gender identity. 5. Group identity. 6. Masculinity (Psychology). 7. Body image. I. Title.
HQ76.W75 1997
305.38'9664–dc21

96-46281
CIP

To the memory of members of my gay family–friends, lovers, colleagues, roommates, peers, and mentors–who have preceded me in the epidemic:

Skip Aiken, Monty Allport, Bart Amarillas, C.D. ("Charlie")Arnold, Allen Barnett, Crawford Barton, John Benes, Jim Berg, Bob Bishop, Mark Borrowman, John Brinson, Tony Buck, Skip Byron, Gary Capps, Tom Castro, Robert Chesley, Mark Confer, Jeremy Costy, Jim Crecca, Ray Cude, Fernando Delgado, Joe Eaton, Carl Forster, Eric Garber, Kendrick Gifford, Gary Griffith, Garth Gwinn, Rev. Virgil Hall, Don Haney, Steve Harris, Bill Hartman, Rev. Peter Hayn, Ron Hendricks, Pete Hopkins, Jerry Houston, Mark Johnson, Paul Karnet, Dennis Kaster, Mike Keating, Billy Komasa, Jason Lazzari, Dale Leach, David Lourea, Pierre Luddington, Michael Lynch, Lee Margerum, Jim Mcguire, John Middlebrook, Chris Minor, Doug Moorman, Robert Musgrave, Mike Napoleon, Mark Nathan, Derek Noakes, Ted Parry, John Preston, John Price, Gary Prutsman, Phil Quattrociocchi, Geoff Mains, Alex Rankin, Rick Redewill, Ed Reidy, Charles Reis, Clint Royce, Vito Russo, Larry Salmon, Kent Seidl, Tom Smith, MD, Nigel Smith, Dan Stardig, Steve Sutton, John Swenson, Robin Townsend, Bud Vadon, Link Webb, Walt Westman, Mark Wheeler, KeithWilson, Carl Wittman, Doug Woodyard, as well as Bill, Bill, Brian, Charlie, Derek, Kit, Rob, Tom, Worth, and the hundreds of others whose names I obliterated from my private records in 1987 because I could not tolerate the mounting horror and the burden of so many to remember at that time.

CONTENTS

ABOUT THE EDITOR

Les Wright, PhD, is an activist and scholar who has been involved in gay studies since the 1970s. Currently an Assistant Professor at Mount Ida College in Boston, he teaches humanities, film, cultural studies, and writing. The founder and curator of the Bear History Project, he has published extensively on the bear phenomenon. Among the few surviving "Castro clones," Professor Wright is a long-term survivor of HIV and is currently conducting two studies, one on the popular history of The Castro and another on trauma, community, and imagination. The founding editor of *Our Stories*, his writing has appeared in collections such as *Hometown: Gay Men Write About Where They Belong; Out in the Workplace;* and *AIDS: The Literary Response*. He is a founding member of the Lesbian and Gay History Project. He is also Co-Chair of the Committee for the Lesbian and Gay History caucus of the American History Association.

CONTRIBUTORS

Pierre De Mey, PhD, is an oceanographer living in Toulouse, France. He was born on the northern coast of France into a working class family from which he obtained what he considers to be a solid set of values and the tools to enjoy life. From 1983 to 1987 he was a postdoctoral research fellow at Harvard University, where he discovered bears. Meetings often bring him to the United States, which he considers his second home.

Bob Donahue, PhD, has been involved as part of the online bear community since its very beginnings, as an early participant on the Bears Mailing List, and by starting the first bear channel on IRC ("2327"), and co-writing "bearcode." At present, he works as a research scientist, and on the side is the owner of "Skepsis Research and Development," which is home to the popular "Resources for Bears" archive on the World Wide Web (http://www.skepsis.com/bears/). He and his husband live in the Boston area.

Steve Dyer has played a leading role since the early 1980s in the formation of electronic communities for lesbian and gay people. In 1983, in the early days of the Internet, he successfully argued for and created the first USENET newsgroup for the discussion of gay and lesbian issues, now known as "soc.motss." In 1988, with Brian Gollum in San Francisco, he started an electronic mail digest for the (then) nascent bear community known as the Bears Mailing list, or BML, which was distributed over the Internet and other electronic mail systems. He handed over responsibility for the digest in late 1994, and it continues, arguably more popular than ever, with over 3,000 subscribers. Steve has been a volunteer and a member of the Board of Directors for Boston's *Gay Community News* and is a member of the New England Bears. He works as a system architect in the area of distributed operating systems and computer networks. He and his partner live in Cambridge, Massachusetts.

Van Lynn Floyd resides in Denver, Colorado.

Sam Ganczaruk co-founded "Bear Hug" in June, 1987, and served on the boards of Bear Expo '92, '93, and '94. Born in Cambridge, Massachusetts, in 1942, he holds a BA from Northeastern University and pursued graduate studies at the University of Chicago. He has worked as a librarian in New York City, as an accountant in San Francisco, and is an expert on rail and mass transit. He has published articles in *The New Electric Railway Journal* and *Transit California*, served as an advisor to the Oakland (CA) Metropolitan Transportation Committee, published a series of rail and trolley postcards, and has been a staunch advocate of the annual San Francisco Historic Trolleys Festival. He currently resides in Santa Rosa, California with his partner Edwin Orrick.

Bob Hay, JP, BA, MSc, was secretary of the now-defunct Ozbears Australia for four of its five years and took on the presidency in 1995 knowing he would have to close the club down. He is presently the coordinator of Bears Down Under (a "virtual" club for Australian bears) and, in 1995, was voted an honorary life member of WOMBATS in recognition of his dedicated service to the Bears Movement. He is also one of the "grand old men" of the Sydney and Australian gay community with a quarter of a century's involvement in gay welfare (particularly gay counseling) and gay publishing. Formerly a professional psychologist specializing in cross-cultural and gay counseling, he "retired" at 50 and went to sculpture school. One of the most published of all Australian gay authors, Bob now divides his time among sculpture, writing, and research into Australian gay history.

Scott Hill was one of the two founders of the Burgh Bears. Still active in the bear community, he volunteers his time in various endeavors. One endeavor is helping to maintain the Skepsis bear site located at http://skepsis.com/.glbo. He is a graduate of the University of Pittsburgh in the field of Electrical Engineering. He presently works for a high-tech company as Manager of Information Systems. The club's other founder is his husbear Rick. Scott and Rick have been together since 1989. Scott views the bear movement as an opportunity to dismiss the stereotypical view of gay life and culture. "The destiny of every bear should be to offer an alternative view of gay men. A show of diversity yet similarity. A portrayal of interests and passions. We should be an example of tolerance, acceptance, and community."

Philip Locke has a Master's degree in Television/Radio/Film, doctoral studies in Communications Technologies, and a lifelong interest in hairy men. Phil's work in this book represents an intersection between two of his main interests: looking at bears and examining the effects the mass media have on our lives. His previous research includes looking at how and why people use online communications, and the ways in which new media can provide a sense of community to geographically separated members of nonethnic minority groups. Phil currently works as a technical writer in the San Francisco Bay Area, and has published fiction in *BEAR* and *American Bear* magazines.

Luke Mauerman, originally from the Pacific Northwest, now lives in San Francisco. He spent over five years on staff at *BEAR* Magazine/Brush Creek Media, and was editor of *BEAR* for a year and a half. With a strong interest in publishing, Luke hopes to keep working on various projects until his old age or first million–whichever comes first.

Tommy McCann, PhD, was born in 1959, in Dublin, and is a geologist working in research. He has studied and conducted research in Dublin, Canada, Alaska, England, Wales and now in Berlin. He has been involved in Berlin Bears since his arrival in Cover Berlin. Other interests include buddying, cooking, ballroom dancing, geology, hiking, reading, opera, gay stuff. He lives with his partner, is happy, and is currently exploring links between gay men and opera.

Rychard G. Powers attended various colleges for nine years as a student of philosophy, and lacks any sort of substantial degree. He claims to be a freelance philosopher, and therefore has no qualifications or business writing academic papers. As a monkey, he aspires to that which he is not–a bear. He resides in Los Alamitos, California, with his television set, absence of wit, and lack of personality.

Lars Rains is pursuing a PhD in Music Theory at the City University of New York. He holds an MA degree in Music Criticism from McMaster University and an MMus degree in Music Theory from the University of Western Ontario. Lars lives in Massillon, Ohio, with his polar bear partner for life, Herman Gaffney. Their rottweiler, Sarah, kind of looks like a little bear, too.

Michael S. Ramsey, PhD, currently a research associate in the Department of Geology at Arizona State University, received his PhD from the university in early 1996. He has authored over a dozen publications on remote sensing and volcanic eruption monitoring. A lifelong interest since his early years in Alaska, the protection and preservation of bears and their habitat has become an integral part of his life. Dr. Ramsey is currently an active member of The Great Bear Foundation, The Wilderness Society, and American Rivers. The significance of the bear to the Native American and its role in their spirituality is a recent area of study since his relocation to Arizona. His participation within gay society's bear community has increased over the past several years, bringing together his love of both animal and human bears. He currently maintains an on-line website archive of pictures and clip art of bears, and volunteers his time to assist in the operations of the Resources for Bears website at skepsis.com. Mike is also one of the founding members of the Phoenix Bears group, and a member of the Human Rights Campaign. As a certified whitewater river guide, he spends his down-time navigating the currents and "river-hopping" throughout the west.

John Rand holds an MFA from UC Irvine, a BFA from CSU Fullerton, and has done postgraduate work at Louisiana State University and UCLA. He is engaged in a visual study to show the ideal Bear, which represents an important step in personal growth–an extension of self, a finding of self through the camaraderie of bears. The Bear Scene importantly represents the need for greater diversity in the state of maleness as a quintessential form. "My own coming out was very much hindered by the cultural imposition of twinkies and beefcakes. Thus, I am compelled in the pursuit of bear photography. My work demonstrates a greater breadth of maleness, the Bear."

Robert B. Marks Ridinger was born in the bear-infested hills of western Pennsylvania, attended the University of Pittsburgh (BA, 1972; MLS, 1973) and Case Western Reserve (MA, 1976, Anthropology). Three years as a librarian in the Peace Corps in Lesotho were followed by a job at Northern Illinois University, where as a comfortably open gay faculty member he began to assemble a collection of the gay and lesbian press of the Midwest. This led to a project to index the *Advocate* and from there to an expanding interest in documenting the homosexual history of the Midwest. Discovering the Bears Mailing List during its early years, a "nom de pelt" was quickly adopted, and soon the messages of The Hidden Paw were familiar reading to many cubs and bruins of all ages across the world. "My article combines my academic training as an anthropologist with a taste for pelt grooming and a determination to help in the growth and flourishing of the bear community."

Eric Rofes is an instructor and doctoral student in Social and Cultural Studies at the University of California at Berkeley's Graduate School of Education. He is the author of *Reviving the Tribe: Regenerating Gay Men's Sexuality and Culture in the Ongoing Epidemic* published by The Haworth Press in 1996.

Jeff Stoner is a 30-something astronomer and computer hack, currently living in Tucson, Arizona with his archaeologist husbear of 7 years, Bob, and their cat Dizzie. When not chasing bears, Jeff chases interesting new technologies on the Internet, computer geeks a little, and also writes fiction, does photography, and likes traveling.

Ron Suresha studied Creative Writing at the University of Michigan at Ann Arbor where he won several writing awards, coordinated a poetry reading series, and co-founded and co-edited two alternative magazines. In the mid-to-late 1980s, he lived in the San Francisco Bay Area, where he worked as a freelance promotional writer and designer. There he became involved with the early San Francisco Bear movement and created promotional materials for the Lone Star Saloon, among other clients. In 1993, he moved to Boston to work at Shambhala Publications, a small book publisher specializing in Eastern studies and philosophy. He currently works as a freelance editor, writer, and calligrapher, and serves on the board of directors of the *Harvard Gay and Lesbian Review.*

John Webster was born, and has always lived, in New Zealand. His education followed the normal school systems operating in the country. However, he did not attend university or attain an academic degree by any other means before joining the civilian workforce of the New Zealand Navy. His present employment is with a nationwide historical trust. This satisfies his wide-ranging historical interests and has resulted in several articles for historical publications and two booklets of historical nonfiction. John knew he was gay from his teens (he is now 51), but also was aware he differed from the perceived gay categories because of his weight and hirsute body. Chris Nelson's *Bear Cult* book was the catalyst for recognizing his bear identity, and joining the local Kiwibears in 1993 consolidated this self-acceptance. After years of trying to fit in, he now is delighted to find he is part of a worldwide phenomenon.

Foreword

"What is a bear?" he asks with confusion in his eyes, wondering if he fits the description. This question has been put to me hundreds of times. One assumes the publisher/editor of a magazine for Bears would have an articulate, if not rehearsed, clear and concise response to this perennial mystery, but I do not. Why? It becomes apparent in this book. (On an occasion or two my response was, "Remember EST, that California-based, New Age quasi-philosophy/religion/psychology from the 1970s? It's like that. You just know if you have it.") We are not dealing with a well-organized, members-only, card-carrying association, but instead the advent of a pervading spirit that is often more a shared personal experience. Even after you have digested these pages the answer remains somewhat elusive. It is not a simple question and neither is the response. This book provides some understanding of the complexity of the issue and will surely help those who inquire to come to a better grasp of the knowledge they seek. For those who believe they have the answer, this book should broaden their perspective. For those who already have the answer and those who will take advantage of "bear" popularity, commercial potential, and marketability, yet knowing little about it, this book could put them on the right track.

The Bear movement is a critical development in our gay male subculture and therefore warrants a treatise of this kind. This phenomenon confronts some of the most basic gay male stereotypes and attitudes on which many of us have based our own identities. The speed at which this subculture has developed and spread globally is a clear indication that it speaks to a real need for many of us in the social and psychological fabric of our lives. We are not dealing with some fad here, though there are fad-like elements, but rather a real development in how many gay men see themselves. Nor are we dealing with some issue of physical taste. The Bear subculture goes deeper than skin and body hair.

Many men are coming out of their second closets and are now proud to admit that what they are attracted to is not the traditional gay stereotypes. Others are finding a new self-awareness that they are desirable and acceptable as they are and not as traditional gay models would have them be. Gay men are finding a home.

If there is anyone who can speak with authority on the birth and evolution of the Bear subculture it would be Les Wright. His passion for this subject and his scholarly attention to its inception and growth are widely known among his peers. Significant social developments need those who are willing to tell its story and Les, with the assistance of several other authors, does this in a compelling and scholarly way. By doing so, they take the heretofore undefined social, psychological, and political threads of the Bear phenomenon and weave them into a very readable and often humorous tome that puts it into its rightful perspective as a force not to be overlooked or taken lightly in the gay community. But more important, we see how this subculture is affecting people on a personal level and helping them come to grips with their own identities.

What will become of the Bear subculture and how it will evolve as it becomes more mainstream and absorbed into the everyday fabric of the gay male community is unknown. But one thing is certain, this emerging Bear phenomenon is already having a profound effect on gay male culture.

Tim Martin
Publisher and Editor
The American Bear

Acknowledgments

I would like to express my deeply felt gratitude and say thank-you to the many people who helped make this book happen, who encouraged, supported, or promoted my thinking about bears, community, self-worth, and to the project of grassroots-based historiography; to:

Bill Palmer, Managing Editor at The Haworth Press for his enthusiastic, wholehearted support of this project; Steve Klein and Eric Rofes who, independent of each other, brought Bill and me together; members of the Gay and Lesbian Historical Society of Northern California and the former Lesbian and Gay History Project of San Francisco, especially my friends and colleagues: Allan Bérubé, Kate Brandt, John De Cecco, Mildred Dickeman, Eric Garber, Tom Holt, Hubert Kennedy, Paula Lichtenberg, Ruth Mahaney, Will Roscoe, and Bill Walker;

Academic peers and mentors: Roland Barthes, Walter Benjamin, John D'Emilio, Terry Eagleton, Michel Foucault, Sander Gilman, Erving Goffman, Frederic Jameson, Jonathan Ned Katz, Theo van der Meer, Gayle Rubin, Ed Schur, Klaus Theweleit; Mount Ida College for a generous Faculty Development Grant (1993-1994), which supported the creation of the Bear History Project archives;

All the bears, especially my dear friends Sam Ganczaruk, Carl Lawrence, Ben Bruner and Bill Martin, John Musselman, Dave Gan, Mel Baker, Luke Mauerman, Ron Suresha, Josef Altenbuchner, and David Bergman who encouraged me to write about the bear phenomenon; the many, many members of the bear community and bear clubs around the world who have shared their ideas, experiences, and resources with me and/or donated contributions to the BHP archives;

And, most of all, to my steadfast, loving partner, Dale Wehrle.

Introduction

Theoretical Bears

Les Wright

> These cells of the inner self are worse than the deepest stone dungeon and as long as they are locked all your revolution remains only a prison mutiny to be put down by corrupted fellow-prisoners.
>
> –Sade to Marat, *Marat/Sade*, Peter Weiss

INTRODUCTION

In this book bears speak for themselves. This is in keeping with current postmodern sentiment that natives can and must be allowed to speak for themselves. Ideally, when the native speaks to the anthropologist, the native and the anthropologist converse in a common language. The problem is that there is no such common language wherein vastly differing values and assumptions are somehow rendered equally neutral, value-free, or transparent to the other. Not just between different groups, say humanists and social scientists or heterosexuals and homosexuals, but among each group there is no longer a cohesive set of shared assumptions. The question of what a bear is, is very much unresolved. The relationship of bears to the gay community at large is just beginning to be worked out. In bringing together this collection of subjective voices from the bear world, I have sought to strike a balance between academic disciplines, between the abstractions of scholarship and the psychological, if not always the empirical groundedness of lived experience, between the givenness of homosexuality and the malleability of socially constructed identities.

The sometimes fractious, sometimes epistemologically productive rivalries between scholars of academic knowledge and adepts of political knowledge has been articulated by Bob Connell, and Lisa Duggin has outlined the consequences of it in her article "The Discipline Problem." Truces and even fruitful syntheses have been attained in the British school of cultural studies and post-postmodern queer studies in the United States. The scholar is repeatedly challenged to separate the emotional from the political. This newly perceived need to separate formal systems of knowledge from a kind of ontological "street smarts," which derives from the participant's understanding of how these systems actually function, and resynthesize them represents an important shift in perspective. It is a step away from the anthropologist's "participant observer" of, say Laud Humphreys' *Tearoom Trade* or Margaret Mead's *Coming of Age in Samoa*, and a step in the direction of a postmodernist's exploration of the interactive web of material, symbolic, social, and other spheres of humanity.

What is a bear? Among the natives there is much disputation. For some it is an attitude (or better, a lack of "attitude"), for some it is an image, a gay sexual icon of desirability. For some it is parts of both, for some the absolute refusal to submit to categorization is the essence of being a bear. The underlying theoretical starting point is the notion of "a bear": as a Saussurian or Barthian empty signifier. Each self-identifying bear, over the last ten years, has filled in his own definition and meaning. From the experiential base of gay male subjectivities the gay mass media has taken over, selling to the bears consumable, standardized images of "real" bears and broadcasting these images and attendant values to society at large. The political shift has been from anarchic to authoritarian. In this new configuration, many bears have created their image as a polarization from "twinks"–the gay mainstream image of the young, blond, smooth-skinned, gym-buffed, presumably shallow and air-headed Southern California "surfer" or *GQ* model type.

There has been much discussion recently about the dead end of social identity politics in America. The essentialist versus social constructionist debate seems fairly settled–it's a bit of both. While same-sex attraction may prove to have more of a biological base than some would wish to be true, the realization, the expression of such desires is clearly socially constructed. The coming-out process itself is the creation of an (on-going) narrative of self. It is part biologically defined gender, it is part claiming a sexual orientation and a politics of attraction, it is part gender politics, psychological and sociological cause-and-effect: "masculine" or "feminine" or "androgynous"? "Beautiful," "sexually attractive," to oneself, to others, in what age range, and through which secondary sexual characteristics? What role does the media play? And what do we make of the fact that a gay social identity has been based, not on a shared sexual attraction, but rather on society's stigmatization of that trait? To borrow from structural linguistics, an unmarked morpheme, an otherwise empty signifier, has been chosen to bear signification: being attracted to members of one's own sex is not something that is a given, but is transformed into a signification laden with the heavy weight of negative meaning. Coming out becomes a mechanism to embrace and work with this meaning, channeling it to the bearer's advantage, rather than being victimized and crushed by the weight of an externally imposed burden.

What the bear phenomenon brings to this dynamic is an active, conscious experiment of challenging the fact or the perception that mainstream gay society, increasingly, imposes what the experience of being gay is or should be about. "Masculine" gay men have existed all along, though only the violators of gender identity have been remembered by mainstream history, no doubt for their usefulness in admonishing would-be gender "waverers" from "turning queer." In *Gay New York* George Chauncey has brought to light the gender polarity within gay circles, between fairies and wolves. By the 1960s, the polarization was expressed as "queens" and "leathermen." The Stonewall rebellion, often thought of in gay folklore as drag-queens-of-color in protest, erupted in a style of hippie-inspired androgyny. It is striking that this initial impulse gave way to the compulsory "clone" look of the 1970s, part all-American middle class, part "butchified" by the blue-collar-coded embellishments.

Obviously, these polarizations represent only the extreme. There are homosexualities in between and outside of such linear pairings. The bear phenomenon manifests both tendencies, arising originally out of an impulse to create "safe spaces" for a wide range of homosocial identifications, and currently coagulating into a new polarity of "bears" and "twinks."

THE INDETERMINACY OF SOCIAL IDENTITY

Much has been penned on the topic of identity formation. To consider "what is a bear," we must separate three subsets: identity formation as males, as homosexuals, and as self-identifying "masculine" gay men.

Freud suggested masculinity was a construction. Jung sought to explain it as a balance between (masculine) persona and (feminine) anima, individual and collective archetype. Radical analysis begins with Alfred Adler's "masculine protest," which posits that children, because of their weaker position vis-à-vis adults, acculturate the "feminine" position. Adult males are in part motivated to resist this internalized sense of "inferiority." Guy Hocquenghem's analysis understands homosexuality as a rejection of phallic sexuality (Lacan) and Oedipal repression. "The male sex role approach, then, is fundamentally reactive. It does not generate a strategic politics of masculinity" (Connell, 1995: 27). Change is a *dialectic* within gender relations–less male/female, than intragay subgenders. Any gender analysis must also include interactivity with race, engenderment, and the power structures of sex roles.

The rise of normative sex roles in the nineteenth century follows the Foucaultian shift from external to internal self-policing. These roles, while touted as universal and eternal, actually change over time and vary from place to place. The rise of a categorically distinguished (biological) third sex or (psychopathological) homosexual deviance rested upon unconsciously normativizing scientific theories, the same sort which sought to justify racial prejudices as objective fact. This is well understood today.

Gay social identity arises from the stigmatization of a perceived difference, not the difference per se. To explain this difference in rational terms a range of philosophies and politics, roughly from separatist to assimilationist tendencies, have been engendered. The inherent dichotomy finds itself expressed in the gradual polarization within the bear subculture into the extremes: from the idea that a bear is an independent spirit, a free thinker who is also simply a man who loves other men to the opposite extreme that bears are a new locus of gay male beauty with all the individual submission to group pressure and conservative, commercialized hierarchies of power which that implies.

> With homosexuality, because the disgrace is geared toward behavior, the level of shame and collapse of self-esteem may be more intractable [than in the case of racial prejudice]. To reach puberty and find oneself falling in love with members of one's own sex is to experience a mixture of self-discovery and self-disgust that never leaves a human consciousness. If the stigma is attached . . . to the deepest desires of the human heart, then it can eat away at a person's sense of his or her own dignity with peculiar ferocity. (Sullivan, 1995: 154-155)

> The shame attached to homosexuality is also different from that attached to race because it attacks the very heart of what makes a human being human: the ability to love and be loved. (Sullivan, 1995: 155)

> This, Orwell intuits, is how you finally break a human spirit: by getting him to betray the integrity of his love. But the prohibition against homosexuality *begins* with such a repression. (Sullivan, 1995: 156)

"The choice of a man as sexual object is not just the choice of a-body-with-a-penis, it is the choice of embodied-masculinity. The cultural meanings of masculinity are, generally, part of the package. Most gays are in this sense 'very straight.' It is not just a question of middle-class respectability. Similar positions were taken by working-class men outside the gay community" (Connell, 1995: 156). Some self-identifying bears are actively engaged in shaping this change in notions of a hegemonic, quintessentially middle-class gay masculinity. It has created a new space where the "very straight" and the very iconoclastic can create social identity and establish membership in the same subculture or community.

The very reification of homosexual men which is intended as a means to control us, as "effeminate," is undone by such counter-production of gay masculinity. Asserting that it is "natural" is a moment of nationalistic politics, both romanticizing and delineating one's (sexual/cultural) political boundaries, bringing a new social arrangement into being. This study of bears focuses on "the construction of masculinity in everyday [gay] life, the importance of economic and institutional structures, the significance of differences among masculinities and the contradictory and dynamic character of gender" (Connell, 1995: 35).

Bears are fully engaged with hegemonic masculinity, seeking an alternative answer, both accepting some of the trappings while rejecting others. Self-identifying bears often embody the gay contradiction (masculine *and* nurturing), the science and the politics of being (gender identity), what Connell calls "rival knowledges." This could be put as a maturing in gay men's self-understanding. For many bears, coming out as a bear represents a major step, from mimesis ("acting myself") to authenticity ("being myself"). Coming out serves as an ongoing narrative constructing of self. To the extent that what a bear "is" has remained indeterminate, to that extent embracing and creating a bear identity serves as a map through life, that is, a diversified nonregimented sexual attraction, a rhizomal rather than a pyramidical power structure, has created an at least temporary space in which many gay men have been able to explore who they are. In this sense, "to tell the truth" is part essentialist revelation, and part active construction.

UTOPIA, QUEER NATIONALISM, AND BEARS IN COMMUNITY

Each generation of gay men, at least during the twentieth century, has reinvented the same wheel. If we consider the appellation of Queer Nationalism to its inferred source, eighteenth-century European nationalism, then we may call upon the internally conflicted impulses: a progressive thrust toward autonomy, individualism, the power to name and define oneself as rational undertakings (as the United States Constitution phrases it, "the right to life, liberty, and the pursuit of happiness"). Simultaneously, we are caught up in the nostalgic, backward-looking romantic impulses: to build upon even slight evidence a heroic past out of our history as the spurned "other" and of an appeal to our empirically-defined "naturalness" (as in the "natural" borders of France, Germany, or the United States) in such a self-evidently conscious artifice.

The United States has a history of utopianism and experiments in intentional communities. Research into gay history reveals a process of self-invention, over and over, in community or in social isolation. The 1960s saw a rebirth of "hippie communes" and the like. Many bears, now in their forties, are of this generation, and there have been numerous reports of intentional "bear families" being established.

My own, oft-repeated definition of a bear is "a gay man who is as comfortable being a man as he is being gay, and who has a good heart." The reworking of masculinity makes bears producers of history, and not merely reactive victims. It would be overdetermined to label the bear subculture a "movement," since there is no agreed upon or articulated program for social change. Bears began as a "politics of pure possibility" (Connell, 1995: 243). Its gender politics have played out in the realm of intramasculine relational politics and social practice.

This dialectical and ethical striving to overcome internalized homophobia and patriarchalism is epitomized in the split camps of bears–defined by (lack of) attitude or by (body) image. In our culture masculinity has been defined as having power and as being *not*-homosexual. As Tony Kushner has Roy Cohn say in *Angels in America*, "*[W]hat* I am is defined entirely by *who* I am. Roy Cohn is not a homosexual. Roy Cohn is a heterosexual man, Henry, who fucks around with guys" (Kushner, 1993: 46). This kind of queer nationalism seeks to lay claim and colonize the previously exclusively heterosexual male domain, within the arena of intramasculine politics.

To live in a state of beardom is to embrace dialectically unresolved tensions between, as expressed in a recent study, McWorld, the modernizing forces of the world leading to global sameness, and Jihad, a kind of tribalism. A bear is an identity in contrast to other homosexualities, with certain alliances or crossovers to hegemonic masculinity as well as with feminism. Within beardom, there is an array of subtypes of bears. As bears build a common culture there is need for citizenship in this new community. We must find a balance between individualism, alliances with like-minded or like-appearing bears, and the diversity within the bear community, the queer community, and mainstream society. Bears represent a threshold in going from an even more specialized self-identity which simultaneously seeks through that identity to bridge back to mainstream heterosexual society.

BEARS AND THE BEAUTY MYTH

Any overview history of art or fashion will quickly reveal that standards of beauty are not fixed Platonic ideals. They have changed dramatically over time and vary from place to place. It is important to keep in mind the functions of standardized beauty in our present consumer capitalist society and the role played by mass media. As Naomi Wolf points out, "The beauty myth is not about women at all. It is about men's institutions and institutional power" (Wolf, 1991: 13). Gay men, to the extent that we have fallen for mass media images of what we *should* consider the gay male ideal beauty, have acquiesced or collaborated in our own subjugation as quasi-women. In this way we subjugate each other, acting out both the dominant male role (you must be attractive to me) and the submissive female role (I must appear attractive to be of any value to you). In the words of John Berger, "men act, women appear."

"The beauty myth is always actually prescribing behavior and not appearance" (Wolf, 1991: 14). This encompasses emotional distance, politics, finance, and sexual repression. "Glamor"–which is the propagandistic language of media images–is, in the famous words of Berger, "the happiness of being envied" (Berger, 1972: 132). The power of being glamorous is in the presumed happiness that comes with being envied. Power comes from possessing the quantified quality of "beauty," and the freedom that comes from having a kind of surplus capital which one may invest as one wishes.

The social construction of bears' bodies is of supreme importance, since this is the essence of sexual capital in the gay male world (not unlike the social hierarchy within African-American circles based on skin tone. The lighter the skin, the closer to being "white" and hence of higher social standing). At one end of the bear spectrum, the "natural"-bodied man is likely to be heavyset or even extremely obese, drawing from the "girth-and-mirth" crowd. Another "natural" bear body may be from the biker/hippie set, with an emphasis on long, flowing beards and hair. When a bear makes such a counter-statement, that he is not a "woman," not a "twink," not a "heterosexual," he is using his body to participate in changing social practice and challenging hegemonic power.

At the opposite end of this spectrum we find, not surprisingly, the "glamor bear" set, often models for bear-oriented publications who embody the emergent consensus of bear beauty, and their affluent patrons, other bears, often in high-tech industries, who have the money and therefore power to project their glamor and hence be envied. Or at least, that is the principle involved. Such practice runs counter to the original impulses of a collective bear phenomenon in the mid-1980s, and it is a capitulation to the symbolic feminization of the gay male body. "Glamor bears" reassert themselves as objects which embody the "symbolic practice and power" of patriarchalism, while devaluing their authenticity by assuming the role of bear, of "acting themselves" rather than "being themselves."

The more masculine, the more powerful? Again, it is not that simple. Connell comments on a "threefold structure of gender"–power, production, and cathexis, or emotional attachment (Connell, 1995: 73). The emphasis on beauty blocks the path to male-male intimacy. The original impulse of the bears, again, was to create a new way to express and find intimacy, emotional and sexual. Hence the emphasis on nurturing qualities, hence the idea of embraceable "teddy bears," hence the effort to create "safe spaces" à la previous generation of feminist practitioners.

Nonetheless, the promulgation of idealizing bears in the gay mass media, for better or worse, is the single most powerful force in the current construction of "bears." The explicit, often intense, and ubiquitous sexual imagery of the gay media and advertising has undoubtedly had tremendous influence in shaping many gay men's sexuality. To the extent that this media speaks with the voice of gendered authority, it speaks a dialect of the mainstream media, as if to women, dictating how they should appear, and, as if to men, (which gay men often internalize as heterosexist) stirring up anxieties over sexual performance and self-acceptance. The promise, the hypothetical never-arrived-at future of advertising, addresses gay men as both agent and receptor, never to be fulfilled. Orgasms are junk food. You can't stop at just one.

Part of this appeal plays on the apparently biologically male predatory appetite for sex. One function of the bearish call for encouraging nurturing behavior in bears is to bring balance. Competition with other gay men for sex partners and the depersonalizing effects of a steady stream of sexually consumed bodies is balanced by the humanizing effort to transform competition into collective sharing and to counteract the alienated consumerism by slowing down enough to establish contact with the person inside of each of those bodies. In essence, a bear attitude in the sexual arena seeks out and promotes emotional intimacy in sexual encounters and a Realpolitik of sustained primary relationships while accommodating the realities of casual sex–fuck buddies, tricks, play partners, and the like. This is a tactic which socializes gay men simultaneously into both traditional male and female roles.

Hegemonic masculinity, as Connell would say, is always in flux. This is why the question of what is "masculine" in the gay community is never settled. It is, underneath it all, a power play for supremacy. This is how any group, in Gramsci's analysis, claims and sustains a leading position in social life. Bear beauty is about consolidating a new power hierarchy. Bear beauty contests, which started up around 1990, began as a camp, parodying the established traditions of gay beauty pageants. Over time this has elided, for many in the bear community, into serious competition. The prize is, if not fortune, at least fame and entry into the ethereal realm of glamor bears.

I must confess to painting these dynamics in highly polarized terms. In actuality, these poles represent the extreme ends of the spectrum. Most bears may tend more in one direction than another, but feelings of ambivalence and a heightened awareness of the inherent contradictions at work inform most bears' consciousness. Advertising rides piggybacked to the main message: bear-oriented magazines, bear-oriented publicity in mainstream gay media, bear listservers and the present anarchy of the Internet all actively carry the message of the existence of bears. The fundamental forum of open communication has itself been perhaps the most significant force in creating and dispersing the bear idea.

Whether one grows up gay or comes to this realization as an adult, most gay men develop a "double vision." Sullivan comments on the "aestheticization of pain as a basis for camp"–and for leather-sex–which is an "ability to see agony and enjoy its form while ignoring its contents" (Sullivan, 1995: 200). Bear camp, as it were, may play on the incongruities of undeniably male bodies speaking in nonmasculine ways. Or, bears may flirt a bit more seriously (because "more masculine") with the trappings of leather. Interestingly, in some places bears and leatherfolk are synergistically aligned. In other places, bears distance themselves from the leather community, seeing themselves as the "alternative" to sadomasochism.

BEARS AMONG THE SOCIAL CLASSES

The "naturalness" of bears expresses a position in a complex web: bears are "naturally" men (and not women or queens), bears are "natural" (as opposed to the ritual and artifices of leathersex or gym-buffed "twinks"). Bears are engaged in staking their claim in the social hierarchy of the gay community-at-large. "Out" gays inhabit at least two distinct, though interrelated social worlds, of the dominant society and of the gay community.

Gays may well inhabit one or more other subcultures, e.g., racial, ethnic, religious, professional, special needs, or class. The semiotics of "naturalness," in this context, also takes in (dominant society's) social class and race structures. Gay social discourses are fundamentally middle class, and include the middle class's pressures, in this case to conform to traditional gay "nonconformity."

To talk about social class in the United States is extremely difficult. Not only does it go against the grain of our public discourse, which seeks to generate the impression of equality and hence absence of social classes, the entire world is undergoing a profound change. Traditional nineteenth and early twentieth-century class distinctions no longer apply. There is as yet no consistent vocabulary to articulate the new categories and distinctions in social hierarchies. So, let us proceed slowly with the consideration of bears and social class.

Bears' "naturalness" registers in the key of "blue collar." In the late 1980s, at least in San Francisco, and some other places, a bear-identified "social space" meant the congregation of several sub-subcultures—bikers, chubbies, leathermen, Radical Faeries, long hairs, "regular" guys, a few people of color, fetishists (beards, body hair, boots, cigars, etc.), rural and urban, and a range of nonconformists and other men who did not identify with the "gay community." One common element was a relaxed, "come as you are" dress code. The semiotics spanned the range of industrial blue collar (urban) and country (farm, ranch, cowboy, rural poor, aka "white trash").

If we define "blue collar" as semiskilled factory workers, we no longer have a working class worth mentioning. In that sense, the bears' appeal to working-class values and dress may be a romanticizing longing for a mythical past. If we define "blue collar" as unskilled or semiskilled labor of every sort, we can talk about the present-day lower-middle-classes. The factory worker of yore may today be doing data entry in a corporate environment, working in a service industry, in retail sales, in construction, as a waiter, a hairdresser, a day laborer, or serve in the military. In terms of dress code, either casual street clothes or a specific uniform, in the traditional sense, is worn. Blue-collar men who do manual labor will have built-up muscles based on "honest work," rather than artificial sculpting at the gym. Those with a sedentary lifestyle will not have developed bodies.

There are new professional classes, as well, which may require a great deal of training, but do not lead to correspondingly higher income. For example, a college instructor, who has completed graduate school to qualify for a professional position, nonetheless will earn less than a building contractor, a plumber, or an electrician (skilled blue-collar professions). The receptionist, the orderly, the nurse's aide, are now team players along with RNs, GPs, and MDs. Yet, in terms of authority, the hospital administrators stand at the pinnacle of the power structure. Among bears, there seems to be a pronounced presence of professional caretakers (from the hospital orderly to the MD) and workers in the computer industry.

Computer enthusiasts, aka "tekkies," represent another spin on class. They are predominantly male, computer work is sufficiently "masculine enough" (drawing from math, engineering, drafting, etc.), and yet the profession allows for a great deal of creativity and individual quirkiness (cf. the mad scientist or the absentminded professor).

Going "natural" is also taken directly from the feminist work of Andrea Dworkin, Mary Daly, and others. It is a transformative action on the part of the oppressed to reject being dominated by the beauty myth, to direct our anger at our oppressors, not ourselves, and to build community with like-minded fellows. In this sense, bears address the issue of class strictures based on looks-ism and fat discrimination. Heavy, unattractive people are discriminated against in our society, which often has direct economic consequences–being forced to take lower-end jobs, being shunned professionally and socially, being dismissed as asexual or unworthy of intimate affection.

The emphasis on stockiness and, especially, substantial body hair echoes "blue collar" in another way. While large bodies suggest manual labor, furriness is most associated with certain ethnic strains–Irish, Italian, Armenian, Jewish, Scandinavian men. At the height of factory labor a hundred years ago, these ethnic groups *were* the poor immigrants. By society's standards of the day these were *not* "white." Racial biology of the day further suggested that working-class men were prone to an excess of atavistic "masculine tendencies," including excessive body hair, overdeveloped muscles, sweat and body odors, and low intelligence level. Even today, conservative social scientists such as Richard Herrnstein and Charles Murray have tried to argue (in *The Bell Curve*) for a shockingly, naively reductionist biological basis to social class.

Within the gay community we must consider another web of social hierarchies. Most important is the "newly arrived middle-class" sensibility that permeates the gay community. This includes the sense of security to be achieved by "passing" as middle-of-the-road gay–dress right, work out, do some community volunteer work, socialize on the gay circuit, vacation at gay spots, hold down a gay-acceptable job. In addition to the usual middle-class occupations, this latter includes being a waiter, a bartender in a gay bar, a hairdresser, a model, an artist, a sex-industry worker, a nurse, a computer programmer, etc. In other words, there is another gay-class hierarchy to take into consideration.

The whole gamut is run among bears. An increasing number of bears are comfortable being themselves as middle-class professionals, who proudly work out, engage in conspicuous consumption, and may even shun their social inferiors in bear circles. If being "natural" is valid, then, it follows, it must apply to everyone equally.

A new gay generation emerges roughly every ten years. While bears began in the over-35 generation (which includes both the Stonewall and pre-Stonewall generations), in part as a coming out in middle age and the community shutdown in the wake of the initial AIDS panic, the community now spans the AIDS divide. Stonewallers still alive are in their forties and fifties. The thirtysomething generation is finding itself rapidly aging as the present post-X-generation comes of age. These twentysomethings bring an entirely different sense of being gay and of being a bear to the community. Most recently, there have been encouraging moves to draw female-to-male transsexuals into the fold of bears.

BEARS AS A RESPONSE TO AIDS

Shortly before AIDS erupted in the gay community, an important trend toward mental and physical health, nurturing and community-building had begun to blossom. By the mid-1980s sobriety, meaning getting and staying clean and sober through Alcoholics Anonymous and other twelve-step programs, had become extremely popular, even heralded as "politically correct," a step in the direction of taking control over one's life.

When AIDS hit, gay men flocked to AA meetings, either to face their illness clean and sober or as "bargaining" maneuver: if they get sober, then maybe, just maybe they will avoid getting infected. AA, for many in the gay community, became a second home, the nurturing community they had longed for, but did not quite find in the gay community at large. As Walt Odets remarks in his book *In the Shadow of the Epidemic*,

> Because of the social and psychological gains made by the gay liberation movement in the 1970s, it is easy to overlook the depression, anxiety, isolation, and loneliness that were experienced routinely by a majority of homosexual men twenty-five years ago. (Odets, 1995: 121)

If fact, such feelings are still manifest throughout the gay community. By the late 1980s, the emergent bears phenomenon was drawing up the spirit, if not the direct example, of such a nurturing community. To some extent, no doubt, bears were reinventing the same wheel–cohesion, nurturance, and mutual aid as a response to the acute sense of isolation and alienation they had experienced. The Ur-bear-coming-out narrative would follow a rocky path, overcoming numerous obstacles: societal rejection for being gay and coming to some terms of self-acceptance, coming out into the gay community and being rejected for not fitting the gay-dominant image (too heavy, too hairy, too old, too odd), coming out into the AIDS epidemic where everyone is afraid of sex and withdrawn in a state of fear or paranoia.

As AIDS became a huge private hell for gay men, the bear phenomenon proved one of the first rustlings of a rebirth of spirit and community. It began as a simple, straightforward approach to reconnecting with life in general and with gay life, social and sexual. So we add to this highly complex concoction yet another layer to the social web. The rise of a bear community is inseparable from the AIDS epidemic. This includes the first broadly accepted sexualization of abundant body weight; in the early days thin equaled sick or dying from AIDS, while fat equaled healthy, uninfected. In the early days, the lack of response from the dominant society forced the gay community to generate community-based institutions to deal with the health crisis, and associated economic and mental health crises as well. AIDS has called upon gay men to develop their nurturing side, to make conscious decisions about striving for intimacy, commitment, and life plans. AIDS, when it seemed as if it would destroy the gay community altogether by sheer attrition, required us to think through what being gay and what living in gay community mean.

> I now understand that our central problem is not depression, but the profound and destructive effects of denial and repression that we are erecting against fear, grief, and depression. These defenses are leaving too many of us in isolation from our own internal lives and feelings, in isolation from one another, and without the capacity for emotional or physical intimacy. (Odets, 1995: 123)

Nowadays, coming out means coming to terms with AIDS, it means learning to live with loss, possibly with multiple loss and living in a constant state of mourning. Beardom has been for some a compensation for these losses. For some it has been a way to address, if not to resolve, fundamental challenges to create a meaningful life. As the gay community has now divided up into HIV-positive and HIV-negative camps, bear spaces have been one place where the two can come together again, heal together, pursue a life of authenticity. Bears potentially offer the spirit of survivorship and, to be true to their romantic roots, a way to transcend the hell of AIDS by joyfully seizing the day.

BIBLIOGRAPHY

Ablelove, Henry, Michèle Aina Barale, and David M. Halperin (eds.). *The Lesbian and Gay Studies Reader.* New York: Routledge, 1993.

Anderson, William. *Green Man: The Archetype of Our Oneness with the Earth.* San Francisco: Harper Collins, 1990.

Barber, Benjamin R. *Jihad vs. McWorld.* New York: Times Books, 1995.

Bem, Sandra Lipsitz. *The Lenses of Gender: Transforming the Debate on Sexual Inequality.* New Haven: Yale University Press, 1993.

Berger, John. *Ways of Seeing.* London: BBC and Penguin, 1972.

Berger, Maurice, Brian Wallis, and Simon Watney (eds.). *Constructing Masculinity.* New York: Routledge, 1995.

Browning, Frank. *A Queer Geography.* New York: Crown, 1996.

Chauncey, George. *Gay New York: Gender, Urban Culture, and the Making of the Gay Male World, 1890-1940.* New York: Basic Books, 1994.

Connell, R.W. *Masculinities.* Berkeley: University of California Press, 1995.

D'Emilio, John. *Sexual Politics, Sexual Communities: The Making of a Homosexual Minority in the United States, 1940-1970.* Chicago: University of Chicago Press, 1983.

D'Emilio, John and Estelle Freedman. *Intimate Matters: A History of Sexuality in America.* New York: Harper and Row, 1988.

Duggan, Lisa (1995). The Discipline Problem: Queer Theory Meets Lesbian and Gay History, *GLQ: A Journal of Lesbian and Gay Studies* 2:3 (179-191).

Dworkin, Andrea. *Pornography: Men Possessing Women.* New York: Dutton, 1989.

Fiedler, Leslie. *Freaks: Myths and Images of the Secret Self.* New York: Anchor, 1978.

Fisher, Hal. *Gay Semiotics: A Photographic Study of Visual Coding Among Homosexual Men.* San Francisco: NFS Press, 1977.

Fritscher, Jack. *Some Dance to Remember.* Stamford, CT: Knights Press, 1990.

Gitlin, Todd. *The Twilight of Common Dreams: Why America Is Wracked by Culture Wars.* New York: H. Holt, 1995.

Goffman, Erving. *Stigma: Notes in the Management of Spoiled Identity.* New York: Touchstone, 1963.

Guarneri, Carl J. *The Utopian Alternative: Fourierism in Nineteenth-Century America*. Ithaca, NY: Cornell University Press, 1991.

Hopcke, Robert H. *Persona: Where Sacred Meets Profane*. Boston: Shambhala, 1995.

Kimmel, Michael. *Manhood in America: A Cultural History*. New York: Free Press, 1996.

Kimmel, Michael S. (ed.). *The Politics of Manhood: Profeminist Men Respond to the Mythopoetic Men's Movement (And the Mythopoetic Leaders Answer)*. Philadelphia: Temple University Press, 1995.

Kushner, Tony. *Angels in America, Part One: Millenium Approaches*. New York: Theatre Communications Group, 1993.

Lewes, Kenneth. The *Psychoanalytic Theory of Male Homosexuality*. New York: New American Library, 1988.

Lorbeer, Judith. *Paradoxes of Gender*. New Haven: Yale University Press, 1994.

Mosse, George L. *The Image of Man: The Creation of Modern Masculinity*. London: Oxford University Press, 1995.

Murray, Stephen O. *American Gay*. Chicago: University of Chicago Press, 1996.

Odets, Walt. *In the Shadow of the Epidemic: Being HIV-Negative in the Age of AIDS*. Durham, NC: Duke University Press, 1995.

Perchuk, Andrew and Helaine Posner (eds.). *The Masculine Masquerade: Masculinity and Representation*. Cambridge, MA: MIT Press, 1995.

Preston, John (ed.). *Hometowns: Gay Men Write About Where They Belong*. New York: Dutton, 1991

___. *A Member of the Family: Gay Men Write About Their Families*. New York: Dutton, 1992.

___. *Sister and Brother: Lesbians and Gay Men Write About Their Lives Together*. New York: Dutton, 1994.

___. *Friends and Lovers: Gay Men Write About the Families They Create*. New York: Dutton, 1995.

Rofes, Eric. *Reviving the Tribe: Regenerating Gay Men's Sexuality and Culture in the Ongoing Epidemic*. Binghamton, NY: Harrington Park Press, 1995.

Ryan, Jake and Charles Sackrey. *Strangers in Paradise: Academics from the Working Class*. Boston: South End Press, 1984.

Sullivan, Andrew. *Virtually Normal: An Argument About Homosexuality*. New York: Knopf, 1995.

Thompson, Mark (ed.). *Leatherfolk: Radical Sex, People, Politics, and Practice*. Boston: Alyson, 1991.

Weeks, Jeffrey. *Coming Out: Homosexual Politics in Britain, from the Nineteenth Century to the Present*. London: Quartet, 1977.

Weiss, Peter. *The Persecution and Assassination of Jean-Paul Marat As Performed by the Inmates of the Asylum of Charenton Under the Direction of The Marquis de Sade*. New York: Atheneum, 1965.

Wolf, Naomi. *The Beauty Myth: How Images of Beauty Are Used Against Women*. New York: Anchor, 1991.

Young, Ian. *The Stonewall Experiment: A Gay Psychohistory*. London: Cassell, 1995.

SECTION I: HISTORY

Chapter 1

A Concise History of Self-Identifying Bears

Les Wright

The origins of homosexual men self-identifying as bears is obscure. There are two entries from 1966 in the minutes of the Satyrs, a Los Angeles-based MC club, noting the formation of a "bear club." Eyewitness accounts from Dallas, Miami, and elsewhere describe the use of the term by self-identifying bears in common usage during the 1970s. The Miami informant reports that while "bears" were well known in Miami, on trips to San Francisco the term was not known there until 1986. Nonetheless, by 1980 individual gay men in San Francisco, New York, Miami, Toronto, and elsewhere, are reported to have taken to placing a small teddy bear in a shirt or hip pocket, some of them with the intent of refuting the clone colored-hanky code, to emphasize being into "cuddling," that is resisting being objectified and reduced to preferred sex acts.

Since the term "bear" *is* applied in a self-defining manner, it is vaguely defined, sometimes in self-contradicting ways, and is interpreted variously. Human identification with totemic, symbolic, and physical attributes of bears has a long history and plays a key role in the specifically gay male adoption of the term. It may describe physical size, refer to male secondary sex characteristics, to alleged behaviors or personality traits of bears, or to metaphysical, supernatural, or other symbolic attributes of bears. Thus, it is impossible to answer the question "What is a bear?" in any definitive way, beyond the array of *connotative* associations in our culture, suggesting a large or husky body, heavy body hair, a lumbering gait, an epicurean appetite, an attitude of imperturbability, a contented self-acceptance of his own masculinity (however that may be defined). The debate, generally framed as bear-as-image versus bear-as-attitude, is as unresolved as ever.

The rise of self-identifying bears as a social phenomenon has followed striking parallels with the gay liberation movement. The Stonewall riots of 1969, usually celebrated as the birth of the gay movement, did not appear out of nowhere. There had been a long, albeit often hidden and isolated, collective political resistance by lesbians and gay men. Mattachine and the Daughters of Bilitis had existed since the dawn of the Cold War era. The philosophies and political strategies of Stonewall modeled themselves at least somewhat consciously upon the civil rights, women's, black, and antiwar movements of the 1970s.

Similarly, an idea of bears was clearly circulating in the gay communities (whether urban enclaves, private network of friends, or organized social clubs) at the same time. It drew upon the representational values described above. It also drew upon, probably quite unconsciously, the gay liberationist tactic of "coming out" as a bear. This would require an internal self-identification, most likely followed by public expression of that identity, and possibly voluntary association with a group of like-minded individuals, i.e., a community, a circle of friends, or an organized club.

Stonewall rapidly became a symbol, "the shot heard round the world," that acted as a catalyst to galvanize individuals and smaller groups into a much larger social movement, social identity, and at least the appearance of cohesiveness. Erroneously, New York City became literally, rather than symbolically, identified as the birthplace of gay liberation. Self-identifying bears underwent just such a moment of titration. The birth of the bear "movement" is generally set at 1986. At this time "bear talk" began taking on concrete shapes and modes of communication. A year later, there was more than one computer bulletin board dedicated to "bears," a group of friends started holding private play parties for "bears" in the Bay Area, and a local underground magazine, called *BEAR* had been launched in San Francisco. There was a certain amount of overlap between the participants in each of these activities and, because self-advertising is the common factor in all three, the news of "bears" spread to increasingly larger audiences. Inevitably, much disputation has arisen over whether San Francisco is the symbolic or literal birthplace of "bears." Because of San Francisco's unique gay community, some believe it should be disregarded as unrepresentative of bear "community." Present-day resentment of "bearish" San Francisco parallels the resistance of a generation ago to the idea that everything important in the gay world happens in New York.

Just as the hippies of the 1960s became the yuppies of the 1980s, the original gay liberationist impulse underwent a radical transformation, from androgynous radical to gay yuppie, or "guppie." So, too, whatever "inclusionary" desires of bears had been present a decade ago have been largely displaced by gay-mainstream values—a tendency to elaborate a hierarchy of "bearishness," to organize in private membership clubs, rallying around images and icons of sexually desirable bears, and the creation of bears as a niche market in the domestic consumer economy.

Simultaneously, "bears" represent a link in the historical continuity of masculine-identified gay men. George Chauncey's exploration of turn-of-the-century gay male subcultures in New York City reveal that, at least among the working classes, there could be found such masculine-identified man-loving men, known as "wolves." This bifurcated engenderment among gay male subcultures has persisted ever since. Wolves and fairies (and punks) mixed with each other or amongst themselves. Following the social clampdown on overtly homosexual behavior in public in the 1930s, the post-World War II era saw the public reemergence of this bifurcation. Nellie queens' effeminate engenderment was book-ended by butch leathermen. By the early 1960s a complex leather subculture had come into being, as Gayle Rubin's research has documented. The emergence of bears in the subsequent decade, and "going public" in the 1980s after the first shock waves of the AIDS epidemic, expresses a renewed engagement with gay male engenderment. (See the Introduction for a discussion of this.) What is of particular interest to me is the grappling with self-identification and elaboration of a consciously masculine gay male identity among increasing numbers of gay men, individually and in community, with this totemic persona of "bear."

ROOTS

In his 1991 introduction to *The Bear Cult: Photographs by Chris Nelson,*[1] Edward Lucie-Smith attributes iconographic sources of bears to the 1950s gladiator movies starring bodybuilder Steve Reeves. Gay "physique studios" of the time reflected the predominant fashion of closely shaven faces and bodies. "Old Reliable," a Los Angeles-based photographer of homoerotic wrestling, specialized in "natural" men, soliciting hustlers, punks, ex-cons, and other truly "rough trade" types off the streets (from the 1950s-1990s) to pose for his camera. Old Reliable's models were always chosen for the "attitude" they embodied, tough, street-smart scrappers, perhaps shabby, perhaps defiant, unquestionably blue-collar, or lower, class. A fat cigar in one hand and the middle finger of the other hand thrust into the camera's face is the signature pose for Old Reliable's models. John Rechy's novels, especially the 1963 best-seller *City of Night*, serve as a record of gay male engenderment of this particular type in the urban subcultures of the late 1950s and 1960s.

Another informant, living in the Miami, Florida, area during the 1970s, reports that when he first started coming out into the bar scene in his mid-twenties he encountered a cluster of "bears" that congregated in the Tool Room, a back bar area of Warehouse VIII, a "disco palace."

> [i]n the meantime, some counter-culture tabloid I read occasionally ran a cryptic personal ad for a Bears party, which would gather at a men's bar called The Ramrod on a particular evening and time, so I bit. Not knowing the bar's whereabouts, then learning the address and trying to find the unmarked place in the downtown darkness, I was late but not too late. A dozen or so men with beards, most of them husky, were piling out of the bar door as I was walking in. Two of them grabbed me by each arm, and one said "Great! You're the even number!" Now I was just in the first stages of coming out, even to myself, but I let myself get swept away (with an alarmed smile on my face). I thought I was headed for my first orgy (gay or straight), but it turned out to be a real party at a home on one of the causeway islands between Miami and Miami Beach. Real men having a hell of a good time without a woman in sight.

Imagine!! We watched the second half of the Dolphins game, played some cards, then sat outside under the moonlight, slowly pairing off and disappearing back indoors or off into tropical hiding places beyond the patio.

I was out. I started hanging out regularly at the Ramrod, where any bearded local was greeted as "Hey, Brother Bear!" I checked out The Rack, a leather saloon, but the bear camaraderie was not present. A few Rack regulars were good-looking, beefy, bearded guys, but their bikes and image were their focus, not the bears among them. The bears continued to patronize the Ramrod and the Tool Room, or a large bar in Fort Lauderdale called Tacky's, but could be found in lots of neighborhood bars, too, like The Hamlet and The Everglades. Not only did we refer to ourselves as bears, but the term caught on among non-bears too.

It was too early in beardom, I guess, to have a Bears club or organization of any kind. Nobody thought of it. There were spontaneous parties arranged by word-of-mouth, picnics, beach volleyball. We even loaded three vans full of bears and invaded Key West.

You might think of Florida as an unlikely place to find bears, but bearded men were very common there in the 60s and 70s. When the disco era steamrollered fashion for straight and queer alike, it became less common. Many bears kept our beards, many left only a moustache. The Ramrod faltered and closed, 13 Buttons and The Copa flourished, as did all the big discos of the day. I became more private with three bear affairs over five years, then finally met a cowboy in New Orleans one Mardi Gras and left Florida forever. We moved to Colorado in 1981 and had five great years together. I've been in Denver since 1986 and was later a founding member of one of the oldest bear clubs in the country, Front Range Bears.

But that's another story.[2]

Larry Reams has unearthed the first documented apparent uses of "bear" in the current sense. He has found among records of the Los Angeles-based Satyrs' MC club the formation of a "bear" club mentioned in two entries from 1966.[3] Another source cites anecdotally a group of lovers of a "Papa Bear" in Dallas, Texas, as the start of "the bear community" "well before 1975."[4] Several undocumented sources have related similar anecdotes of private circle or bar circles of self-identifying bears.

The first published description of gay "bears" appeared in a whimsical article called "Who's Who in the Zoo: A Glossary of Gay Animals," penned by George Mazzei in the *Advocate,* July 26, 1979. Larry Reams reports that he and his friend, the author,

> were standing in Griffs', a Los Angeles leather bar, one evening discussing the types of men we were and those to whom we were attracted. We decided we were Bears and continued on to formulate what we thought constitutes a Bear. Once we had described Bears it was an easy step to look around the bar and create the rest of the article.[5]

Because the type so strongly suggests aspects of both bear attitude and bear image, it is worth quoting in its entirety:

> Bears are usually hunky, chunky types reminiscent of railroad engineers and former football greats. They have larger chests and bellies than average, and notably muscular legs. Some Italian-American Bears, however, are leaner and smaller; it's attitude that makes a Bear.
>
> *General Characteristics:* Hair. Their tangled beards often present no discernable place to insert a comb. Laughter. Bears laugh a lot and are generally good natured. They make wonderful companions since they are prone to reach for the check, buy the next round and keep abreast of when the Trocadero is dancing this season. Their good humor can turn threatening if you attempt to cruise their trick and you will hear about it for weeks afterward.
>
> *What They Eat:* Beer is their favorite food. When they stay out past their hibernation time on weeknights, their lower Bear nature takes over and they drink more Scotch and water than is good for them. Then they will often perform hilariously, trying

to dance in time to the disco beat, providing entertainment for all around.

> *Mating Peculiarities:* Before asking you home, Bears ascertain that you will stay and cuddle all night even if nothing else happens. They may wear full leather at all times, but Bears are usually not kinky. They are fascinated by nipples–others' as well as their own–and spend hours playing with them. Bears always have lovers to whom they are loyal, even though they don't sleep together much anymore.
>
> *Natural Habitat:* Bears are fascinated by motorcycle runs–possibly because it provides an excuse to keep a can of beer in their paws at all times. Although titillated by the motorcycle mystique, they prefer to let other woodland creatures ride in competitions. And as for fixing a disabled bike, they wouldn't know a clutch cable from a zippered pocket.
>
> *Domestic Rating:* Bears are wonderful around the house since they don't need much exercise to keep their distinctive shape and are extremely loving, loyal and dependable. The most affable of pets, they do require constant reassurance and, like some large dogs, tend to shed on the furniture.[6]

Jack Fritscher was creating and documenting a similar impulse in San Francisco contemporaneous to this Los Angeles subculture. Those pre-AIDS years in the Castro and South-of-Market subculture are documented in the roman à clef *Some Dance to Remember.* Recorded in the novel is an account of Fritscher's short-lived underground magazine called *Man2Man*, a direct precursor to the first incarnation of *BEAR* magazine. The "homomasculinity" of Fritscher's philosophical quest was summed up in the magazine's subtitle: "What you're looking for is looking for you!"

FIRST-WAVE BEARS OF THE ZEITGEIST, 1986-1989

The energy that called itself "bear" appeared as one of the signs of reemerging gay communal life following the arrival of AIDS in the 1980s. After several years in a state of shock, emotional devastation, eating more, perhaps exercising less, continuing to age, and ready for a somewhat slower and more compassionate pace of gay sex and gay social life, "hibernating" clones, leathermen, and many other self-identifying types came back to gay public spheres as "bears." AIDS led many of us to put on extra padding and to eroticize (or publicly admit to our erotic desire for) male bulk. Feminists, such as Andrea Dworkin and Mary Daly, had articulated the mechanisms of patriarchal/capitalist subjugation through the "beauty myth." The tyranny of the "Castro (or Christopher) Street clone" had been breached.

Since the late 1970s, in counterpoint to the "endless party" spirit of gay life, increasing numbers of gay men were burning out on the alcohol and recreational drugs. Alcoholism has been, and remains, a serious problem in the gay community. The drug experimentation of the "love generation" had turned into a nightmare before AIDS arrived. Now, for the first time, many were experiencing another sense of self, a "sober self," a discovery of self-respect, which allowed them to bring to a halt these self-destructive behaviors. Across the country sobriety became not only fashionable, but even "politically correct." Discussion of the uses and misuses of the principles of Alcoholics Anonymous belongs elsewhere. Relevant to bears is the rise of self-esteem among gays–whether through sexual "liberation" or adoption of cultural norms of the moment.

The self-empowerment movements of the 1970s, the nurturance and "safe space" strategies of 1970s feminism, the ever greener alternative impulses of rural gays, Radical Faeries, and nongay-identifying men-loving men (as disseminated, for example, through *RFD* magazine), and the fundamental strategy of Stonewall politics–coming out–prepared the way. For gay men, who had come out as gay, as sober, as HIV positive, as leathermen, it would seem "natural" to come out–yet again–as a bear. On the one hand, Stonewall-era identity politics shaped the Zeitgeist. On the other hand, for many men-loving men who did not identify with any of the images of gay men in the gay press or with (usually) urban gay men they had encountered on trips to a city, their first encounter with the idea or an embodiment of a "bear" would strike pay dirt. Many have reported immediate identification, sometimes after years or decades of not "fitting in." Twelve-stepping and two-stepping were new venues for socializing, for being in community without an explicit exhortation to sex. It gave us another chance, a utopian moment, in which to reinvent ourselves and our community.

"Bears" have been emerging as successor to the "clone" and as transmutated variant of "leatherman," as an integration into gay mainstream social life of "girth-and-mirthers." In many ways, it was a humanizing response to what clones had been. Martin P. Levine, in his study "The Life and Death of Gay Clones," focuses on the urban enclave of West Village clones (Manhattan), noting that "AIDS, gay liberation, male gender roles, and the ethics of self-fulfillment, constraint, and commitment"[7] were the sociocultural shapers, creating and destroying this gay male subculture. Bears, during the 1980s, represented a break with the competitive and objectifying tendencies which had alienated so many Stonewall-era gay men. Bears continued the tradition of masculine identification, the social identity politics of gay liberation, and basic Enlightenment values of equality, self-determination, and self-fulfillment. Bears sought to ameliorate between socially isolating cliques and creating safe social spaces, comingling social and sexual spheres, merging rough, unkempt masculine iconography with the emotional nurturing lacking in the clone subculture and the caretaking many gay men felt called to as a direct result of the AIDS epidemic.

The point of titration came in 1987. The "Bear Hugs" parties, the advent of *BEAR* magazine, and developments in electronic communications were the catalysts that sparked the concept of the self-aware, self-identifying bear across communities. First, computer bulletin boards and then listservers and moderated mailing lists made communications instantaneous and were collectively dubbed "cy*bear*space." All three significant events took place or are traceable back to San Francisco, independent of each other but with an unexpectedly synergistic effect all together. All three represented, each in its own way, a "safe space" for bears.

PLAY PARTIES

A group of friends began organizing private "play parties" in Berkeley and San Francisco in 1987, as safe and warm gatherings—

social and sexual–for their friends and friends of friends. Private, invitation-only "jack-off circles" became popular during the AIDS sexual freeze, but these were an alternative social and sexual space for gay men who felt "left out"–out because they did not fit, or felt like they did not fit, the gay media images of "beauty"–young, tanned, smooth-skinned, blond LA surfer boy "twinks." Their "difference" was both physical and perceptual, and was expressed through a social and sexual inclusiveness–men in their thirties, forties, and fifties, ranging from slender to stocky to chubby (though generally on the heavier side), usually with beards and perhaps body hair, and from a range of social classes. The common mold was a warm, nurturing, affectionate attitude toward each other. The intimacy of the early days changed, however, when the gatherings grew to over 100. By 1989, a larger space and a more formalized "guest list" became necessary.

This San Francisco group was the spawning ground for several later developments. Among them were Bear Fax Enterprises, a business privately owned by Ben Bruner and Bill Martin. The International Bear Expo, which ran for three years in San Francisco (1992, 1993, and 1994), the effort of dozens of local bears, was overseen by a steering committee, many of whom later founded the Bears of San Francisco and the International Bear Rendezvous. The "International Mr. Bear" competition and title were introduced at Expo '92; John Caldera, the first titleholder, eventually acquired ownership of the tile, and the contest has been held annually ever since.

"Bear soup" became a widely adopted idea. In many places it refers specifically to hot tub parties, though often with the implication of an orgy or private sexual pairings later in the evening. Sometimes "bear soup" seems to refer merely to a crowded space full of bears. The Bear Hugs group in Great Britain is a strictly social organization.

Similar groups, such as the OzBears of Sydney, Australia, and the Bear Cave parties in Manhattan, had started up for purposes of private socializing, and formed the basis of new groups that developed into bear clubs dedicated to social activities or even community work. As organized bear clubs have arisen and sex clubs started advertising a weekly "bear night," these play parties have all but disappeared.

BEAR *MAGAZINE*

At about the same time, Bart Thomas began putting together a small, photocopied underground magazine he called *BEAR*. The magazine was, at first, local to San Francisco. It consisted of jack-off photos and personal ads. The reader could send in appropriate photos of himself or stop by the *BEAR* office and pose for the magazine. In some ways, *BEAR* may be seen as the direct successor of Jack Fritscher's *Man2Man* underground magazine of nearly a decade before. Before he could actually launch the magazine, Thomas succumbed to complications from AIDS, but not before passing the torch to his friend Richard Bulger.

Bulger's vision of a lifestyle magazine, articulating this masculinity, with a leftist sexual political slant, and embedded anthropological underpinnings, not to wax abstractly, but to act, to embody the principles through practice and a level of discourse clear to any blue-collar man. In a few years' time the magazine expanded in size and status, and from word-of-mouth circulation to international commercial distribution, with a full line of videotapes, photo sets, and accessories.

In his 1993 study of *BEAR* magazine, Joe Policarpio describes the dual aspects of image and attitude stressed by publisher Richard Bulger through his choice of models and editorial content. The general profile of a "bear" includes at least some facial hair and some body hair ("usually the more the better"), a "musky animality," a blend of traditionally masculine aggressiveness and (feminine) desire to cuddle, muscles by Nautilus or physical labor, and a tendency to be older than the models found in most other gay male porn magazines. "The most important point is these men are presented as fitting an ideological pattern the magazine espouses. This is one of freewheeling, playful and positive attitude toward sexuality between men. He is comfortable in his body and exudes a sense of self-assurance."[8]

Because of personal ties, *BEAR* magazine was from the start intimately connected with the South-of-Market bar scene. The original Lone Star Saloon was the first "bear bar," and followed the tradition of the Ambush and the Balcony, both of which had gone out of business early in the AIDS epidemic. These "sleaze bars" all developed an international reputation. They all offered a free-spirited, anarchic, anything-goes ambience, drawing in blue-collar types who disdained the middle-class pretensions of mainstream gay culture, those whose sensibilities combined social rough edges with the loyalty ethic of the American lower classes, and misfits, eccentrics, and other "rugged individual" types historically drawn to frontier towns and their saloons.

"CYBEARSPACE"

Direct electronic communications over the Internet developed and proliferated during the 1980s and 1990s. Word-of-mouth knowledge of bears spread very rapidly across the Internet. The preponderance of bears on-line or in computer fields is traceable back, in part, to this. One of the most often used private or personal uses of the Internet, regardless of sexual orientation, is for communications of a sexual nature. The lines of communication are numerous and diverse: live chat lines (IRC), BBS (electronic bulletin boards), unmoderated (echoed) and moderated mailing lists, websites, CU See ME (live video transmission), and e-mail. Altogether an individual can transmit or receive text, images (such as gif or jpeg), sound, and video images (nearly) instantaneously. The Internet allows for establishing and maintaining contact anonymously, for uncensored communication, for the exchange of visual images (yourself, your friends, your favorite sexual icon), and for echoed messages (broadcasting to all subscribers of a mailing list or a global mailing to everyone in your e-mail address book). Certain mediums (such as the IRC) can guarantee anonymity (no clues as to personal identity or physical appearance). The question of subverting prejudgment on the basis of appearance becomes moot, however, when we consider the proliferation of visual mediums, such as webpages, archived gif and jpegs, or CU SeeMe, which permit blatant self-advertising based on one's appearance without revealing one's name or location.

Early on, circa 1985-1988, there were several bear-dedicated bulletin boards, such as the PC Bear's Lair (sysop Les Kooyman). The bearcave chat room on the IRC has been a very popular site in cybearspace for live conversation. While the option of remaining anonymous is always available (everyone uses a "handle," or pseudonym), cyber-communities have evolved over time. This may range from sexual encounters to personal friendships to life partners.

By far the most popular cybearspace is the Bears Mailing List, or BML. Founded by Steve Dyer and Brian Gollum in 1988, it grew from a small, friendly, safe-feeling cybergathering of several dozen bears to a heavily subscribed, largely anonymous, and often fractious, moderated exchange of over 3,000 subscribers. Since 1995 Henry Mensch and Roger Klorese have been moderating the BML and introducing changes to accommodate the dramatic shift in tenor and purpose of the list. Subscribers are drawn from all fifty states and several dozen nations worldwide. English is the lingua franca although everything, including whether to have and who should determine a common language (and how), has been brought up for discussion. Bob Donahue's somewhat tongue-in-cheek rough guide to "bear codes," which was accessible from the BML archives, is the source of subspecies terminology within the bear community, such as cub, otter, behr, and the like. Numerous individuals have taken the code in all seriousness and this has become a source of contention, quoted by both sides in disputes over what is a "real" bear. (The code appears as Chapter X.)

Although not the only cybear group to do so, the BML has staged several informal, in-person gatherings of its subscribers. During Stonewall 25 in New York City, for example, some sixty to seventy BMLers gathered at Bethesda Fountain in Central Park on the day before the parade. Consensus determined the group should form a spontaneous contingent and march in the parade. And thus on Sunday, Stonewall 25 included a sizable contingent of mostly bearded, bearish-appearing gay men from all across the country and from abroad.

SECOND WAVE: FORMALIZING, 1989-1994

Bear Clubs

As the concept of bears circulated between gay communities across the country and "news of recent developments in the gay capital" was drawing more comers to San Francisco, localized efforts to promote and organize bears appeared everywhere. The Bear Paws of Iowa, co-founded by Dave Annis and Larry Toothman in 1989, was the first bear club. By 1992, Bear Expo organizers were aware of four such clubs. Two years later, there were forty. According to the *International Directory of Bear Organizations* maintained by The Tidewater Bears (Virginia), as of January 1996, there were 137 bear clubs or explicitly bear-friendly (girth-and-mirth and leather) clubs worldwide.

Bear clubs have generally followed along the lines of their older cousins, the leather motorcycle clubs. In some places this means an informal club that schedules periodic social events. In other places, this has translated into a great deal of fundraising and gay community civic activities. As the club model has gained wider acceptance, it has drawn long-standing problems endemic throughout the gay community into its sphere.

A formal club membership structure creates automatically an insider/outsider division, even if membership is "open to all" (usually defined as "bears and their admirers"). Having a club also invites quibbling over definitions of who is a "real" bear. (This is borne out by regional differences, whether emphasis has been placed on body hair, on body weight, or on "attitude," though a beard or moustache seems to be universally required). Clubs and organizers of events, such as the OctoBearFest (Denver), Orlando Bear Bust, Bear Pride (Chicago), European Big Men's Conference, or the International Bear Rendezvous (San Francisco) have created bear contests, which engenders the very hierarchical system the earlier bear impulse had been resisting.

Finally, the disjunctive ideals of bears as working-class masculinity and bears as an increasingly distinct subculture within mainstream gay culture bring into sharp relief the larger issues of gay community. If bears began in a spirit of inclusiveness and egalitarian-mindedness, sex positive and relatively "anti-looks-ist," then what is to be made of the increasingly conformist, consumerist, competitiveness that has taken over? As the idea of bears has spread, the opportunities to travel far and wide, to purchase ever more and ever more costly bearphernalia, to update and expand one's computer resources are generating another, unanticipated dividing line–between bear haves and bear have-nots. To what extent does having money now calculate into the formulas of who is a "real" bear?

Expanded Print Media

As *BEAR* magazine rapidly grew in format, production values, and circulation, reception among gay mainstream media remained very low. The first published serious essay on bears was a piece I wrote in 1989. It appeared in its entirety in *Seattle Gay News*, an abbreviated version in the *San Francisco Sentinel*, and *Drummer* magazine carried the "Sociology of the Urban Bear" as the first bear cover story in 1990. (It was reprinted in *Classic Bear*, February 1996.)

What became known as bear types had been featured, in one way or another, in *RFD* (rural), in *Chiron Rising* ("mature"), in leather/SM-oriented, and girth-and-mirth publications. Numerous niche-crossover magazines sprang up in the early 1990s–*Bulk Male*, *The Big Ad*, *Husky*, *Daddy*, *Daddybear*, *GRUF*. Bearish models began staring back at the reader from the pages of *Advocate Men*, *Honcho*, *In Touch*, and other gay mainstream glossies. *BEAR* magazine's direct competitor *American Bear*, published by Tim Martin (Louisville, KY) took advantage of a lacuna left by *BEAR* magazine's retreat from Bulger's philosophical lifestyle magazine publishing. With the establishment of the bear icon in the gay community and the world of mainstream-gay print advertising, gay bears had become a local presence everywhere (not just in San Francisco). And with interests, at least sometimes, beyond immediate sexual gratification, this translated into new niche markets. While *American Bear* features a regular column on dissonant (HIV-positive/negative) couples (Bulger adamantly refused to mention AIDS in his magazine), a how-to column on accessing the Internet, and other features, none of the bear magazines have attained *Playboy*-calibre intellectual content.

In the early 1990s "bear war" broke out when Bulger, then owner-publisher of *BEAR,* sought to gain sole ownership of the word "bear" as his company's trademark. Needless to say, this led to a lot of bad feelings and was widely followed and criticized in cybear-space. The *Advocate* even mentioned it in print. At the time, the Bear Hug group's informal newsletter the *Bear Fax* had been expanded into a full-fledged magazine by Bill Martin. The lingering legacy of this "war" was a schism, based on a difference in basic body types typically portrayed in each magazine, between "fat bears" and "skinny bears." Since this time, personals ads have proven far more profitable, and the bulk of the magazine currently consists of personals ads, photo spreads, and commercial advertising.[9] The magazine was sold to Bear-Dog Hoffman in 1994 and is currently under Joseph Bean's editorship. It is not clear which direction the magazine will go. It *is* clear that *BEAR* is the voice of authority in matters of bear community and sensibility.

Print media has gone a long way in generating a prototypical bear icon–full-bearded, fairly to very hairy, beefy to chunky GWM baby-boomer, probably of Irish, Jewish, Italian, Scandinavian, or Armenian heritage. In reality, the question of race, presence or absence of body hair, body build, social class, or outlook on life is anything but so neatly compartmentalized. *BEAR* magazine introduced the serious photographic work of Chris Nelson (as Brahma Studio) and Steve Sutton (who succumbed to complications from AIDS in 1994). Lynn Ludwig has established himself as the documenter of the San Francisco bear community. And, perhaps, the most gifted photographer of bears is Los Angeles-based John Rand, whose work is included in this book.

Bear Contests

The bear calendar includes many regional gatherings, as mentioned above, as well as annual bear contests at the local club level. The highlight of such events is often the bear contest. As Lurch, a popular bear icon, stand-up comic, TV actor, and psychiatric nurse, has put it, "I prefer to say 'titleholder.' 'Winner' implies 'losers,' and none of us are losers."[10] Successful bear contest titleholders may be expected to organize or work a number of fund-raisers, go on public speaking engagements and represent their hometown or club on the road. In other places, the local bear club may be one of the few, or even the only social outlet, and merely being a known presence in the local community is the extent of the titleholder's "duties."

The emergence of bear contests has tended to straddle the fence between two sides–parodying traditional gay ideals of beauty while striving to establish a new, legitimate bear ideal. The International

Mr. Bear contest, a component part of the San Francisco-based International Bear Expo, evolved in its first three years from poking somewhat self-conscious fun at traditional gay values to striving in an increasingly serious manner to project an image of a self-confident bear ideal, a new icon assuming its place among the archetypes of male beauty. From the beginning there has been an emphasis on personal warmth, a compassionate nature, civic-mindedness in the gay community, and spiritual playfulness. Titleholders John Caldera (IMB '92) and Steve Heyl (IMB '93) worked hard during their "reign," and have remained genuinely and deeply committed to the bear community. Yet, in the progression of titleholders and the proliferation of bear contests in recent years, there has been an increasing tendency toward consolidating a bear image, and away from qualities intangible or at least invisible to the camera.

A DECADE OF BEARS: GLOBALIZATION OR TRIBALISM?

Several efforts to document the steadily growing bear phenomenon have been undertaken. Joe Policarpio prepared a two-year study of "*BEAR* Magazine: Masculinity, Men's Bodies and the Imagination" and preserved it as a videotaped slide show/lecture, but ultimately decided not to pursue it as a dissertation in cultural anthropology. As a film archivist, Vic De La Rosa presented screenings of his work-in-progress *Lions & Tigers & Chubs & Bears* (1994), a collection of bear-related films and clips, to audiences in San Francisco, Los Angeles, and Houston. John Outcalt has spent several years filming for his documentary on body image in the gay male world, called *Chubs and Bears*. John Topping filmed some forty interviews with bears before abandoning his project. Copies of selected interviews have been deposited with the Bear History Project archives. Perhaps the most ambitious effort is the Bear History Project, which I founded in 1993, and have modeled after similar projects for preserving gay and lesbian history. Currently housed in a private home in the Boston area, it is ultimately intended to be preserved in perpetuity as part of the History of Sexuality Collection at Cornell University.

The emergence and development of bears as a gay male subculture, and the ability to capture its unfolding from an early point onward offers an unusual opportunity to study how a subculture forms, its mutability by internal and external forces, and how a code of social values develops and changes. Bears are clearly a new icon within the self-identifying gay community. It is still too early to say whether bears represent a phenomenon, a movement, or a community.

Potentially, bears represent a new option, rather the reverse of androgyny. Instead of a "neutral" engenderment as devoid of either gender as possible, the bear ideal embodies positive qualities of both masculine and feminine, uniting traditional gender polarities—strong and sensitive, gruff and affectionate, independent-minded and nurturing. In reality, bears collectively harbor all the same problems as before. To what extent are bears caught up in a utopian-romantic impulse to reinvent themselves, to what extent are bears merely exploited consumers in a highly fragmented niche market system? To what extent can anyone find social liberation through enslavement to one's sexual passions? Conversely, to what extent can bears render powerless social forces that seek to control them by manipulating terms of erotic attraction by declaring their actual preferences and fostering new anti-ideal ideals, insisting on what is, rather than what should be? In microcosm we find in the bear phenomenon an expression of the contemporary dialectically opposed forces of globalism (instant communication and a homogeneity in style of thought and behavior) and tribalism (the banding together, for any given reason, of smallish, overseeable numbers of people into an identifiable group). And this leaves us with the oddest of dialectical questions: what happens when first-world tribalism encounters the global village?

NOTES

1. Chris Nelson, under the name Brahma Studio, was the original staff photographer of *BEAR* magazine, as well as the lover of then-owner/publisher Richard Bulger.

2. E-mail to the author, Bear Sawkins, February 10, 1996.

3. Letter to the author, Larry Reams, July 17, 1995. "The minutes of February 11, 1966 make notes of the fact that the Bear Club in San Francisco is having their first open meeting February 24, 1966. The minutes of March 11, 1966 mentions

that the Koalas of San Francisco will have an open meeting on March 18 (Are they one and the same? I don't know.) The Koalas put out a newsletter called *The Bear Facts*. They were into leather and rode buddy on motorcycles and carried tiny teddy bears in their hip pockets."

4. Letter to the author, Tom Poindexter, February 10, 1994.

5. Letter to the author, Larry Reams, May 27, 1995. The other "gay animals" described are owls, gazelles, cygnet swans, pussycats, marmosets, and pekes and afghans.

6. George Mazzei, Who's Who in the Zoo? A Glossary of Gay Animals, *Advocate* (July 26, 1979) 42.

7. Martin P. Levine, The Life and Death of Gay Clones, in *Gay Culture in America*, Gilbert Herdt (ed.). Boston: Beacon Press, 1992:82.

8. Joe Policarpio, *BEAR* Magazine: Masculinity, Men's Bodies and the Imagination, Madison, WI: Media PUP, [1993]:25.

9. An informal sampling of two recent issues each of *BEAR* and *American Bear* yield the following:

10. An oft-repeated phrase of Lurch's, most recently heard at IBR 96 in San Francisco, February 1996.

Chapter 2

Bear Roots

Ron Suresha

Before the dozens of Bear clubs across the United States and abroad, before the Bear phone chat lines and computer bulletin boards, before the regional Bear conventions and international Mr. Bear competitions, before the plethora of slick magazines, where were the Bears? The Bear phenomenon did not simply spring up overnight on the gay cultural plateau, as a colleague wrote, "from a fortuitous conjunction of three events in San Francisco in 1987," without any precedent. That's simply not the way history in general, and culture in particular, work evolves.

Personally speaking, Beardom has almost always been a fact of life. I've lived as an openly gay Bear (or at least a bearishly open gay man) as long as I can recall, or at least since my early pubescence in the early 1970s. I've always been a hairy guy loving other hairy guys. I recall when in 1987 a friend first showed me a copy of *BEAR* magazine: it confirmed that I was not alone in my attraction to hairy, masculine men. Unsurprisingly, after *BEAR* began publishing, they discovered that there were already many men of the same persuasion, scattered around the country and the world, who mailed letters and photographs to the editor, claiming the same lifelong affinity to facial and body hair. In many ways it was a matter of the publisher providing for an already-existing need, that of gay men who could not fit in with or did not desire the then-popular gay cultural models.

A much shorter version of this chapter appeared in the February 1995 (Vol 2: No 3) edition of the *New England Bears Newsletter*. Thanks to Jeb Bates, Eric Rofes, Mike Frisch, Alan Troxler, and Jim LaBonté for their insightful comments on earlier drafts.

As much an anomaly as Bears may have seemed at its inception in relation to gay (and mainstream) sexuality, fashion, and culture, there were, I contend, several solidly identifiable cultural streams from which the early Bear groups drank.

For certain, bearded, hairy, big homosexual men existed before 1987. We can look to Walt Whitman, that foremost gay American poet whose image should be familiar to every gay American, as perhaps being the first Bear. Although Whitman seemed to carry no particular physical preference or "type" as far as his comrades were concerned, he embodied many of the ideals that we now ascribe to Bears: bearded, hairy-chested, above-average weight, sensual, strong, earthy, yet spiritual.

From Whitman's time in the mid-nineteenth century, however, there seem to be few others who could be looked upon as Bear icons. For the most part, the gay Euro-American culture (as well as the larger straight culture) of the past 100 years or so has placed on its fashion pedestal the clean-shaven, smooth, slim male model for consumer consumption.

In *The Bear Cult*, the 1991 book of photographs taken by *BEAR* magazine's co-creator and first photographer Chris Nelson (and incidentally, the only book to date about Bears), Edward Lucie-Smith states in his introduction that the Bear concept began as early as the mid-1950s, when American muscleman and peplum actor Steve Reeves began "experimenting with a beard. For the role of the legendary Greek strongman, facial hair was more or less obligatory, and both he and his rivals grew what was required." Lucie-Smith then quickly admits that such films rarely depicted body hair and that they were only "briefly popular . . . more or less over by the mid-1960s" (Lucie-Smith, p. 6).

Although Reeves' short-lived yet successful film career may have held more appeal for gay men than for the straight American culture of the time (for the basic attraction of Reeves' stunning physique), it seems, rather, that it is something of a misinterpretation to perceive Reeves as an early Bear icon: if he was gay, he kept himself completely closeted about it; if indeed he was able to grow body hair, he kept his body completely shaved and smooth-appearing; and although we know he could grow facial hair, he regularly appeared on- and off-screen *sans* beard. Granted he may have been a gay icon at the time, but his outward Bear characteristics were the exception, not the rule, and his influence on the gay culture over time, and specifically to the generation that gave birth to the Bear movement, was negligible.

In the 1950s appeared yet another American poet whose presence was unmistakably Bearish: Allen Ginsberg, the preeminent Buddhist/Beat poet and poetics teacher. His homosexuality was never concealed in either his writing or his politics, and he indeed served as a Bear role model for many young gay men who would later come of age at the time the Bear movement surfaced.

The foremost cultural influence, however, that led to the Bears' emergence is the Radical Faerie movement. Over twenty years ago, a humble group of homespun gay men, largely dedicated to gender equality, sexual freedom, and nonurban living, started a collective publishing venture in Iowa. They chronicled their ideas of democratic gay living, as well as other aspects of their radical but very real sexuality, in their long-running magazine, *RFD: A Country Journal for Gay Men Everywhere*. Over the course of its history, the group eventually centered itself out of a gay commune/community, the Short Mountain Collective in Tennessee. The editorial and production work for *RFD* has moved from place to place, yet the collective continues to publish its quarterly collection of generally high-quality features, including in-depth news articles, AIDS research, astrology and gardening columns, reports of local Faerie gatherings, contact letters from prisoners, poetry, and photographs and illustrations of (often naked or semiclad) men. It certainly helped to create a contemporary iconography of the hairy "natural man." In issues going as far back as the late 1970s–indeed, way ahead of their time in gay publishing–there are unposed photos of nude and semiclad bearded, hairy men.

This publication, while not devoted exclusively to the hairy or oversized ideal, created a unique medium in which the "alternative" male body could be romanticized and adored. The faeries began as an original gay expression with distinct ties to the hippie movement. On a physical level, the expression manifested in ways including long hair, beards, and colorful clothes. On a social level, the faeries embraced the ideas of "free" love and alternate family structures, including communal living. On a political level, they sought to employ the ideas of democracy, cooperativism, and ecological responsibility in their own lives. And on the spiritual level, the Faeries sought to attain to higher consciousness through such means as pagan ritual, Goddess worship, and Eastern meditation and tantra.

To be sure, many of the Radical Faeries participated in urban as well as rural lifestyles. Beards and body hair were not necessarily worn to the exclusion of jewelry, makeup, or women's clothing. It was from this movement that the term "genderfuck," meaning the apparent contradiction of traditional masculine and feminine attributes, was born.

There are some distinct differences between the Faerie and Bear movements. For one, the Bear cult, as coined by Lucie-Smith, originated in the gay Mecca of San Francisco. It has based itself primarily in city settings. Conversely, the Faerie movement sprang from and still largely defines and confines itself by its affinity to country life and spirit. In general, Bears imbibe the values of urban gay life, which emphasizes looks, money, and status. Faeries tend to eschew materialism and classism. Also, Bears tend to be more involved in the leather scene, which bases itself primarily in cities, than their Faerie counterparts, who are usually content with softer fiber clothing or with nudism.

This is not to say that there aren't Bears who cross-dress, farm, and worship Pan, or that there aren't Faeries who have heavy leather gear, live in gay ghettoes, and participate in S&M rituals. Based on my experience with both of these communities, I envision a sort of continuum, where many of these seemingly opposed values (urban/rural, status-conscious/democratic, and so on) can be placed at opposite ends of a spectrum that includes both the nature-based ideal of the Faerie and the city-based ideal of the Bear.

One may well postulate that, because of the Faeries' existence prior to the Bears, and based on the cultural evolutionary concept that the natural precedes the artificial, that the Bear culture took the ideal of the "natural man" from the Faeries, applied an urban spin to it, and produced a cult that espouses a so-called natural-man ideal while in actuality embodies its opposite. Or perhaps the Bear movement in general subscribes to the superficial aspects of natural masculinity–secondary gender characteristics such as abundant facial and body hair, and body weight, strength, and maturity. Given that two of the founding fathers of the Bear movement–Rick Redewill, proprietor of the Lone Star Saloon in San Francisco (considered by many to be Bear Mecca), and Richard Bulger, co-creator and publisher of *BEAR* magazine–began their businesses with capitalistic rather than community service-oriented motives, this postulation seems plausible but casts an unfavorable light of classism on Bear orientation in relation to the Faeries.

Although where a culture emerges from and where it leads are not necessarily the same place, if one examines the overall population of Bear-identified men, it is clear that the majority of Bears are white, upper-middle class, white-collar professionals. Examining the structure of Bear clubs, too, indicates the pervasive presence of a good-ol'-boy (in some cases, even frat-boy) mentality.

As we have seen, although not all Bears define themselves or are defined by these characteristics, it is apparent that the closer to an urban environment that a Bear lives, the more likely it is that he will be identified with such upper-middle class characteristics. Conversely, the further away from an urban setting that a Bear lives, the more likely it is that he will identify with Faerie-type values. The common thread running through the lives of such disparate kinds of gay men is the self-perception of "naturalness," whether it be in physical appearance, personality, sexuality, or lifestyle.

In sharp contrast with the "good ol' boy" mentality that some Bears have developed, another major constituent of the Bear movement that I would posit is radical lesbianism. But where the Radical Faeries were quietly creating their own democratic sexuality, the lesbian movement of the late 1970s and early 1980s was political and vocal about its models for cultural sexuality. These efforts were part of a larger feminist movement, in which women of all types, shapes, and colors began to reclaim their own bodies from the dominant straight white patriarchy and redefine their own sense of self from the inside out.

Among these were radical, Rubenesque lesbians who, like Bears, were disparaged and fed up with the stereotypes and offensive role-playing presented for common consumption by the traditional heterosexist mainstream. In essence, these women's message loudly proclaimed: "Hey! We're big, fat, (below-) average-looking people who love others of the same sex–and we're just as worthy of love and respect as anyone else in this world." These sisters in the early movement made a radical proclamation of their own intrinsic self-worth and challenged the accepted norms of beauty, paving important cultural inroads for the Bear movement to come.

Coincident with, or perhaps emergent from, the dyke liberation politics of the early 1980s was the primarily nonstraight, nonwhite, nonpatriarchical idea of political correctness, which values diversity and personal differences and which supports the idea that language and practices that offend others' personal and political sensibilities should be eliminated. Thus also began the larger cultural process of destigmatizing that which was previously held by the popular culture to be shameful or taboo. Not only did some American English usage change, and not merely by a marginalized minority, but an even greater change in attitude and action was attained by American society. This increased value on diversity was especially profound in the countersexual culture.

This significant sociocultural shift–from the establishment and emulation of certain narrowly defined physical stereotypes and models toward the introduction and acceptance of a broader and more eclectic set of norms–now allowed a place at the table for people of color, religious and spiritual minorities, deaf and differently-abled ("handicapped" and "disabled") people, and others with specialized traits, orientations, and interests. Indeed, as anyone who has witnessed the day-long San Francisco Pride Parade can attest to, there is a seemingly endless stream of special-interest contingents that cater to every conceivable whim.

This emphasis in the countersexual culture on specialization is also reflected in the plethora of publications, ranging from the pornographic to the poetic, that has emerged since the late 1980s: in the gay male market alone, the are 'zines for Bears, Chubbies, Brainies, gay Hippies, Latinos, Asians, PWAs, men into foreskins, men with small penises, and computer nerds, to name but a few. Indeed, *BEAR* magazine must be credited with being one of the first of these special-interest publications. Its success has encouraged many other gay publishers and writers to pursue material that speaks to their own hearts, minds, and bodies. The magazine's prominence and editorial independence has also helped to break through the pervasive clone-ism of gay male culture and the looksism of the gay-fashion culture at large.

On the trade fashion front, it's interesting to observe that "big-boned gals" began to make national fashion spreads not too long before bearded men also started appearing as fashion models. "Big and Tall" clothing stores starting emerging in the sixties, first for women, then for men. Bearded men emerged as models and product spokespersons in the early 1980s, first in L.L. Bean and similar outdoor clothing catalogs, but then becoming quite common in the mass media by the later part of the decade. By the early nineties, beards were commonly seen in mass-market culture: print and TV advertising spokespersons; sitcom, soap opera, and movie stars; talk-show moderators, newsmen, and sportscasters.

Currently, although the clean-shaven look is still emphasized in Euro-American fashion, beards and facial hair are now accepted to a degree not known for over a century. Today we see beards on men from walks of life that used to stigmatize–indeed, prohibit–facial hair of any sort (the so-called establishment types), including corporate lawyers, politicians, CEOs, national news anchors, policemen and firemen (in major urban areas), and even FBI and CIA agents. Additionally, over the past two decades, public exposure to and acceptance of overweight men and women has increased markedly.

Suddenly, it seemed, by the mid-1980s, the slim-waisted look became quite unfashionable, as the lives of most gay urban Americans had been touched by the loss of loved ones to AIDS. In those days, if someone confessed to losing weight, one would more likely urge the individual to see a doctor rather than congratulate him or her on the opportunity to shop for new clothes.

Somehow, this "slim-phobia" was eventually translated in the minds of most gay men to mean that it was actually unhealthy to be of even average weight. This paranoia coupled with a rejection of what many considered the gay male physical ideal–that of the body-sculpted, slim-waisted, smooth-chested, perfectly coiffed young male–and built up to the point that a new cultural model was ready to spawn. To some extent, however, it was the same old fetishism simply transferred to a new set of superficial images.

What the Bear movement helped to create was a sort of "reverse discrimination" in gay culture. For perhaps the first time, instead of

Bears not fitting in with the typical gay scene, the roles were reversed, at least in Bear spaces such as the Lone Star Saloon or the Bear Hugs social/sex events. The gay clone or tanned, buffed twinkie type, should he find himself in a Bear crowd among mature, heavy, hairy, bearded men, might feel singularly unpopular.

At some point in the early San Francisco Bear years–around 1990, when the first Girth-and-Mirth groups appeared to infiltrate the Lone Star Saloon crowd and to intermingle with the Bear Hug sex groups–there was a noticeable shift in the way that the local community defined Bears, and in the way Bears defined themselves. It was only later that the basic defining characteristic of a Bear as having abundant facial or body hair changed to an equal if not greater emphasis on body weight.

So, from becoming an untrue marker of good health, being overweight became a Bear fashion statement. People's attitudes in this regard are amazingly regimented. Even now, there are many proto-Bears that remark: "I can't be a Bear–I'm not fat!" This indicates a great misconception in the gay culture at large about which characteristics, be they physical, social, or otherwise, constitute Beardom. Ironically, one may observe a significant number of men who use the "Bear" label as an excuse for being overweight, out of shape, and unkempt.

Nevertheless, the Bear movement was the first sex-positive cultural phenomena to spring up following the advent of AIDS. This is one of the most exciting and inspiring aspects of the Bear subculture: its freewheeling, openminded, and democratic sexual mores. Perhaps one could epitomize Bear spirit as this feeling of loving openness, which as often as not manifests in sexual promiscuity as it does in monogamy. Considering three of the initial primary venues for popularization of the Bear cult–the often-sleazy Lone Star Saloon, the erotica of *BEAR* magazine, and the Bear Hug sex parties–it is remarkable that a single, distinct group of gay and bisexual men created such emotionally and psychically positive activity in the face of such devastation of its ranks.

However, Bears are no more immune to AIDS than anyone else. In the five years that I lived in San Francisco and was active in the early Bear community, I lost to AIDS dozens of Bear friends and lovers. It is the enduring legacy of those Bears that continues to this day, and flourishes with the proliferation of the many popular and successful Bear clubs, organizations, events, and businesses. To those first Bears, who embodied the natural and irrepressible love of comrades, this article is dedicated.

REFERENCES

The Lone Star Gazette, (1:1-3 and 2:1-3), R. Suresha, (ed.). San Francisco: The Lone Star Saloon, 1991-1993.

Lucie-Smith, Edward, "The Cult of the Bear," in *The Bear Cult*, Chris Nelson (London: Gay Men's Press, 1991) 6-8.

Thompson, Mark, "This Gay Tribe: A Brief History of Faeries," in *Gay Spirit: Myth and Meaning*, M. Thompson, (ed.). (New York: St. Martin's Press, 1987) 260-278.

Chapter 3

The Bear Clan: North American Totemic Mythology, Belief, and Legend

Michael S. Ramsey

Throughout human history, perhaps no other animal has inspired the numerous stories, instilled such primal fear, or given us quite so many fond childhood memories as the bear. In our modern society, it is often anthropomorphized, first being transformed into a lovable and cute character with the creation of the "teddy bear." The bear has now come to symbolize something very different in the twentieth century than it did throughout humankind's past. Today, the free roaming and truly wild bear is all but a memory for most Americans. Due largely to an effective extermination effort of the early pioneers in conjunction with today's constant pressure of expanding urbanism, the grizzly bear (*Ursus arctos horribilis*) now only resides within the most inhospitable, mountainous regions of the continental United States. However, prior to the coming of the European to North America, the natives had a very different relationship with the bear. To them it was one of the most powerful totemic spirits in all of nature. The unique similarity to man in many ways, coupled with the animal's strength and knowledge of the land, imparted within Native Americans a great respect. In response

---

This chapter is by no means an exhaustive or complete review of the mythology of the bear. Rather, it is meant as a cursory summary of the significance of this animal to humankind. The topics touched on are further elaborated in the listed sources. In general, these references are summaries in themselves and contain extensive bibliographies on this subject for the interested reader. Unique to this work, however, is the reexamination of bear mythology in the light of the modern gay community that *bears* its name.

to this, the native peoples of North America and other circumpolar tribes of the world evolved similar myths and legends regarding the bears present in their respective lands. While certainly differing in degree, depending on the people and the aspect of the animal being celebrated, these legends often told of a similar bear-mother creation myth, bear-wife story, and hero-hunter tale. This intertwined relationship of human and animal has continued from the earliest cave-dwellers through today in many of the Native American tribes still practicing their traditional religions.

Today, the bear still holds a significant place in our culture. No longer seen strictly as a wild and fearsome animal, it has become the fuzzy childhood toy, the oafish cartoon character, and the leading symbol of forest fire prevention. Often given loveable names such as "Yogi," "Winnie," or "Smokey," this bear character is stripped of those qualities that made it so important among the Native Americans. However, giving the bear human qualities and thereby relating to it more easily, is perhaps not so very different from what the Native Americans did centuries prior. In both cases, humans are creating logical or spiritual ways to coexist with an animal easily able to kill with one swift blow of its paw. In order to represent such a presence, an elaborate and rich history of bear symbology has evolved. This symbolism illustrates the animal to others and connects one's self to the spirit of the bear, providing a constant reminder of the relationship between human and animal. Today it is manifested in the form of the stuffed animal, the photographic picture book, and the carved figurine on our shelves while that of the Native American took the form of pictographs, twig figures, stone carvings, and bone weaponry.

In an attempt to better relate to the bear, members of both past and present cultures have also projected ursine qualities onto themselves and others. For example, prior to the New Year celebration or before a hunt, Bear Clan members of the Yuchi tribe of the southeastern United States prayed and danced to the bear. Members of clans such as these often adorned themselves with bearskins, necklaces of claws, red face paint, and distinct hairstyles in order to physically become more bear-like. Today, rather than relating strictly to the animal, humans identify more with their own interpretation and characterization of the bear. It is perhaps not all that surprising that as the bear in our storybooks has come to more resemble humans, many men in our society were recognized as having bear-like qualities. A hirsute man of formidable size and strength is often given the nickname, "Bear," for example. So, while the relationship of man and bear has persisted throughout human history, a distinct shift in the expression of that relationship has occurred over the last century. No longer looked upon in a mystical and religious sense, the spirit of the bear in man has become more of a physical and, to some degree, mental state.

In today's world, the bearish man is perhaps most evident and well-organized within the bear community that exists in gay America and throughout the world. This subgroup of gay society owes its formation to several factors, each of which will be explored further in this book. The most obvious and relevant to the discussion here is the celebration of the physical attributes of these men. Clearly, qualities such as body fur, beards, masculinity, and larger frames are not typically associated with the gay mainstream, and to a large degree, are still shunned by that majority. In part, this outward rejection galvanized many gay men, causing them to form a new group consisting of men who were both appealing to and accepting of them. What defined a man as a bear was not solely dominated by the outward appearance, however. Less tangible aspects such as friendliness, affection, and persona also formed the ideal of what it was to be a bear. Beginning as a small group, it has expanded tremendously over the past decade. With bears clubs in most major cities, thousands of members worldwide, and several magazines catering to them, bears have come into their own and now represent more than just a small outcast, splinter of the gay culture. The success and popularity of the bear community, due mainly to the freedom of outwardly expressing one's masculinity, has clearly filled a void that had previously existed in the gay world.

The questions then arise, "What factors existed between man and bear in the past to foster such a unique relationship?" and, "Do those factors have any impact on the formation and success of the modern bear clan?" Unlike any other, the association of man and bear has had a rich and long history. In the bear we see a mirror of our animalistic side, the epitome of all that is wildness. To the Native American, this represented power, spirituality, and nature.

To modern man, the freedom, strength, and playfulness are its virtues. In either case, the recognition of the animal's inherent qualities are at the core of the human-bear mythos. The purpose of this chapter, therefore, is to explore the past in an attempt to understand early human's totemic relationship with the bear by relating their stories, myths, and legends, and in so doing, hopefully point out several of the commonalities between the past and present bear clans.

Native American bear societies mainly evolved and persisted for the sole purpose of celebrating the religious significance of the animal. This totemism of the bear was so strong and so far reaching that it has persisted throughout the greater portion of humankind's written history. The Neanderthals, living in Europe and Asia 50,000 years ago, respected the great size, strength, and power of the now extinct cave bear, *Ursus spelaeus*. These early humans formulated primitive religious practices with the cave bear at their core. The primary connection to death and renewal became evident with the unearthing of Neanderthal and cave bear bones together in caves throughout Europe. These beliefs were carried in the minds of the humans who ventured over the Ice Age land bridge that once connected Asia to North America. Taking root in what was to become the Native American population, the bear cult became truly circumpolar at this point. Also making the journey over that land bridge long before humans was the common ancestor of the varied species of bears that would come to populate the Western Hemisphere. The lifeways of North America's bears and humans have been intimately linked for at least 20,000 years as both species evolved together on the continent. The native peoples that inhabited north and eastern Siberia, northern Japan, and North and Central America saw the same qualities in the brown (*Ursus arctos*), polar (*Ursus maritimus*), and American black (*Ursus americanus*) bears that were evidenced long before in the ancient cave bear. For the Native Americans, who believed all animals were sacred and possessing of individual spiritual powers, the bear held a very special place in their religious belief system. Almost every Native American culture that lived in proximity to major bear populations of North America had a commonality of customs, mythology, legends, and ceremonies involving the animal. In part, this similarity and strong presence of the bear as a powerful totem sprang from the knowledge that it was one of the few animals that could easily kill human beings. Fear-inspired respect such as this was reserved for only the strongest of spirits. This respect often manifested itself as taboos and ritualistic practices. For instance, upon slaying a bear, many northern hunting tribes would cut off the paws and poke out the eyes in order to protect themselves from the anger of the dead animal's spirit. With increased observation of the bears around them, fear slowly began to give way to the recognition of the bear's unique ability of "rebirth" after hibernation, its superior aptitude at locating food, and its strong maternal instincts. These characteristics were greatly revered and respected by Native Americans and elevated the bear to one of the most powerful religious symbols in many indigenous cultures.

Because of these physical abilities, the Native Americans believed the bear to be something very much more than a powerful animal that conjured fear. To them he was a brother, a kindred spirit, and a teacher. They saw in the bear an animal that had amazingly similar traits to themselves. These included physical attributes such as the ability to walk upright for periods of time, the human-like mannerisms, as well as the striking similarity of its skinned body to that of their own. The bear was believed to be half human, a kinsman. In fact, many tribes referred to the bear with the same term they used for man or relative. To the Cree of eastern California, a bear is "a furry person, a relative, that goes underground when the earth sleeps and emerges when it awakes."

From this respect and kinship with the animal grew a rich and elaborate system of representation. As with any totemic animal, symbology played an integral part of the ceremonies and even the daily lives of the Native Americans who cohabitated with bears. This symbolism ranged from the fetish sculptures of the Pueblo Zuni of New Mexico to the elegantly carved totem poles of Pacific Northwest tribes such as the Tlingit and Haida. The Lakota of the northern plains painted pictographic representations on shields carried into battle and on the teepees of their shaman. Tribes of the southeastern United States, on the other hand, performed bear dances in honor of the New Year. Individuals, especially during religious and hunting ceremonies would "become bear" through adornments such as bearskins and face paint. The purpose of these symbols, like those of any modern religion, was to bring the individual closer to that which he worshiped and even more important, join the spirits of bear and human through a connection to the spirit world. To Native Americans, many animals had very strong spiritual forms and bestowed their powers at certain times to humans. For the shaman, receiving these powers through a vision was a guarantee that he would practice good medicine. Among the northern plains tribes, spiritual gifts came during the vision quest, a time of isolation and meditation. Once an individual returned, he was often asked to reenact or recount the events of the quest to the elders. The visions were interpreted and the individual informed of their meaning. At this time, a medicine bundle, containing various relics, sacred objects, and symbols, was created and carried from that point onward. The bundle had the sole purpose of joining the owner to his spiritual guardian. In some cases, the link between the individual and his totem was so strong, as with the shaman, that it was believed he could transform himself physically into his guardian animal for the purposes of spiritual journeys and insights.

Clearly, not all members of a given tribe had this level of connectedness to their spirit guide. It was only attained by a select and powerful few. Almost all individuals could, however, have a guardian spirit. Whether one's spirit was revealed through a dream or vision, as was the practice of many of the Athabascan-speaking tribes of the plains and Canada, or bestowed at birth, as was believed in Central American cultures, that guide was there for a specific reason. Exactly what that purpose was and how the person expressed his totem was, to a large extent, a function of the tribe but also the individual's choice. The external symbols chosen had to be understood by others and typically followed long established traditions rooted in geographical location and religious beliefs. However, the objects carried in a bear medicine bundle or displayed in a private dwelling certainly took on a more personal nature. They expressed the intimate and private relationship that existed between the guardian spirit and the individual. Totem animal spirits were always associated with certain characteristics and knowledge that was beyond the individual and therefore sought by him. Common throughout most of North America's native population, the bear for example, was connected to the powers of healing and shamanism, rebirth and renewal from death, fighting, and creation. A more detailed examination of these four attributes reveals the primary reasons why this animal in particular was so significant to the Native Americans.

THE BEAR AS "HEALER"

To the Native Americans, the bear was a master gatherer, a knower of herbs and medicines, and a healer. Existing on a diet of nuts, berries, roots, and meat, it was the only large omnivore familiar to them. Further, they observed the bear's seemingly remarkable ability to heal itself from injuries, often covering a wound with mud in an attempt, it was believed, to keep out infection. Actions such as these elevated the bear to the rank of shaman of all the animal spirits. As such, it was devoutly pursued by human shamans as their totem. Often a common "gift" of the bear to a seeker of a spiritual vision was a previously unknown herb for medicinal purposes.

The bear as a curing animal was practically universal among Native Americans regardless of geographic location and societal structure. They observed the bears digging for roots, eating various parts of particular plants, and moving with the seasonal food supply just as humans did. Many tribes such as the Cheyenne, Cree, and Penobscot regarded the bear as physician. In fact, the Tewa word *kieh* means both bear and doctor. The Canadian Eskimos called upon the bear spirit whenever performing healing ceremonies, while the Cherokee of the southeastern United States performed a bear dance to protect the tribe against disease brought by the Europeans. The Oglala Sioux of the northern plains have one of the most elaborate and well-documented belief systems concerning animal spirituality. Two Shields, a Lakota shaman, observed:

> We consider the bear as chief of all the animals in regards to herb medicine, and therefore it is understood that if a man dreams of a bear he will be expert in the use of herbs for curing illness. The bear is regarded as an animal well acquainted with herbs because no other animal has such good claws for digging roots.[1]

Many of the native plants and herbs used for healing such common illnesses as headaches, coughs, heart trouble, diarrhea, sore throats, and swellings had names derived from the word bear. These plants were favorites of the animal, which was often observed by Native Americans eating them in times of distress or sickness. The bearberry, bear grass, bear's foot, and bear's tail are a few of the several dozen plants routinely utilized by the Native Americans to help cure the sick. The combination of such medicines together with the invocation of the bear spirit by the tribe's shaman was the most powerful cure available.

THE BEAR AS "CREATOR"

For Native Americans, the bear existed both in the physical world, gathering plants and passing on medicinal wisdom, and also in folklore, as the primary character in their creation myths. The link established between the creation of life and the bear doubtlessly evolved from the relationship of the mother and her cubs. Female bears often emerged from the long winter's hibernation with one to several cubs in tow. They had a strong maternal devotion to their young that endured for at least two years. The cubs stayed with their mothers, being fiercely protected, while undergoing a period of learning and growth. This close relationship, unusual for the typically antisocial bear, was observed by Native Americans and the bear became a metaphor for the universal mother, the giver of all life.

A culture's creation legends are some of the most fundamental and significant foundations on which that society forms itself. Fables such as these have a grounding effect giving members of the society insights as to how and why they exist. Among the many roles the bear played in Native American religions, the one of creation character is perhaps the least universal among the tribes of North America. There was a wide disparity on how men and women came into being and why they were put on the earth. What was shared, however, was the common principle that human beings were but another piece of nature, and in the case of many groups, not even the most significant part. Nature was not given to human beings for their sole use, as believed in the Judeo-Christian tradition. Rather, it existed as an interconnected whole of which humans were a part.

The Bear Mother story was very similar among the many tribes who had the bear linked to the creation of humankind. In fact, it is the oldest and most persistent story ever told by human beings. It speaks of a time before humans existed in their current spiritual and moral state. In the myth a young, blasphemous girl is often depicted gathering berries. She does little work, constantly babbles, and shows no signs of respect for nature and, in particular, the bears. Overheard by the bear spirits, they assume human form and lead her away. She is married to a chief's son, and lives among the bear-people for many years giving birth to several sons. One day her human brothers come to look for their sister, and she lets them know of her location through various signs. The Bear Husband knows he must give up his life to the hunters and teaches her the way to properly hunt, kill, and dispose of his remains. The woman and her sons go to live with her former people and instruct them in the important lessons learned. The Bear Sons eventually become great hunters and the progenitors of the modern human race. This myth has its roots in the earliest hunting and gathering societies of ancient Europe, and its basic premise has stayed fundamentally constant for at least fifty-thousand years. The shamanistic cultures that followed from those early hunters passed along this creation story, perpetuating the bear cult. When cast in this historical framework, its significance to humankind cannot be underestimated. At the very least, one must look critically upon the precepts and vitality of modern religions. By comparison, the creation myth of Adam, Eve, the apple, and the serpent are a mere several-thousand years old!

Through the Bear Mother creation story, the kinship of bear and human is established. The Bear Mother, elevated from a blasphemous child to that of divine creator, becomes the root of the civilization tree. The Bear Father dies for the welfare of the people and his sons are the intermediaries between the human and the divine. This belief of direct descent made all other aspects and gifts of the bear even more significant to Native Americans.

THE BEAR AS "WARRIOR"

The bear as healer and creator involved the intellectual and emotional aspects of the animal. Typically, the first impression for anyone seeing a bear in nature is that of its strength, size, and power. This physical prowess, especially when protecting its young, gave rise to the bear totem as one of the most powerful fighters. For many tribes, a young warrior could do no better than to carry the spirit of the bear with him into battle. His animal totem was usually manifested in symbolic war paint and perhaps the brandishing of a weapon made from the bones of a bear. However, not all tribes believed that for battle, the power of the bear was good. For the Tlingit, the bear was too unpredictable. Having it as one's totem in war might prove to be a hindrance since its rampant spirit was too difficult to control and master. For the Shoshoni of the central Rocky Mountains, the anger of the bear also made it undesirable for a family man. Having it would cause him to get angry and lose control over nothing.

Nevertheless, the bear as a fighter and his resistance to injury made him the guardian for the warriors of the Blackfoot tribe. Perhaps one of the most powerful object that a Blackfoot man could possess was the bear knife bundle. Made from the jawbone of a grizzly and adorned with sacred objects and feathers, the bear knife was thought to protect the one carrying it even in the most brutal of battles. The bundle was either fashioned by the warrior after instruction learned during a dream or vision quest, or it could be purchased from a current owner. The transfer of such a powerful object involved long and elaborate rituals that entailed tremendous work on the part of the knife's seeker. Typically, the often brutal ceremony ended with the owner throwing the knife as hard as possible at the buyer, who was required to catch it. Any injury sustained during this transfer proved that he was not worthy of carrying such a powerful totem. A missed catch usually involved serious wounds that often led to death not long afterward. Bear warriors of the Crow tribe of the northwest plains and neighbors of the Blackfeet, often prepared for war by covering their bodies with mud and bunching their hair to resemble bear ears. During battle, they vowed to walk straight into an enemy's camp and not retreat, fully relying on the powers of the bear spirit for protection. The sight of a Crow bear warrior often struck tremendous fear into their enemies.

THE BEAR AS "RENEWER"

The one ursine attribute that drew the most attention and elevated the bear to the pinnacle of the underground Spirit Realm was not that of healer or warrior, but rather its ability to hibernate. In fact, to several tribes the bear was smarter than man because it knew how to survive all winter long without eating or having to hunt for food. Arguably, hibernation spawned some of the most culturally significant folklore among the Native Americans and crystallized within them the deepest levels of spiritual belief. It gave rise, for example, to such fundamental societal customs as initiation ceremonies and life and death rituals, and linked the bear to the change of seasons and the coming of spring.

All of these practices have as their major underlying theme the act of death and rebirth. Just as the earth itself died with the coming of winter, so did the bear. It prepared its den for several weeks, during which time it added a tremendous amount of body weight in order to survive the coming cold. As the days began to grow longer, signaling the end of winter, the bear would emerge from the den oftentimes with newborn cubs. To Native Americans, this rebirth was significant in three important ways. First, the sight of the bear was an indication of the nearness of spring. He brought with him life and the earth's rebirth after the cold death of winter. Second, the bear itself was reborn after as much as six months in the den. Without food, water, or others of its kind, bears are able to seemingly die in isolation and then return with the arrival of spring. And finally, in the case of cubs, there was yet further new life seemingly created in the midst of death. All of these factors combined to become the underlying themes in ceremonial traditions that involved death and the hope of rebirth. Without doubt, the most widespread of these were initiation rituals. Initiations, whether puberty rites, shamanistic inductions, or entrance into certain secret societies, all had a similar structural pattern. When the initiate was ready to enter into a new phase of his or her life their old self had to undergo a ceremonial death in order for their new self to be born. Rituals such as these invariably involved a prolonged isolation and fasting, a death, and finally a rebirth and subsequent celebration. The imitative aspect of these ceremonies to the bear's preparation for hibernation, long isolation, and eventual renewal is easy to comprehend. Many, however, went beyond mere imitation and involved the initiate or the participants actually becoming a bear.

The puberty ceremony of the Pomo tribe of California, for example, involved one of the elders wearing a bearskin and acting like a bear. During the ritual, the children were shoved in the bear's path, to be knocked down and eventually "killed." The boys were then taken by relatives, cleaned, given new clothes, and sent into isolation for a period of time. In their absence, the "bear" went into the lodge, removed his skin and prayed for the initiates. For the Pomo, the "making of a bear" entailed an all-night dance followed by rituals and culminating in the return of the youth to village. Their return signified a rebirth into adulthood, emerging from the forest as men. Other tribes had similar initiations that lasted days or weeks. The length of time the individual was isolated and "dead" was a function of the purpose of the initiation, the depth of the spiritual significance, and the amount of learning that was required. It was during these periods of fasting and solitude that visions were sought and elders came to teach the neophyte the ways of the society. In all of these varied practices involving the bear, the initiate's death came without sorrow or fear, for they knew they were like the bear and had his power of rebirth.

Native Americans of many different tribes organized and belonged to bear societies that celebrated the bear as healer, progenitor, or warrior. The purpose of these groups, while mainly to pass along traditions, was also to bring individuals together for a common purpose. Typically these groups, such as the Bear Dreamer Society of the Lakota, were open only to those who had visions or dreams of the animal. Further, because of the respected place of the bear as healer, members of the Society were the shamans of the tribe and often performed public curing ceremonies. The group would share plant remedies, teach ritual songs and tell stories, and became almost fraternalistic in its initiation practices and secretive codes. As for other Native American tribes such as the Western Yokuts, the Bear Society was responsible for the celebrations of spring and good harvests. Members would participate in the planning and organization of the bear dance following the acorn harvest. Performed only once a year, it consisted of four men and one woman, and ensured continued abundance of acorns in future years.

Across the continent, the bear societies were very prominent and their members greatly respected. While their principles and practices varied from place to place, members dressed, ate, and oftentimes acted like the bear in order to gain favor with its spirit. Many of these bear rituals clearly show a depth of understanding of the bear's daily life, in addition to the spiritual connotation. To carry the bear as one's guardian spirit was truly respected, to become a bear either metaphorically or physically gave insight and power from the Spirit World.

With the onslaught of Euro-American culture and religion, many Native American cultures with their secret societies began to disappear. The ceremonies of some tribes, most notably the Sioux and the tribes of the Pacific Northwest, have been well documented and preserved. But even among these culturally vibrant tribes, the native language is rarely spoken and ceremonial rituals, including those related to the bear, haven't been performed since the mid-nineteenth century. For other groups no longer in existence, like the many tribes of California, specific human/bear myths have had to be deciphered through careful study of the remaining symbols and artifacts. Such interpretation surely lacks important information and is unable to recapture the vital human element so necessary in translating these traditions and stories.

As the early pioneers moved westward across North America they encountered not only Native Americans and their legends, but the bear itself. Its size, power, and resistance to death fostered an abundance of fables, exaggerations, and legends like that of Grizzly Adams. Rather than live in coexistence with the animal, these pioneers and their descendants opted for the domination and extermination of the bear. Through these actions, the west was "made safe" for man and cattle and the bear was relegated to isolated tracts of land and city zoos. Despite this change, our view of the truly wild bear has changed very little in 20,000 years. Perhaps no longer seen in such a spiritual light, the animal still stirs a certain anxiety, respect, and awe deep within us.

The linkage of the modern bear clan in the gay community to the many and varied ancient bear societies that have existed over the past tens of thousands of years seems tenuous at best. Both share a common name derived from the animal itself, but differ in the perception of that animal. Both also consist of smaller subgroups within a larger social structure, with obviously different purposes, however. Perhaps the most direct connection that can be drawn between the two is the use of symbology to express one's love of, and membership within, the given group. Many bear clubs in today's gay society use both abstract and realistic representations of the bear, its paw print, and vocalizations as symbols for the group and their upcoming gatherings. Individuals within these clubs, while also utilizing these symbols, are often more personalized in their expression of the bear. This form of symbology is a matter of one's personal taste and often spans a wide range from Native American emblems and icons to modern representations of the bear to more specifically homoerotic forms. These are expressed in a number of ways, but primarily through the wearing of bear jewelry, clothing, and tattoos. However, no matter how far-afield, the basic and continued realization of the similarities between humans and bears is the strongest premise that binds the ancient bear cults with those of today. It is no wonder that because of this connection, and enriched with a great tradition of native North American myth, a fascination with the bear continues today and will surely continue into the next millennium.

REFERENCES

Brown, Joseph Epes. *Animals of the Soul: Sacred Animals of the Oglala Sioux*. Rockport, MA: Element, 1992.

Hallowell, A. Irving. *Bear Ceremonialism in the Northern Hemisphere*. Philadelphia: University of Pennsylvania Press, 1924.

McCraken, Harold. *The Beast That Walks Like a Man*. Garden City: Doubleday, 1955.

Rockwell, David. *Giving Voice to Bear: North American Indian Rituals, Myths, and Images of the Bear*. Niwot, CO: Roberts Rinehart, 1991.

Shepard, Paul, and Barry Sanders. *The Sacred Paw: The Bear in Nature, Myth, and Legend*. New York: Viking Penguin, 1985.

Versluis, Arthur. *The Elements of Native American Traditions*. Rockport, MA: Element, 1992.

Chapter 4

Aroused from Hibernation

Scott Hill

The emergence of self-identity often eludes those of us in the minority, any minority, be it sexual, racial, political, take your pick. We grow up deprived of the familiar role models that the remainder of society has taken for granted, followed, and relied upon for centuries, crucial examples that form your perspective, your worth, your sense of independence, your place in the world.

There comes a time however, when society–whether in one great flash or piece by piece–affords us a glimpse of a world of our own, a world where our values and identities are not only shared, but valued and encouraged. For the fortunate, we can discover a world where we finally feel at ease, content to be ourselves, and able to truly appreciate one another. For me, this is the world of Bears.

Bears are living contradictions to the gay stereotypes that still permeate today's society. Our mere existence erodes the portrayals of effeminate sinners, recruiting young children, a portrayal still perpetuated by the religious right in such a "matter of fact" manner. Don't forget too the stereotypes of our own making, images of the attractive, blond clone with his smooth gym-toned body. We are none of these. Nor do we fit the mold of the typical straight man, for some of the most endearing qualities of a Bear are of a feminine nature.

We are a community woven together by an appreciation of masculinity and genuineness in a man. This is what really makes a Bear. The most apparent of bear traits is masculinity, a trait for which we are obviously known. The emergence of a true Bear actually takes years, a culmination of experiences, attitudes, and self-discovery. A

Bear is more than a look, it is an attitude, an almost instinctive desire to include other like souls into a sort of adopted family. Though some can agree on general traits, inevitably, there are personal nuances to each individual's definition.

My definition was cultivated in the lush region of western Pennsylvania, a generally blue-collar area, its landscape scattered with steel mills and manufacturing facilities, heavily forested, and rural. Pittsburgh, my actual birthplace and again my primary residence, is a city of small houses nestled on its rolling, wooded slopes. The downtown business district, its monolithic steel sentinels guarding the river valley, is the only contrast to the green hills that surround it. These hills and winding rivers continue to keep the ethnic neighborhoods within the same boundaries set more than a hundred years ago. Unavoidably corralled inside, an attitude of narrow-mindedness was perpetuated in the neighborhoods my parents came from.

We moved about in the early years, finally settling in a small town of about 5,000, Ridgway, three hours north of Pittsburgh–East Bum Fuck, as it was often referred to by our city relatives. Gone was the connection to opportunities the city offered, my relatives, and the potential to discover who I really was. The town was predominantly Catholic since many of its residents were Italian-Americans. Social events mainly centered around organized sports, church events, the fireman's carnival, hunting, and the escape to local bars and clubs that exist in ungodly numbers. Its men–mostly blue-collar men–worked in factories, lumber, or construction. The availability for viewing was never a problem. The sight of bearded, husky men in jeans, T-shirts, or flannel shirts, and work boots driving logging trucks or 4×4s was par for the course. These men were obvious descendants from a long line of healthy laboring stock, an image which today, closely describes myself.

Bears do tend to have an overall look. Generally we're furry in some respect, most often with a beard or nice stache; we tend to dress more casually. Jeans and flannel shirts, T-shirts and boots are typical after-work attire for the masculine Bear, though, during the day you'll find us sporting whatever our job requires. For me it's the business Bear attire, for my husbear, Rick, it's landscaper's garb.

I was one of two sons born to an ex-Marine, now a retired state cop, a man who could never get enough of two things–alcohol and subservience. His career choice fueled the demand for both, and then some. He was a man who could never show emotion, except to the dog, the source of my disdain for all our family pets. He was a bitter man around whom our whole being and household revolved. He issued irrational proclamations from the haze of his drunken stupor while reclining on his throne, the couch, his scepter, the all-powerful instrument of change, the remote control. My mother, the ever-loyal and devoted spouse who never had a say in any matter, dotes on the miserable fuck still. His macho image now, ironically, exists only in his mind. The repercussions of his addiction have certainly taken their toll. He has irrevocably sentenced himself and, by association, my mother to a life of loneliness, not a solitude of choice but an abandoned loneliness. Relatives endured him only for my mother's sake. As a result, gone are the family gatherings at Christmas and the faint family ties we did once have. My father did provide me with one truly important example, the image of the kind of man I didn't want to be, an example of what a life of manipulation, bigotry, and self-righteousness returns—nothing but the stark reality of an empty life. Fortunately, for my family the theory that "opposites attract" was valid.

My mother, the product of twelve years of Catholic schooling, was highly intelligent, resourceful, and flexible. Her caring demeanor, gift of gab, and girlish innocence endeared her to all. She volunteered for school events, shuttled our friends to various destinations, and, as we lived a mile from any other children, was our best friend. She was open to new ideas, her heart to even more. She was physically affectionate and never had a problem vocalizing the words, "I love you." She was an individual who derived her own satisfaction in the act of pleasing others, your success and accomplishments were hers, too. Her encouragement was lavished on whatever your fancy was at the time. She had an appreciation of my artistic and musical abilities, traits that my dad said were only for faggots. In my case, his bigoted attitude was right on the mark, though he wouldn't know "how right" for quite a few years. The trumpet was my forte, and to this day I can still blow out a pretty good tune. I finally realized the depth of my mother's devotion to us, after one of my father's tyrades. Who knows what it was about. She stood by the sink as we washed dishes crying. "I wish it would be different," she said, "I wanted it to be different but it isn't. It's the same." You could just see something terribly sad in her eyes, the realization that it truly wasn't different. But different from what? She was referring to her own father and how he had put her and her three siblings through the same kind of crap. I realized for the first time what a great effort she made for us. How Freudian that these traits of my mother are the qualities which I find so common in Bears; the desire to please, the sincerity, the ability to build a friendship on the basis of who the person really is, rather than what you want them to be.

I went to kindergarten in the Burgh but I remember very little except for the walk to school on the city streets. The next year we moved to the sticks where I was enrolled in a Catholic school. My class of about twenty-three was evenly split between boys and girls. We wore uniforms, the boys in navy pants, a standard issue clip-on tie, and light blue shirt, the girls in plaid skirts with suspenders and a light blue or yellow shirt beneath. In the regimen of Catholic school, only jackets and lunchboxes were a sign of personal individuality. I had a Road Runner lunchbox. Mom made a hit at show and tell when we had a guest appearance by my rabbit, Peter, and one of our no-name chickens.

Nuns and female lay teachers dominated the school. The only men we had contact with were the parish priests. The pastor was somewhat pretentious and set in his ways. His main job was to be late for Mass and wolf down those baked goods the parish women whipped up for church raffles. We did however have a lot of new priests sent in for training. Always wanting to make a good impression, they were all more than friendly and attentive. I became an altar boy, as was expected, and I was able to spend time with some of the priests. I grew to like the experience, not for any sexual excitement, but for the companionship, the inclusion, and the camaraderie. One priest took to my mother and, in turn, to us. He used to put his hands on my shoulders and rub them while he talked to mom. He was a caring man, not afraid to show affection through physical contact. I knew at an early age that I preferred the attention of a man. Even in first grade, I spent a good deal of time at lunch watching the men working on the school grounds. I'd wait anxiously for the school bus, occupying my time until it's arrival by watching the men at the gas station that also served as the bus stop. I'd sit in the front seat and admire the bus driver who sported a big, thick, black Fu Manchu a good several inches wide. He had nice thick masculine hands, too. I knew something was up but couldn't quite figure it out. But over the period of about four years I slowly realized the story. Believe it or not it all came together at the YMCA. Being from a small town, most of the weekend's activities took place at the Y. This was, coincidentally, where the local men had meetings, organized sports, lifted weights, shot hoops, and–most importantly–showered. I knew then that my confusing preoccupation was centered around what I specifically saw in the showers–naked men. My preference was for those who leaned toward the husky and hairy. I specifically remember going to a particular locker that had an open view of the showers, but where I couldn't easily be seen. Many a fantasy raced through my head there. I guess when I was about ten I realized there was a word for it: gay. I learned this word courtesy of *Playboy*, a magazine my father kept hidden under the couch, away from the eyes of impressionable youth. I can still remember, after verifying that my parents' car was clearly down the drive, anxiously reading the forbidden magazine for any mention of homosexuality. It distinctly told me who I was, generally what we did, and being the 1970s, that we homosexuals preferred to be called gay. Of course, every other month they did have that long-awaited coed pictorial. The rest you can probably take from there. Through my teens I realized that this subject wasn't the best thing to talk about in my house. I just kept quiet.

I had very few sexual experiences while in high school and look back at all on it as experimentation. The encounters tended to be more odd and perplexing than sexually exciting. You know the feeling. . . . you really wanted "it" bad but actually had no idea of what "it" entailed. Most of my energy was spent fitting in and not making a big deal out of what I subconsciously knew I really wanted. I did the dating thing and excelled in football. I played for a year but quit the next year to join the band. Dad wasn't happy. I went to the prom and just once, experimented with heterosexuality. For me, it was all or nothing. I guess I had to get over that, "Well, am I really gay?" thing. The answer came as a resounding "Yes." My ideas of what to do sexually were inspired by numerous shots in

Playboy. I had one hand in her panties and while she moaned, she proceeded to stick her tongue down my throat. The whole time all I could think of was how long it would be before I threw up. I could hear that little man running around in my head yelling "Fag, fag, fag!" That man has since taken up permanent residence in a masculine but fabulously decorated psyche. It was proof by trial and error. I knew right then and there that this small town, whose residents were sworn to marry young, to their cousins if necessary, was not the place for me to stay.

I really looked forward to the opportunity to be out on my own. And my chance came, in an envelope disguised as my acceptance to the University of Pittsburgh. I had $5,000 willed to me by my father's Aunt Jule so I was definitely going. What I needed now was a really good summer job. Mom came through with a job in her employer's factory, a major company that made brake linings. Back then the recipe included fiberglass, carbon, brass filings, and a bunch of other nasty things all nicely cooked in pressure ovens at unbearable temperatures. If you were the child of an office employee and not a factory worker–their children were placed in more desirable finishing jobs–you had two options. You could fill the forms, which required wearing a mask all day and being totally covered in the mixture. Or you could load the premade forms into the ovens one by one, and remove them when the ovens popped open. They were both shit jobs. If you signed up for overtime you eventually ended up doing both. Previously having little social interaction with men I now found myself in a factory with 300 of them. Wow, instant reality and a peculiar mixture of excitement and fear. I was put on a line of eight ovens, one of the worst jobs in the factory.

The first two weeks were hell. The brass filings burrowed themselves into my hands and the fiberglass itched like crazy. The forms were hard to load and even harder to pry from the molds. This was done with a bar, about twelve inches long, shaped like the letter T. It was like prying bread from a toaster with a piece of dental floss. I ended up breaking the tool. The guy in the next row said to take it down to the maintenance department where they would make me a new one. They were willing to customize it any way I wanted and it was returned within several hours lengthened by two feet and the end sharpened into something of a chisel. That day I easily made rate and then some. And since the machine had such low output, the rate paid per piece was exceptional. I ended up being one of the best-paid students that summer. The guy in the next row of furnaces wanted me to show him how to work my oven, so, on several occasions, when on overtime, he visited me and watched how I did it.

I was a prime target for various pranks. I wasn't as easily suckered as my friend Steve, who they once had running around for an hour trying to get a wheezbob for his furnace. But my turn was sure to come. My lunch always consisted of four McDonald's cheeseburgers packed frozen, thawed, and then microwaved. One day as I was washing the first few bites down with juice, I realized they were way ahead of me. A few sizable globs of Murphy's oil soap, used to lube the ovens, had found their way into my thermos. It was absolutely disgusting. I swallowed this first mouthful and pretended to take a few more gulps. I killed the taste with the last three burgers and faked another few swallows of juice. I made small talk until the break bell rang and left like nothing had happened. I did notice how intently several people were watching me and knew by the look on one face that I had the perpetrator. Later that week his snuff can was laced with cinnamon oil used to make fireball candy. He was running for the water fountain. His lips burned slightly for days. I presented him with the remaining oil the next week during lunch.

I'm still amazed that most men continue to show their affection through pranks, other forms of ribbing, or just plain harassment. It's just the "way" that most men say they like you. Some gay people are put off or take offense to this. Some of the more pretentious come off as being better than the average man, as if the world owes them some sort of special treatment, just because they're gay. The Bears aren't really like this. If you respect us for who we are and treat us fairly, that's all we ask. We fit in more easily, which allows straight people to see us as individuals as opposed to just homosexuals. Instead of throwing my homosexuality in their face, I adapt to them and wait for opportunities where I can educate them. For me this works to my advantage.

I feel it's better to let others figure out my story for themselves. People are then more accepting and supportive of who you are. I never did see the benefit of shoving the fact of my sexuality in anyone's face. I'm just like anyone else except for that "dick" thing.

If other men can adapt to me, then I can roll with their punches, too. Everyone has their own way and that's fine but when working in the world, you have to adapt. This is what I think Bears are best at.

We're very flexible and open minded. I'd like to think that Bears are the bridge between stereotypical gays and your average straight person, not that our acceptability to straights makes us better than more obvious gays. Everyone is equal. But as Bears, we are afforded a better chance to prove ourselves. We aren't prejudged based on our looks, quite the opposite. We're judged by our personality. On numerous occasions, usually during a long flight conversing with a fellow passenger, a question arises where my answer makes it clear that I'm gay. The reactions of people vary greatly but generally are very positive. You know you changed someone's perception of what a gay person is just by the look on their face. I also make it a point to help people on the road. They'll always, in some way or another, ask what they can do for me. I always say, "First, the next time you see someone on the roadside who needs help at least stop." And, "See, gay people aren't as bad as you're lead to believe. We're really quite friendly."

That summer my factory friends were easy going men, many of whom sported beards or a hefty stache and a somewhat dumb look. Like Julie Brown says in her song, I like them big and stupid. I gravitated to their personality first and then to their looks, but I will admit that I particularly liked being around the bearish ones.

That summer made me realize for the first time that I really wasn't all that different from other men and that acceptance wasn't that hard to find. I was just one of the guys, a person who, just like anyone else, needs to prove to themselves and others who they really are and what they are capable of. I realized I was someone who learned about life as they went along, just like everyone else. Well, except for that "dick" thing again . . . that was a side of me yet to explore.

I majored in Electrical Engineering and remember my mom telling me years after I graduated that when they dropped me off at the University, I didn't even look back. It was more true than she could have imagined. I could finally start to discover who I was, where I fit in, and what life had to offer this burly fag from the sticks. One of my first acts was to grow a beard. Call it an act of rebellion, the search for a "look," or mere curiosity. Whatever the reason, I wanted it, I grew it, and I still have it, being without it only once, for two weeks, in the last twelve years. As I've seen on someone's e-mail, "Razors. Just say no." In some ways I now identify with my beard. It's a part of me, a form of personal expression. Many times people stop and ask me for directions or strike up a conversation saying that I look friendly. You'd also be surprised how often bearded men check each other out. It's like some instinct. Over the years, if another bearded man isn't shy about looking too long, I'll stroke my beard, nod my head, and compliment him saying, "Nice." It inevitably gets a smile or some sign of recognition. The biker types will sometimes even strike up a conversation. I can pick a beard out anywhere, a studio audience, the grandstand at a football game, even in opposing traffic. I think that's the seventh sense Bears have. The sixth sense, gaydar, is the unique ability of one gay person to know that the other one "is" too. The seventh, for Bears, is furdar. If someone is sporting it on their face we'll spot them. In college the viewing was quite good on a campus of 20,000. Lots of Middle Eastern and Mediterranean types and some nice local men too.

The first year went fast and I lived with my dad's sister, MJ, short for Mary Janet. Her mother, Nana as she liked to be addressed, had been living with her for years. Nana took charge of the household, and my aunt had a career at AT&T. Nana always had dinner ready and the only rule in the house was to call if you weren't coming home. A house with only one rule, amazing. My aunt was always encouraging me to go and do everything I wanted. She always had my best interest at heart and wanted me to get out and take advantage of all those opportunities. She was doing this for as long as I could remember. One year she signed for a rental car, since three of us college guys had not a credit card between us. We squished ourselves into their smallest car and headed for Ocean City, each with a gym bag of clothes and very little money. My aunt's place was nice but I still needed more freedom.

By the winter semester of my sophomore year I had moved into an apartment in Shady Side with three male classmates. I remember how funny my mom's voice sounded when I called to tell her, excitedly, where I was moving. It took a while for me to realize that many of *us* lived in the neighborhood, a fact that obviously went through her head long before I figured what kind of neighborhood I had moved into. It was a neighborhood quite different from Mr. Roger's–which is filmed about a mile down the road. The area was predominantly upper middle class with a heavy mixture of artists and gays. This explained the sometimes long glances some of the people on the street gave me. You know the "look," that cruisy look that now is so easy to recognize no matter how subtle, the look that slightly extends normal allowable eye contact. One of my roommates was an obnoxious self-proclaimed playboy, Tim. Ironically it later turned out that Tim's best friend was being kept by a Pittsburgh businessman. Getting along with three totally different personalities, their friends, and their habits was another learning experience.

The first morning of winter semester found me talking to a friendly guy at the bus stop and three days later, Saturday morning at five, I was working with him at the Red Bull Inn as a prep cook. If you want a learning experience, take a job where you have to deal with the public. I started picking up overtime as a lunch waiter and coming in on weekends to do the books. They knew I was an engineering student and we geeks know our math. I started to become caught up in one of those family type circle things that form with restaurant staff. My co-workers were very sociable. They went out together, vacationed together . . . they did everything together. For me it was another lesson in making good friends and sharing in their camaraderie. And where there are restaurants, there are fags. There just seems to be a higher percentage of us in the industry. So, I got to know some other gay people, where they went, and what was happening around Pittsburgh. Another of life's educational adventures. I started tagging along when the clan went bar hopping after the restaurant closed. We even went to the occasional gay bar. We wanted to be fair and after all, we were out to have fun. What I saw in the two gay bars we visited was definitely not for me. Unappealing were the red satin walls, the pretentious attitude, and the people who lisped more about you than to you. I absolutely could not see myself in this atmosphere. Had I waited all my life for this? It was depressing. I was just beinning to feel comfortable with my homosexuality and was thinking of coming out, but if this was what gay life was like, would I really fit in? And, if I did, would I even want to? Well, nineteen years had already passed, so what would an additional delay hurt?

I met an attractive girl, Carole, while working at the restaurant. She was a tad shorter than average, with long blonde hair. She wore lots of black and was always into something mischievous. She was studying psychology and lived in a house with four other women not but one block from campus central. Shit smack in the middle of everything. Carole and I hit it off just great and when my lease expired several months later she suggested I move in with her. One of her roommates had skipped out and they needed a replacement. My mother thought I was moving into a house with four women specifically for sex. She even mustered up the nerve to ask as much one evening when she called. I told her no and she seemed content but in retrospect, I told her that she may have preferred to hear a yes instead. Back then the "G" word hadn't even been uttered.

I ended up spending a lot of my free time with Carole. She was a person who said exactly what was on her mind, in no uncertain terms, and loved to fuck a person's mind. Her sister Amy worked at a jetset nightclub where bikini-clad models danced with a snake on the balcony. Amy's boyfriend Michael was a bartender there. One night Carole and I watched the two of them fucking through the keyhole between our rooms, high on grass. The show abruptly ended when Carole burst out laughing. Funny, Amy had never really struck me as a verbal person. Live and learn. Nice dick on Mike though!

I often found myself just watching Carole. Her own excitement and exuberance were contagious. I unknowingly became an accomplice in some really weird, but funny, incidents. I also discovered food shopping at 1 a.m., buckled down at the books, and had a great time. And it was through Carole that another world opened up to me, a world where you did what you wanted without regard to anyone else's opinion. I finally got over that nasty military/Catholic mentality where everything is structured or, in some way, involves guilt. I got my first glimpse at the gray area that exists between the black and white view of good and evil. Initially, on many occasions I was utterly embarrassed by some of Carole's antics but as time progressed, I became outgoing and approachable.

Carole showed me how to be happy with myself. My life didn't have to be black and white. I saw in her a perfect example of how to enjoy being yourself. She lived her life for herself, uninhibited by the expectations of others.

One reason I like Bears is that many are comfortable with themselves just as they are, alike in their attitudes toward life while still retaining their individuality. Most don't really see themselves playing a role. There's no dress code, no specific look or attitude. I will admit that a lot of Bears tend to be levi/flannel types, but more out of comfort than looks. Unfortunately, some people are caught up in the thinking that to be a Bear you have to act this way, or look that way, you can't wear deodorant, you must have a beard. These people miss the point that a Bear is a person content with himself, leading a life he's comfortable with by himself or, if he's lucky, together with another humpy bruin. We're just happy being ourselves. For the most part we don't have expectations for fellow Bears either. I've found Bears to be the most accepting subset of gays. We really aren't impressed by where you live or what you drive, or what label is on your shirt. These things are a waste of time. We're much happier engaging in conversation, which ranges from camping to computing and, for a lot of us, food. The one statement I can make that isn't a generalization is that we love to sit down to a really good meal. Step back Julia Child, the Bears are in the kitchen. Invariably, fifteen minutes into any meal involving Bears, the trading of recipes begins!

Carole and another roommate graduated, and I moved in with a Lebanese guy who I hung around with during my last year of college. He had that stereotypical terrorist look which I find sexy. He was well built and furry. Only later did I realize that he had "plans" for me when we first met. Apparently the Lebanese aren't shy when it comes to experimenting. But nothing ever happened and we were friends above all else. I already had a good job, a place to live, and friends that were dependable. I wanted to experience for myself the intimacy others around me had.

I now drove back and forth to the restaurant in a Buick Regal purchased from Carole. She gave me a nice payment deal, a hundred dollars per month. I started noticing that an area I drove through was pretty crowded with cars late at night. I eventually figured out that it was a gay cruising area. Driving through it for months built up my nerve and curiosity. One night, omitting the torrid details, I found myself with a man, with a walrus mustache, in the passenger seat next to me. He told me about a bar on the other side of town, The Crossover. It was a butcher bar, with more blue collar types in the basement of the Buhl mansion. The bar was like a huge dungeon, rock walls, wooden rafters, quite dimly lit and somewhat clammy. I picked up a copy of our local gay rag there and my exploration began. Every bar was the same as the first two I had been in except one, The Pittsburgh Trucking Company. On Friday and Saturday nights the bar attracted people from all over the area. I soon discovered my preference in men definitely tended toward a particular type–the bearish, older masculine man. The next few years found me playing around, discovering what I liked, having a few crushes here and there, but nothing really serious. I did however make some really good friends. One in particular was Keith, a bartender at The Crossover. He was like Carole, but with a dick. He was sarcastically funny and could embellish a story like there was no tomorrow. He grinned from ear to ear while detailing his antics on his trips to DC–clips, fists, chains, whips. I can just imagine the look on my face when he was telling me his stories. It was like Gay Sex 101. By this time I had found my place and was comfortable with my homosexuality, but I still hadn't told any of my relatives.

It all came to a head when I totaled my car coming home from the bar one evening. Doing thirty-five down a hill I decided to take a nap and don't remember a thing until I awoke hours later in the emergency room with a cop requesting my signature for the results of my blood alcohol tests. The frustrations of changing my insurance, finding a new car, and the resulting disruption of my life brought another concern to light. Being closeted had been eating at me for years and it was getting worse. I needed someone to talk to and called my aunt MJ to go to dinner figuring, what could I lose? She was in her mid forties, never been married, and visited the same butch woman every weekend for years. She just had to be a lesbian. I remember the smile on her face when she heard my news. She was ecstatic. She was my favorite aunt and I, her favorite nephew, and we were both queer. Family values 1980s style. Her only warning. Don't ever tell Nana, she'll die. I knew the same would apply to Mom and Dad.

Nevertheless, things were getting easier and I found myself more relaxed. I moved into my other grandmother's house. Her son, my Uncle Rich, had been laid off for a year and decided to take a job in Harrisburg. She kept on asking me to move in, so I did. A tough German woman, extremely independent, she had worked all her life to support herself and four children. It had been a very difficult life but she never complained. She insisted on cooking, did my wash, and always minded her business. Smart and observant, within months she knew my story. She was sort of hip. I was usually in bed early and I could hear her laughing downstairs at David Letterman. I kind of spoiled her by taking her to dinner or out to the movies and I brought her flowers every week from town. For years she had lived in the same drab house, always talking about fixing it up. She received an inheritance and we started our home improvements. After fifty years she had new furniture, carpets, and plaster work. We did her small yard over with hundreds of perennials. She grinned from ear to ear sitting outside in the evenings reading her favorites; *The Globe*, *The National Enquirer*, and *The Star*. I assumed this was her antidote for reading the morning newspaper front to back. She knew everything that happened in Pittsburgh, and took a special interest in the obituaries. In Pittsburgh, we don't have grandmas we have "grandmals." My grandmal was someone who appreciated even the smallest things. She truly enjoyed people and after a few months we were living together quite easily. She expressed opinions to me that her own children never heard, a lot of them about my father. It was kind of funny to hear her make comments in her sly and subtle way. But she had a gentle disposition, and usually chose to express herself through actions rather than words. She was a somewhat private person, too.

In a way grandmal had some essential bearish qualities. Bears too can be really friendly and caring, even gregarious at times. And like Grandmal, they have a private side which they reveal a little at a time. Bears at their best are sensitive, accepting, and thoughtful. And like my grandmother, a Bear mellows with age, becoming more interesting and content with himself, accepting life for what it is.

By now I had a job with a large engineering firm that specialized in systems integration. Field assignments, mostly in Chicago, sucked, though there was the consolation of being on site with 500 steel workers. When I got really dirty I'd hit the showers with the rest of the mill hunkies. WOOF WOOF. Working in the mills and frequenting the gay areas of Chicago made me realize that I had to get out on my own. Being in a different city while coming out gave me the freedom to do what I wanted. I didn't know anyone in the entire city so instead of keeping to myself the way I did in the Burgh I pulled a Carole and socialized with everyone. Chicago was my proving ground and showed me that you could be gay and not have to hide it. When the travel assignments slowed down I spent more time in the Burgh. Now making decent money and saving faithfully, I started looking for a house that would free me from having to live with my family. Though Carole provided a great example of not caring what people thought of you, I still had problems in applying this practice to my family.

Troy Hill is an older depressed section of the city, a family neighborhood of mostly German-Americans. Definitely white trash, but the real estate was affordable and the location was good. I started looking for a house where the first floor could be rented while I fixed up the rest. I eventually found just what I wanted and I thought that my new house was the best thing that could happen to me in 1989. What I didn't know was that the best was yet to come.

Chicago had taught me one thing, you have to make things happen for yourself. Things aren't going to just land in your lap by wishing or fantasizing about them. For the last year or so I had been giving a certain DJ at The Crossover a dollar or two to play a few songs. He was older than me with a thick stocky build, a bushy Vandyke, and big muscular arms, each sporting a tattoo. On one arm a gothic griffin, which I later learned he designed himself, and on the other an eagle. He was five foot eight and weighed in at about 190. He had a wide chest, covered in the winter but quite noticeable in the summer when he wore a tank top. He said he was Polish, and his Slavic traits showed in his thick meaty hands with fingers like sausages. He was really sexy. One Tuesday night in June I got up the nerve, with the help of a few extra beers and went up to ask not for a record but for a date. Three days later, I found myself in a German restaurant eating dinner with Rick, my husbear for the last seven years. Several months later he helped me move into my new house. I always tell people that Rick taught me how to relax. Like many Bears, Rick has an easy going disposition, a classic type-B personality. He balances out those type-A traits I sometimes have. We work quite together and from him I've learned to lose that possessiveness that so many people have for their spouses. It wasn't easy but it seems to have worked out quite well for both of us. Neither of us feels trapped and we have made some really nice friends. Though five years ago I would have never even thought it possible, it's been a pleasure to be allowed to express affection to more than just one person and our relationship is strong enough to allow for this. We have many common interests, and over the years we have learned to be tolerant of the interests we don't share. I will now go to a football game with him but I still hate to watch it on television and he'll even listen to country music and watch *Star Trek* with me. He got me going to the gym, which I needed, and both of us are in the best shape we've ever been. One of the nicest things about Rick is that on cold winter nights I can feel him snuggling up to me under the flannel sheets to warm himself up. He makes a slight whispering noise and I can feel his belly swell in the small of my back. Many nights I lie on the couch, eyes closed, with my head in his lap listening to the TV as he pulls at the triangular patch of hair on my back just about at the belt line. Odd as it sounds, this is very relaxing and I sometimes fall asleep. We enjoy touching and often give each other short rubs or long massages. I've found that it is not a generalization to say that Bears are tactile creatures. Sure, some do it as a prelude to sex but for a lot of us it's just nice to feel the touch of another. A reassuring hug, the rubbing of another's belly, or a paw draped over the back of one's neck are all familiar Bear behaviors. Rick and I always say that Bears are gentlemen. A Bear is eager to interact with his surroundings and always willing to help out, not for personal gain, but just to be nice. A lot of us are rewarded with a simple gesture of gratitude and the satisfaction of knowing that we are giving in some way to another.

My mother visited me in Troy Hill one evening. Even upon her arrival she was somewhat hesitant in her demeanor and gestures. She had that same look she had when less palatable events took place when I was younger. She made small talk and asked general questions about this and that but her conversation slowly began to turn to an event that had occurred about a year earlier, a fight in a gay bar for which I was arrested. A family friend had helped me with legal advice and apparently just couldn't keep his mouth shut, although he had said he would. I knew she was going to approach a subject that wasn't going to be easy.

It must have been something in her voice, a few certain words she spoke or merely a hunch, but I knew that the G-word was about to be discussed. I felt oddly on edge seeing her so uncomfortable and decided to get it all over with once and for all. I looked at her and said, "Are you trying to ask if I'm gay?" She was obviously relieved that she wasn't the one who had to ask, and quickly answered, "Yes!" I told her, "Yes, I am." and she immediately inquired, "Are you seeing someone about it?" "You mean like a doctor?" I asked. She nodded her head in agreement to which I replied, "No!" I could sense that she was way out of her element by the look of confusion on her face, a look of relief, sorrow, and hesitation. I continued to explained that I have known, for as long as I could remember, that I was gay. It wasn't something I was ashamed of and was quite happy with my life. The reason for my silence about it was that I knew it would only bring conflict into my life. I also warned her that if she was going to pray for a cure she was wasting her time. I didn't want to be "cured." I liked who I was and being gay was part of it.

I no longer viewed being gay as a problem, a deficiency, or something about myself that I couldn't face. I had finally discovered who I was, where I fit in, and I liked it. The final deed of telling Mom, which would lead to the rest of the family knowing, was just icing on the cake. I felt relieved. I told her that I understood how the news, or should I say revelation, was most likely a disappointment to her. Obviously you never hear the ladies at bingo saying that they want their children to grow up to be big fags. But I did, and that was that. The conversation continued and after all the tears, answers, and explanations she seemed more at ease and satisfied. Ironically, my atheistic father still thinks it's a "personal choice" that I made to, in some way, spite him. Sure, sure, I chose homosexuality and the difficulties, hate, and bigotry that comes along with it, a package deal, just to be spiteful.

I was however amazed that my own mother would have been so naive about why people are gay. Especially since we know that, deep down inside, all moms "know." You think she would have paid more attention to gay topics. In retrospect, her inquiry as to whether or not I was seeing someone about it, was actually funny. Rick said I should have replied, "Yes, I'm seeing Rick." I even think that I came out in a bearish way. I've found Bears to be very nonconfrontational, more likely to take the high road in situations to avoid unnecessary conflict. However, we will proudly stand up for who we are, explain why, and try to educate anyone who is inquisitive.

I guess my perception of a Bear is always changing but still focuses on the traits that I've valued in others; from the easygoing attitude of Rick to the more gregarious traits of Carole, the nurturing side of Mom, the privacy and pride of Grandmal, and the independence of my Aunt. I'd like to think that Bears are creatures that can see the good qualities in people and learn to use them in their own life. To me a Bear isn't merely a man who has the "look." Though the look is quite pleasant, it is but a small portion of a much bigger picture, an artistic rendering that doesn't fit everyone's expectations but that each Bear paints for himself.

Chapter 5

Bearaphernalia: An Exercise in Social Definition

Robert B. Marks Ridinger

Study of the formation of social subgroupings of any sort involves examination of factors as disparate as historical context, available sources of definitive imagery from which to craft a new identity, and motivation. Such research is particularly complex within the gay and lesbian community, where questions of self-definition have been hotly debated since the beginning of the American homosexual movement in the 1950s. This article will explore the evolution and emergence of what is commonly termed "the bear movement," a phenomenon of the late 1980s which united gay men of a particular physical type,

Personal definition as a member of a specific social group may stem from factors as diverse as individual choice, commitment, or accomplishment (examples being the Veterans of Foreign Wars and the National Peace Corps Association) and ethnic or racial heritage (B'nai B'rith). Following the birth of the contemporary gay and lesbian rights movement at the Stonewall Riots in New York City in June, 1969, a new category was added, that of sexual orientation. Acknowledging one's attraction to members of the same gender, a process popularly termed "coming out of the closet," however, was only the first step in the birth of the highly diverse contemporary gay and lesbian community. Once past the initial emotional turbulence of the coming out process, the newly-awakened individual would next be presented with an array of stereotyped images, each offering a variety of expression of homosexual identity. The oldest and best known of these is that of the archetypal "screaming queens," marked by blatantly effeminate dress, mannerisms, and patterns of speech and exemplified in the closing song of San Francisco's famous Black Cat bar, "God Save Us Nelly Queens." Specializing in sharp and sarcastic verbal game playing, this image of homosexuality was the predominant one spread throughout mainstream American culture during the 1950s via the media of jokes, magazine cartoons, and literature. A notable feature of the Stonewall Riots was the high visibility of these characters and their campy interactions with the police which turned demonstration into street theater.

The advent of gay liberation created a new figure in the homosexual world, the militant who would no longer be satisfied with passive toleration by heterosexuals and made civil rights for homosexuals a matter of public discussion through aggressive protest and propaganda. Rebelling against the assimilationist tactics of the homophile activists of the 1960s, whom they derided as "Uncle Marys" and "Auntie Toms," their image was marked by long hair, beards, and the flamboyantly free styles of dress borrowed from the counterculture. Gay liberation also drew to some degree on the idea of the androgyne, beings whose bodies were neither overtly masculine nor distinctly feminine yet whose character possessed qualities of each, a concept briefly manifested in unisex fashions. Following the mellowing of rabid liberation by the early 1970s (in favor of a revival of the homophile philosophy that gays were "just like everybody else" and so entitled to the same civil rights, protections, and privileges), a new ideal emerged. Young smooth-skinned, tautly-muscled males (the very opposite of the bear) were presented as subcultural icons through such nationally distributed periodicals as the *Advocate* and innumerable pornographic books, magazines, and videos tailored to the gay market. Drawing heavily on the mythical southern California lifestyle of sun, surf, and sex, this new stereotype further expanded the menu of possible identities. In some ways, this image foreshadows a dominant icon of urban gay culture in the later 1970s. This consisted of bodies well-defined and toned by daily workouts and an almost religious obsession with physical perfection, the wearing of close-trimmed hair (extending to mustaches and beards, when present at all) and was termed "the clone," giving due notice of its widespread occurrence in many American cities. The newest model of gay masculinity appeared after 1981 with the impact of the AIDS pandemic, a rebirth of the angry activists of the early liberation days, who retained the short hair of the clone while adding the earrings of the queen along with the slogan "Silence equals death." Men whose physical type did not fit into any of the above categories were often made to feel inferior and told to strive for change through dieting, trimming their hair, and revising their philosophies to be "politically correct."

In the same period as the emergence of AIDS another social force on the American scene achieved national visibility, the "men's movement." Coeval with the women's movement of the early 1970s, when it was known as "men's liberation," it reexamined and explored the definitions of gender, essential qualities of masculinity, and paths to their achievement, development, and maintenance. Discussions of "what it means to be a man" had been ongoing in the gay male community from its very inception in some form, as witness the album *Walls to Roses: Songs of Changing Men* produced in 1979. Indeed, the very concepts of being masculine and homosexual were viewed by many as mutually exclusive, notably psychologists and counselors. The new publicity of the men's movement and its variegated approach to masculinities offered a model of definition to men within the gay community whose physical types and social and spiritual needs were not being reflected by established images such as the queen or the clone. Interest in alternative models of masculine bonding marked out a certain segment of the movement, the mythopoetic branch, symbolized by group rituals and a sense of tribal identity. Animals symbolizing masculine qualities from many cultures gained new popularity as modern totems, among them the bear.

Bears as cultural icons had been part of many cultures over the centuries. The most familiar example of this influence is seen in astronomy, with the names for two circumpolar constellations, the Big and Little Dippers. To classical civilization, they were Ursa Major, "The Great Bear" and Ursa Minor, "The Lesser Bear," while Hindu astronomy referred to the former as "the Seven Bears" from the number of its component stars. World religions and mythologies are replete with bear deities representing qualities as diverse as courage, strength, gentleness, and security. The bear as quarry required special ceremonies upon its death, extending (as in the case of the Ainu of the northern islands of Japan) to the ceremonial slaying of a bear specifically raised for that purpose. A common thread of sending a message home to the ursine spirits runs through these tales, as does the idea of bears as akin to humans, represented in stories of bears who wed and interbreed with mortals, taking on human form and only donning their pelts when leaving their lodges, as in "Bear Mother" tales of Native American folklore. Perhaps the most familiar of all ursine personalities to Americans is the plethora of small stuffed figures which are grouped under the nickname "teddy bear," a reference to a cub spared by Theodore Roosevelt on a hunting trip. By the late 1980s, expressions such as "he's as hairy as a bear" were appropriated to designate a new and distinctive social grouping.

Although presaged by a brief fad in the San Francisco gay community in 1980 of wearing small teddy bears in one's back pocket (intended to send the message "I like to cuddle") as a reaction to the seemingly ubiquitous hanky codes indicating specific sexual proclivities, the "bear movement" itself had its birth in Berkeley and San Francisco in 1987 through the intersection of three events. These were: the holding of private gatherings or "play parties" at which bear-type men could meet and socialize in a judgment-free environment, which were later institutionalized as "Bear Hugs" and, in some cities, formed the basis of "Bear Pride" events and contests; the appearance of a small magazine dedicated to an accurate portrayal of adult males complete with beer bellies, body hair and beards, called simply *BEAR*, which eventually achieved international circulation and spawned successors, *American Bear* and *Daddy Bear;* and the general identification of a disparate group of gay men with the bear as their totem animal.

Gay males choosing to call themselves bears quickly generated lively discussion of the question "what is a bear?" interpreting various aspects of their totem to fit individual natures. Qualities possessed in common were seen to be a predilection for cuddling and being cuddled, the frequent wearing of beards or mustaches (often extremely full by mainstream standards), frank rejoicing and pride in possession of body hair, a stocky or heavily built physical frame, and a willingness to explore the inclusionary possibilities of an alternate male identity. This process was hastened through the construction of such communication channels as the Bearcave BBS (a computer bulletin board) in New York City and the world-spanning BML (Bears Mailing List), first created in 1988 by Steve Dyer and Brian Gollum and later resurrected in 1994 by Henry Mensch and Roger Klorese. Its introductory message to all new members states that "this is a list devoted to the care, feeding and appreciation of ursine men . . . directed to all gay and bisexual men who are bears, arctophiles, or both." By 1995, subscribers to the list numbered some fifteen hundred worldwide, which had become known as "the cyberden," with regular posts appearing under such noms de pelt as ChubbyCub, SFGrizzly, Youngbear, NewDCCub, The Hidden Paw, and Captain Woof. A review of the board archives reveals much discussion on bear identity, with most subscribers gratified to find a group of men where their hirsute qualities were not only accepted but prized. The forum has also served to stimulate and distribute an emerging ursine literature, ranging from a series of poems on "Bear Soup" to the public joint creation in 1995 of a new species of a traditional Japanese genre, "bearku." Perhaps the most baroque affirmation of ursine being was in a poem (written as a burlesque of a well-known Gilbert and Sullivan aria) which begins "I am the very model of a merry hairy fairy bear."

The paths which lie open to the bear movement are many, leading both to reexamination of the Western definition of acceptable male sexual expressions and images and the resurrection, reclamation, and psychological reintegration of ancient images of the bear into the evolving mythos of the gay male. As initiates of a newborn male subculture only eight years of age, the bear men offer a valued voice whose depth will only grow in the coming years.

REFERENCES

Harding, Christopher (ed.). *Wingspan: Inside the Men's Movement*. New York: St. Martin's Press, 1992.

Rockwell, David. *Giving Voice to Bear: North American Indian Myth, Rituals, and Images of the Bear*. Niwot, CO: Roberts Rinehart, 1991.

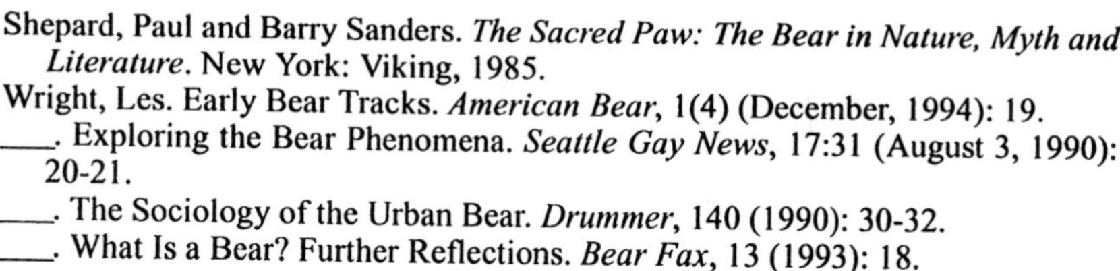

Shepard, Paul and Barry Sanders. *The Sacred Paw: The Bear in Nature, Myth and Literature*. New York: Viking, 1985.

Wright, Les. Early Bear Tracks. *American Bear*, 1(4) (December, 1994): 19.

———. Exploring the Bear Phenomena. *Seattle Gay News*, 17:31 (August 3, 1990): 20-21.

———. The Sociology of the Urban Bear. *Drummer*, 140 (1990): 30-32.

———. What Is a Bear? Further Reflections. *Bear Fax*, 13 (1993): 18.

Chapter 6

Academics as Bears: Thoughts on Middle-Class Eroticization of Workingmen's Bodies

Eric Rofes

I enter the Lone Star on a Saturday evening, wearing blue jeans, black construction boots, and a white T-shirt with "Bear America" emblazoned across the chest. On my head I wear an SF Giants cap. I am chewing gum. My stride is strong, firm–a big guy lumbering across the entryway toward the pool table. A hand reaches out of the dark to tug at my shoulder. I turn abruptly to find Paul greeting me. Paul is wearing a black leather jacket, plaid flannel shirt, blue jeans, black engineer boots. He has a Harley cap pulled over his brown crew-cut.

Paul introduces me to a few friends who are standing in an awkward circle–as bearish guys tend to do–chugging beer from bottles. All of us are bearded and wearing caps (in addition to my SF Giants and Paul's Harley cap, others represent the 49ers, Oakland As, a construction company, and a chainsaw manufacturing firm). All of us wear boots and all the boots are black. Each of us is wearing jeans–some blue, some black, one grey–and most of the jeans are Levi's 501s. One man wears a thermal underwear shirt, two appear to be wearing flannel shirts, and the rest T-shirts. Several men have thick cigars sticking out of the pocket of their leather jackets; two are carrying their motorcycle helmets; one is chomping on chewing tobacco.

My mind suddenly switches to another channel. I am not familiar with each of these men's autobiographies, but I know four of the men pretty well. One man's father was a classmate of my dad's at Harvard. Another is a self-employed computer technotrainer. The fourth works as an aerospace engineer and another is an attorney. I teach college. Most of the men earn an annual salary of over $50,000, some considerably higher. One was raised on New York's Upper East Side and attended prep schools. Most of us were raised in middle-class and upscale suburbs of major metropolitan centers; Larchmont, New York; Princeton, New Jersey; Evanston, Illinois; West Hartford, Connecticut. All of us graduated from college; several have advanced degrees.

I know that the burgeoning spaces designated "Bear" bars, parties, sex club nights, social groups, conventions, and campouts are populated in part by men who were raised under different economic and cultural conditions from my own. One man raised poor in rural Texas, told me the Bear scene offered the only gay spaces in which he'd felt comfortable and accepted without formal education, "proper" manners, and trim beard and body. Another friend, raised in a Midwest trailer park, initially embraced the proliferation of Bear venues and expressed gratitude for an alternative to what had become, in his eyes, a gay male culture saturated with $150-a-plate tuxedo fundraising dinners and leather-chic parties in upscale penthouses thrown by lawyers and physicians playing "dress-up" for the evening. After a few years, however, this man withdrew from the Bear scene, disillusioned and disappointed. He told me he'd found it no different than the leather scene–dominated by upper-middle-class men "slumming" for the evening, before returning to the safety and privilege of silver-spoon lives.

I observe the participation of middle-class, upper-middle-class, and upper-class men in the rapidly expanding and diversifying subcultures of Bears with great interest. How have we come to comprise a large portion of a community whose symbols, rituals, references, and collective culture appear rooted in working-class, white trash, and lower-middle-class populations? What does it mean that we wear grease monkey suits, sleeveless sweatshirts, combat fatigues, thermal underwear, or football jerseys? How have specific artifacts and symbols of white working-class masculinities become a part of the collective landscape of middle-class bears' imaginations?

What has led me–a white, Jewish, Harvard graduate, and college instructor–to incorporate gimme caps and shitkickers in my leisure-time apparel? How does my own confused class background–as well as the confusions and heightened anxieties of many white men of the middle class during this period of intensifying economic stratification–inform my contemporary appropriation of working-class cultures?

What does it mean that key cultural references that have become signifiers of white, working-class men, appear prominently in the everyday social practices and erotic fantasies of men like me? When did I acquire and sexualize a range of gestures, preferences, and activities which appear in the social worlds I have inhabited only as representations of "low-class" behavior? How did country music become my entertainment-of-choice? Why has a man who spits become sexy to me?

Pierre Bourdieu, the French social theorist, discusses "the hidden persuasion of an implicit pedagogy which can instill a whole cosmology . . . and inscribe the most fundamental principles of the arbitrary content of a culture in seemingly innocuous details of bearing or physical and verbal manners."[1] Bourdieu understands the human body and its movements, not as "natural" or genetic, but as constituted through a complex matrix of social and cultural forces:

> Bodily hexis is political mythology realized, turned into a permanent disposition, a durable way of standing, speaking, walking, and thereby of feeling and thinking . . . The manly man who goes straight to his target, without detours, is also a man who refuses twisted and devious looks, words, gestures and blows. He stands up straight and looks straight into the face of the person he approaches or wishes to welcome.[2]

Where did I acquire the language, diction, guttural sounds, and deep tones to sound like an auto mechanic rather than a university teacher? When I "put on" the voice of Bourdieu's "manly man," am I assuming an authentic working-class role or am I only able to perform middle-class representations of working-class men? Why do I feel more comfortable in the clothes of workingmen than in a suit and tie?

Are middle-class Bears imposters, theatrically assuming the costumes and body hexis of working-class men? How do Bears who were raised poor or working class differ from middle-class Bears? Do they look different from me or act differently? Is a contemporary American culture of yuppies in country-western wear, white adolescents in modified gangsta-rap gear, and queer academics and computer technocrats in workingmen's clothing simply sublimating (or exacerbating?) class warfare through masquerade? And what kinds of symbolic violence are visited upon authentically poor and working class men through these attempts at impersonation and ventriloquism?

CLASS, SILENCES, AND URSINE REPRESENTATIONS

The pages of *BEAR* magazine and other discursive materials focused on Bearish men have been filled with editorial commentary and letters to the editor debating questions related to Bear identity, definition, and representation. Key points of controversy have fallen into three broad categories: (1) *Questions of core identity:* Is a Bear defined through appearance or spirit? (2) *Issues of definition:* Must all Bears have a beard? Body hair? Hefty body weight? and (3) *Representational Matters:* Do Bear texts (magazines, newsletters, flyers, social events, sex parties) conflate Bears with chubs? Is the Girth and Mirth crowd a subset of Bears? How do we fit men without facial or body hair into the "Bear community?"

While discussion of weight, hairiness, and size continues to cycle through these publications, thoughtful interrogation of class is almost entirely absent from the pages of Bear discourse. Despite the fact that the commodities of Bear culture–diverse magazines, videos, posters, and T-shirts which have been mass produced over the past decade–consistently valorize images of working-class men, few have examined the meanings and politics of such representations. Porn stories focus upon truckers, gas station attendants, and hick farmers rather than the computer programmers, Silicon Valley executives, and biotech librarians who one-handedly thumb through their pages.

It is not unusual for class and fundamental economic divisions to go unrecognized and unexamined. While a language discussing race and gender has been forced on commentators on American popular culture over the past three decades, issues related to social class and the stratification accompanying late twentieth-century capitalism have been overlooked, avoided, and trivialized. A range of emotions and intense anxieties have attached themselves to questions of money, economic origins, social trajectories, and class mobility, particularly among the middle class. It is not uncommon for friends and lovers to have never discussed one another's class backgrounds and to harbor a range of class-based assumptions about everyday life which go unexamined. In the mindless meritocratic mentality of the Reagan-Bush-Gingrich years, all are made to feel responsible for our class positions and encouraged to deny the existence of powerful structures accompanying capitalism which continuously replicate and deepen class divisions.

Despite body hair, beards, and girth, it somehow has been easy to misrecognize the foundations of Bear discourse and ignore their deep roots in class divisions. A recent issue of *American Bear* features photo spreads which illustrate the eroticization of working-class men. One features Al from Indiana, first posed shaving, then on the toilet in a "Just Do It–USA" cap, and finally naked in the tub. Another focuses on Kevin from Dallas, in cowboy hat, plaid flannel shirt, and torn jeans posed amid bondage ropes in a barn. Amid the "contact file" advertisements and snapshots in the back of the magazine, most men shown wear some kind of hat or cap: Dallas Cowboys, cowboy, hard hat, Confederate, motorcycle, baseball. One photo strikes the eye as oddly out of place: not only is the handsome, bearded man wearing a suit and tie, but the man is also black.[3]

On the rare occasions in which issues of social class are discussed within the "Bear public sphere," a few observations, assumptions, and judgments circulate which may provide clues leading to deeper discussion and insights. Some insist that Bear sites are populated entirely by middle-class men playing dress-up as working-class men; the Bear subculture simply fetishizes signs and symbols of lower-class white masculinities. Others argue that Bear culture is one of the few queer spaces–along with the leather scene and motorcycle clubs–constituted in large part by working-class men. The magazines, gatherings, bars, and social groups supposedly reflect the cultural capital of white working-class and lower-middle-class men–their values, processes, and understandings. Amid a national urban gay scene overrun by West Hollywood pretty boys–smooth, muscled, blond, and (not incidentally) middle class–the emergence of Bear culture is said to provide a blue-collar oasis amid a desert of upscale gyms, RSVP cruises, and "Tzabaco" as *Shocking Grey* has closed catalogues.

There is a dearth of research–quantitative and qualitative–on homosexual men in America. This makes it impossible to confirm, refute, or flush out the fine points of any of these informal theories about social class and Bears. The field is ripe for rich, ethnographic research into Bear subcultures which seeks to trace what is likely to be a complex web of class issues threaded through sites as disparate as local Bear social groups, photographic and illustrative representations of Bears in magazines, and the sexual activities shared by Bears in couple and group encounters.

THE SUBTEXT OF EROTIC CLASS WARFARE

The April/May 1995 issue of *American Bear* offers two pieces of jerk-off fiction with a clear and articulate subtext involving class among Bears. Richard Brazwell's "Son of Dust," provides a beautifully crafted example of a mobile, urban, middle-class white man–in this case a technician from Maryland who overhauls specialized medical equipment–lusting after a rodeo rider who drives a pick-up truck and lives in a small trailer. In the story, the technician's desires are stirred as he surveys the rodeo rider's body after a post-rodeo shower. He recalls:

> Something intense and barely subdued played under [the rodeo rider's] flesh, rippling and hard. His muscles flexed and contracted as he reached for and then put on his jeans. Catching only a glimpse of a thick, yet flaccid cock, I observed his wide, primitive back and thought about being over such an expanse of pure power–and gave some thought to being under it as well.[4]

Do middle-class men invest working-class men's bodies with a range of symbolic meanings emerging out of the class-based contradictions of white, middle-class masculinity? When we see the other as "intense and barely subdued," what fears lurk in the recesses of our minds? How does a wide back become seen as "primitive" and what makes us classify a man's odor as "primitive and raw, man and dust" (p. 20)? How do our yearnings to be "over" or "under" working-class men become the embodiment of imagined working-class threat or middle-class guilt?

Zeke, the rodeo rider, grew up in a small Nevada desert town and describes the construction work which supports his rodeo life as "Sweaty, honest kinda jobs" (p. 20). We're told he has a "full, hearty laugh" and his crotch harbors "the scent of a man." The middle-class man is positioned to service the rodeo rider, and sucks him off in a half-hour of cross-class adoration. The initial encounter finishes with the technician explaining:

> I was strangely content even though I hadn't had an orgasm. With a man like Zeke, I guess just the act of bringing him off was a satisfaction. We drove back to his trailor [sic] while talking about our jobs. Zeke was as intrigued with my line of work as I was with his, though you won't find many novels where being a medical equipment specialist is romanticized. (p. 21)

Things "even out" back at Zeke's trailer, where the technician discovers Zeke to be "a very active bottom," and fucks the man roughly. He confesses, "I'd never gotten so into fucking someone. For a while I became a thing whose sole purpose was to fuck." What kind of power dynamics are inscribed on this sex act and how do class and rural/urban differences between the men inform the encounter? While it is dangerous to simplistically reduce sexual fantasies and root them in social structures, the erotic frame for this story is clearly constructed upon middle-class men's fetishization of workingmen's bodies and the complex power dynamics which operate between men across class lines.

Bill Blodgett's "The Auction," the other piece of fiction in this issue of the magazine, is invested with similar subtexts. The story focuses upon what appears to be a middle-class urban gay man's sexual connection with a rural man who is part of an Amish-type sect living a simple and humble life. The men happen upon one another at an estate sale in the country, which provides an ideal setting for the mixture of classes:

> There was a good mix for people-watching, everyone from farmers to city folks dressed in their chic summer sportswear looking like they stopped off on their way to a tennis match. The men and boys of one of those religious sects that makes you dress like you were living in the nineteenth century were there . . . . They were all wearing homemade flap-front denim trousers, tan work shirts with the sleeves rolled up, and black suspenders. The boys wore felt caps and the men wore modest straw hats and long bushy beards without mustaches.[5]

Class differences and tensions appear frequently within the text. The middle-class urban protagonist comments upon the phony "maitre d' smiles" of the women hosting the auction, and describes the shift in tone at an auction when "the city folks showed they had money" (p. 33). He hooks up with the rural religious sect Bear when he's looking for a place to pee but is nervous about wandering behind the barn because he can't recognize poison ivy. Hence rural man serves as guide to city man, leads him behind the barn, they pee together and start playing around in a friendly Bear-like way.

The urban protagonist romanticizes the poorer rural man as he catches his first glimpse of the man's foreskin:

> I marveled that God should pick a man born to be so unadorned in his life, and give him a penis fancier and more attractive than any budding rose I'd ever seen . . . I felt a rush I can't quite describe. We seemed to find some bond in sharing something that all men do, regardless of their backgrounds. The intimacy excited me. (p. 34)

The erotic success of this story is grounded in the eroticization of class difference, as the urban, gay-identified protagonist sucks off the simple, kind, country bumpkin with the "big, calloused" hands. While distinct from the more typical vision of white masculinities embedded in working-class/middle-class sexual linkages depicted in

"Son of Dust," Blodgett's story again serves as a site for middle-class gay-identified men's service of rural and working-class men's dicks.

BEARS, IDEOLOGY, AND THE URGE FOR REUNIFICATION

In an essay exploring stereotypes of "white trash," Matt Wray explains that in order to understand why stereotypes of white trash are highly sexual, "we need to understand how lower class bodies in general get constructed in the social formation and the class imaginary."[6] Wray writes:

> [i]n the class imaginary, manual labor is deeply connected with and assigned to lower-class bodies, those bodies and the labor they perform are deeply devalued. In extreme cases, that is, in the case of white trash, they become objects of middle-class disgust. I would suggest that all that attaches to or emanates from these bodies is also degraded or, at least, made suspect, by this general devaluation of manual labor and the bodies that perform it. And any cursory reading of popular representations of lower-class whites suggests that the middle classes seem obsessed with what lower-class whites do or threaten to do with their sexual bodies. These bodies, marked as they are by poverty and economic oppression, are at once unsettling and fascinating.[7]

I believe the heightened eroticization of workingmen's bodies and sexuality evident in burgeoning middle-class participation in Bear culture has similar roots. Wray maintains that "in the ideological realm of the class Imaginary, certain economic relations are transcoded as sexual relations, in order to repress the fact of class exploitation." I suggest that middle-class gay white men, who share not only the contemporary middle class's deep anxiety about maintaining economic security and class status, but additional fears based on discrimination on the basis of sexual identity and HIV status, may be drawn to Bear spaces and texts as sites for a reaffirmation of class privilege (and race privilege) through the apparent discovery of "comfort" and erotic fulfillment in the celebration of white working-class masculinities.

In *Picturing the Beast: Animals, Identity and Representation*, Steve Baker poses the question, "How are we to account for the pleasure genuinely taken in representations of animals, and for people's readiness to identify themselves with and through such images?"[8] He asserts:

> the sign of the animal typically operates in the unwritten system of common-sense consciousness, of common knowledge, of stereotypes, where meanings are assumed to be self-evident. Much as with a linguistic sign, where a majority of language-users may know nothing of its etymology, its meaning will nevertheless be known to them in the sense of their knowing when and how to use it, and they will do so quite "naturally" and unthinkingly. Similarly, in the context of its everyday use, there is no need to dwell on the sense of an animal sign–it is part of common sense, part of what everyone already knows, part of everyday reality. (p. 171)

The bear has long served as this kind of animal sign. One writer refers to "the primitive identification of the bear with male sexuality," and cites Winnie-the-Pooh and Christopher Robin as a sign of "a homosexual phase, usually relatively brief, in the life of a child."[9] She traces the medieval use of the bear as "a symbol of evil," and its later association with "impure love." The author credits the Swedish mystic St. Bridget, as claiming the bear "represented both the lusts of the flesh and greed of worldly goods." The bear is further linked to craft and violence, brute force, anger, greediness, and gluttony.[10]

In *The Sacred Paw: The Bear in Nature, Myth, and Literature*, Paul Shepard and Barry Sanders write:

> The bear strikes a chord in us of fear and caution, curiosity and fascination. In self-absorption we may fool ourselves, forgetting his otherness, and feed him in a national park as if he were a pet dog. Perhaps the impulse is the same, whether we invite the bear to share our food or our folklore: the urge to be reunited with something lost and treasured, seen in the animal that most resembles us. It is almost as though in him we can see how great is our loss of contact with ourselves.[11]

Middle-class Bears like myself might ask ourselves some difficult questions when we become drag queens in our performances as working-class men. Do we turn to the bear to reclaim vestiges of ourselves long lost or forgotten? Or do we use Bear culture as a way to transcode highly charged ramifications of economic privilege onto sexual desire? Is our preference for Bear images, and Bear men, a simple fetish or "taste" in men or is it inscribed with deeply embedded cultural cues about class, race, and gender? When I put on my Harley cap and walk into the Lone Star, exactly who am I and what am I doing there?

NOTES

1. Pierre Bourdieu, *The Logic of Practice*. Trans. Richard Nice. Stanford, CA: Stanford University Press, 1990, p. 69.
2. Ibid., p. 69.
3. *American Bear*, 1(6) (April/May 1995).
4. Richard Brazwell, Son of Dust. *American Bear*, 1(6) (April/May 1995), p. 19.
5. Bill Blodgett, The Auction. *American Bear* 1(6) (April/May 1995), p. 32.
6. Matt Wray, Unsettling Sexualities and White Trash Bodies. Presented at White Trash: Reading Poor Whites, sponsored by the American Studies Working Group at University of California at Berkeley. October 10, 1994.
7. Wray, p. 1.
8. Steve Baker. *Picturing the Beast: Animals, Identity and Representation*. Manchester: Manchester University Press, 1993, p. 121.
9. Beryl Rowland. *Animals with Human Faces: A Guide to Animal Symbolism*. Knoxville: University of Tennessee Press, 1973, p. ix.
10. Rowland, p. 33.
11. Paul Shepard and Barry Sanders. *The Sacred Paw–The Bear in Nature, Myth and Literature*. New York: Viking, 1985, p. xii.

SECTION II: BEAR IMAGES

Chapter 7

Male Images in the Gay Mass Media and Bear-Oriented Magazines: Analysis and Contrast

Philip Locke

INTRODUCTION

In our society we are daily bombarded with images from the mass media. The average American watches hours of television daily, every hour of which is filled with images–both within the programs and in the advertisements which sponsor them. Magazines are filled with advertising images and billboards stare down at us from roadsides and urban buildings, showing us more images. Images appear to us in books, newspapers, catalogs, and junk mail. Our brains process many thousands of images daily. Many times we skim over or glance past these images, scarcely noticing them. If that is the case, do these images really have an effect on us, or are they merely scenery fading into the background of our daily activities?

In examining the body of research into mass communications, one is led to believe that media images are more than just glossy wallpaper. Much time and energy has been spent researching the effect that these images have on the viewing public. Some scholars believe that this constant image bombardment can have serious consequences for those exposed to it.

A wide range of possible effects has been attributed to mass media images. Researchers have posited links between television images of violence and real-life violence, between sexually explicit magazine and movie images and violence toward women, and between television portrayals of urban life and a distorted perception of crime rates and personal safety.

There is also a sizable body of research which examines the effect that the portrayal of body images in the mass media has on consumers who view them. The media in our society tend to present an idealized, iconized standard of personal beauty, with little room for those who fall outside this subjective norm. Advertising has been targeted as the worst "offender" in this area, but these beauty standards reach to all areas of the media.

Most of the research on body images in the mass media has focused on the effects that images of the female body in advertising have on women (e.g., Thomas, 1989; Silverstein et al., 1986). Scholars have proposed connections between these idealized images and cases of bulimia, anorexia, low self-esteem, and distorted body image in women. But it is not just women's bodies that are presented in mass media images. Men's bodies are increasingly prevalent, from Calvin Klein ads to the soft-core homoporn of *International Male* catalogs and men's exercise magazines. Just as with images of women, male forms in media images fit within a narrowly defined spectrum of "desirable" male beauty.

When our society looks to the mass media, it sees a distorted view of what a male body should look like. Rather than celebrating the diversity of male body types, the media imply that the range of acceptable types is very limited, and that those who do not fit into this range are less attractive, less sexy, less *worthy* as a result. In our society, which places so much emphasis on personal appearance that dieting, hair replacement, hair coloring, and plastic surgery have become major industries, the effect of falling outside of the acceptable categories of beauty portrayed by the deluge of images in the media can be profound.

The problem is compounded for gay men, who are already marginalized by society as a result of their sexual orientation. For gay men, the obvious solution to feelings of marginalization caused by lack of gay images in the mainstream "straight" media would be to turn to the gay mass media for support and validation. There is not a lot in the way of specifically gay-oriented television, but there is a variety of magazines, including both erotic and nonerotic publications, as well as videos and films. But an examination of male images presented in gay mass media reveals that they do no better than their straight counterparts at presenting an accepting view of male body types that fall outside of a particular standard of beauty. As this is the case, the only solution for marginalized men may be to create their own media to hold a flattering mirror up to themselves and portray themselves as worthwhile and desirable.

The Bear subculture within the gay community has done exactly that. The rise of Bear media (primarily in the form of Bear-oriented magazines, but also videotapes, calendars and greeting cards) has provided Bears with their own media outlets which celebrate Bears' alternate take on acceptable masculine body images.

This chapter begins by looking at the current state of male body images in the mass media, with a focus on magazines aimed at gay men. It will become evident that the range of male body types presented as acceptable and desirable is very limited. The effects of the marginalization of men falling outside these types will be examined in the next sections.

Following this will be a discussion of the rise of Bear media as a voice for men who do not fit the mass media's idealized vision of masculine beauty, and have therefore become an overlooked minority within gay culture. After this, the results of a content analysis of the images presented in Bear-oriented magazines (*BEAR, American Bear; Daddybear*) will be described. This will include a discussion of the common image features which are presented to readers in photo layouts and advertisements.

Additionally, a content analysis of personal ad photographs in these magazines will be included, with the goal of comparing the images which are presented to readers by magazine publishers with the images of themselves that readers have chosen to present.

When a group such as Bears takes control and creates their own media, the question then becomes, "What of the images in these Bear magazines?" If we accept that these magazines arose because of the power and effects of the stereotyped images in more mainstream publications, what effect will these nontraditional images have on their viewers? Will new Bear stereotypes arise and alienate subgroups within the Bear subgroup? This chapter will examine the possibility that Bear magazines can end up being just as damaging to readers' self-esteem and self-images as the "twinkie" (non-Bear) publications.

Finally, the chapter will conclude with a discussion of the facts presented throughout and an examination of areas for potential future research.

MALE BODY IMAGERY IN THE MASS MEDIA

Monica: "Here's a picture of [an old boyfriend] naked."
Rachel: (looking at picture) "He's wearing a sweater."
Monica: "No, he's not."
Rachel and Phoebe: "Ewwwwww . . ."

The above dialogue from NBC's popular television series *Friends*, demonstrates the typical attitude regarding extremely hirsute men presented by the mass media. Body hair is almost always presented as a negative physical attribute. Any time a hairy back is mentioned, whether it be in a Nike commercial from a few years ago, an episode of *The Simpsons* where Homer is worried about growing more back hair, or a sitcom like *Friends*, it is typically used as an example of the worst possible physical feature a man could have. Chest hair, while less commonly derided, is sometimes seen as a negative attribute. In one example, a recent NordicFlex Gold television ad celebrates the transition from an average-proportioned furry torso to a sleek, smooth, and hairless one. The ad clearly suggests a better-looking body is one that is trimmer, more muscular, and hairless.

It is not just television that expresses such narrow views of acceptable male bodies. All of the visual mass media present us with a restricted range of male body images. When alternative body types are included, they are most often presented as "flawed" bodies which can be corrected through diet, exercise, or surgery. People who do not fit into the "slim and trim" mold advocated by the media are usually depicted as bumbling characters of less-than-stellar intelligence who are most often used for comic relief, either through their own actions, or by providing a "butt" for the jokes of others (Moog, 1990, pp. 202-203). Gay men, when they appear on television, are typically portrayed or described as "neat and thin," as on *Seinfeld*, which used this stereotype as a focus for an entire episode.

It is not just alternative body types which are ridiculed by or excluded from media images because they are large or well-furred. Facial hair, particularly beards, are a rare sight in the media. When bearded characters show up in movies, they are most often terrorists, villains, or some other type of "bad guy" (e.g., *True Lies*, *Something Wicked This Way Comes*, or any number of films with bad guy bikers, criminals, etc.). With very rare exceptions (*Four Weddings and a Funeral*, and some "period" films), the concept of presenting positive gay characters with beards seems to have never crossed the minds of mainstream Hollywood producers and casting directors.

On television, beards are also a scarce commodity. There are exceptions, of course–Bear icon Al on *Home Improvement*, James Brolin on *Hotel*–but they are distressingly rare, and beards are rarely seen as sexy and desirable. Look at the number of jokes clean-shaven lead character Tim makes about Al's facial fur on *Home Improvement*.

Normally clean-shaven characters do occasionally appear with beards on television series. Unfortunately, though, this seems to have evolved into some sort of "shorthand" for aiding plot and character development. When a character suddenly starts growing a beard, this is a signal to the viewers that he is going through some sort of serious conflict or turmoil. Whatever this trouble is, it is apparently serious enough that the character is no longer able to be responsible for his own basic hygienic needs, like shaving. The beard indicates the character is going through a "dark night of the soul."

A good example of this was the dark-edged detective series of the late 1980s, *Wiseguy*. At the beginning of the second season, Ken Wahl's normally clean-shaven character, Vinnie, suffered a series of personal crises. During this time he let both his hair and beard grow, until he became quite Bearish-looking (Roush, 1988). By the end of the episode, however, Vinnie had conquered his personal demons. This is revealed to us in a long tracking shot at the close of the episode which ends with Vinnie standing, clean-shaven once again, at his brother's funeral. This is a signal to the audience that Vinnie is once again in control of his life.

A more recent example comes from the January 14, 1996 episode of the CBS series *Cybill*, which included a recurring story line focusing on the character of Ira Woodbine, a professional writer. Earlier in the series, he encountered a serious case of writer's block and went into a prolonged depression. Among other things, this depression resulted in Ira throwing his laptop computer into a canyon and growing a beard, which he kept while the story line continued. The continuing appearance of the beard was a signal to the audience that Ira was still suffering from a debilitating depression.

In the January episode, Ira managed to overcome the writing block, thus ending his "dark night of the soul." Once the block was conquered, Ira shaved off his beard and told the other characters, "I'm shedding all vestiges of darkness and moving into the light." Once again, the beard was a sign of darkness and personal crisis, and its removal let the audience know that Ira had overcome his difficulties.

Beards have even been derided in advertising for children's toys. A recent television advertisement promotes a doll called Shaving Fun Ken, which is part of the Barbie line of dolls. While a voice-over urges youngsters to "shave him really clean," a young doll-owner removes the "beard" with which Ken begins the ad. It is only after the beard is gone that Barbie wants to touch him. Now Ken not only represents a slim, tan, toned, idealized male body, but he also promotes a completely clean-shaven look and presents facial hair as something to be gotten rid of.

A CONTENT ANALYSIS OF GAY MASS MEDIA IMAGES

The above examples from television and movies primarily represent images of straight characters and straight actors. What do gay men see when they turn to gay-oriented mass media? To answer this question, this chapter presents the results of a content analysis of male images presented in gay-oriented mass media magazines.

The focus of this content analysis is on the most widely read and available gay publications, since these reach the most gay men.

Magazines were chosen as the media focus for this analysis because they are the most common specifically gay-oriented mass media sources. As mentioned previously, gay-specific television is limited to occasional special programs, and gay-themed films are relatively few in number and are not often shown outside of the major urban centers. Gay erotic videos represent another possible area for research, but are not included in this particular study.

Other than photo essays, gay-targeted books typically do not contain many, if any, images which could be analyzed. Those which do contain images typically support the same beauty standards as other media. *The Joy of Gay Sex*, which is discussed later, contains many line drawings of gay men. *Why Gay Guys Are a Girl's Best Friend* (Rausch and Fessler, 1995) lists reasons why gay men and straight women get along, and one of the book's chosen reasons is that "Gay guys will say the world would be a far better place if everyone were given a makeover."[1] Accompanying drawings show a male and female character before and after a makeover. The makeover of the male character includes removing all traces of facial hair.

Both nonerotic magazines (hereafter referred to as lifestyle magazines) and erotic magazines are considered in this analysis. Among the lifestyle magazines, the greatest attention was paid to images portrayed in the *Advocate*, which is probably the most widely available gay publication. Multiple issues of the *Advocate* were surveyed to provide a greater amount of data. In addition, issues of *Out*, *Genre,* and *10 Percent* were included in the study. Erotic magazines surveyed include *Inches*, *Torso*, *Honcho*, *Advocate Men*, *Mandate*, and *Playguy*, since they are among the most widely available titles in the genre, as well as being some of the longest running. The goal in choosing both the lifestyle and erotic titles was to select those which would be accessible to the greatest number of gay men, and whose images would therefore have the greatest possibility of affecting gay men.

The focus in the analysis of lifestyle magazines is primarily on those images contained in the advertising in the magazines. The images in advertisements are specifically selected because they match some criteria set by the advertiser, advertising agency, or photographer. Therefore it is these images which would most likely reflect preconceived notions of male beauty. Images in fashion or beauty layouts were also included since they are also presumably chosen to reflect notions of male beauty. Other images of men in the magazines were included in the analysis if it was clear from the context that the men were gay. Thus, photos of Jesse Helms and Robert Dornan were not included, but photos of gay celebrities were included on the grounds that they assist in presenting an image of what gay men look like. The analysis of the erotic magazines included images in advertisements, photo spreads, and articles, since they are almost all related to the idealization of a particular standard of male beauty.

The analyzed sample for the lifestyle magazines consisted of the eight most recent issues of the *Advocate* (issues 674 to 681) at the time of the survey, along with the most current available issue of *Out* (May, 1995), *10 Percent* (vol. 3, issue 13), and *Genre* (No. 27) at the time when that portion of the survey was completed. The sample of erotic magazines consisted of the most recent available issue at the time of the survey of *Mandate* (vol. 19, no. 7), *Torso* (vol. 12, no. 12), *Inches* (vol. 9, no. 12), *Honcho* (vol. 18, no. 7), *Advocate Men* (July, 1995), and *Playguy* (vol. 19, no. 7).

Images in these magazines were examined and classified according to a preset list of criteria. All images containing men's faces and/or bodies were included, as long as the images were large enough and clear enough to be easily classified. Drawings were included if they were clear and life like, under the assumption that life-like drawings are effectively the same as photos in representing a particular type of male form. As with photos accompanying articles, images in advertisements for music albums, movies, political candidates or professional services are included only if context makes it clear that the subject is gay.

For each magazine which was considered, each male image within the photographs was classified according to the criteria in the tables below. Obviously, criteria applying to faces were only used for ads where faces were visible, and criteria applying to bodies were only used for ads where bodies were visible.

During this analysis, models who appeared in more than one photograph in a photo spread were counted once for each appearance. Each photo contributes to the glut of images presented by the magazine, and has the effect of reinforcing the standard of male beauty (positive or negative) which that model represents. Some of the included categories are subjective judgments. In order to keep the statistics accurate and representative, every effort was made to remain consistent when assigning photos to particular categories. Additionally, in order to prevent bias in favor of the researcher's hypotheses, when there was a close call between assigning a photo to one of two categories, the benefit of the doubt went to the category which does *not* support the hypotheses. Thus, the results present the lowest possible level of bias in selection of male images, and the actual level is probably higher.

In terms of specific category definitions, the facial hair classifications include beards, moustaches, clean-shaven and "other," which includes goatees, Vandykes, and other variants. The "Men w/facial fur" column is the sum of the three facial fur columns. "Slimmer" and "heavier" bodies refer to those which were considered to be below or above a subjective range of "normality." Torsos were classified as being either furry or smooth, based on the amount of body hair present on the chest and abdomen. Everything except for very minimal dustings of fur was classified as "furry." "Bald/balding" refers to head hair and "Gray/graying" refers to head and/or facial hair. The results of the analysis of the lifestyle magazines are presented in Table 7.1.

As is evident from these results, there is clearly a bias in the ads in gay lifestyle publications toward an image of men who are younger, clean-cut, smooth-skinned, and slim. If anything, the numbers in Table 7.1 probably underrepresent this fact. Although there are not a lot of men classified as "slimmer," almost all of the men whose bodies show up in these magazines are on the slimmer side of average and would definitely be classified as "trim" and/or "toned" and/or "muscular." There is a dearth of alternative body types. Heavier-than-average men almost never appear in photos. Beards appear infrequently in ads or photo layouts, and these bearded images are outnumbered in some issues by photos of bearded terrorists or bearded antigay congressmen. Images of gay men who are balding or graying are confined almost exclusively to those accompanying stories of aging gay celebrities.

TABLE 7.1. Content Analysis of Male Images in Gay Lifestyle Magazines

Content Analysis of Lifestyle Magazines							
Issue	Clean-shaven men	Men w/ facial fur	Beard	Mustache	Other	Smooth torsos	Furry torsos
Advocate 674	34	5	4	1	0	22	0
Advocate 675	36	8	1	3	4	22	0
Advocate 676	33	3	2	1	0	9	2
Advocate 677	40	8	2	5	1	19	1
Advocate 678	41	3	1	2	0	10	0
Advocate 679	30	6	1	5	0	22	0
Advocate 680	41	12	5	4	3	9	0
Advocate 681	41	6	2	3	1	24	3
Out	62	5	2	2	1	28	0
10 Percent	19	7	0	0	7	4	0
Genre	62	4	3	1	0	27	2

TABLE 7.1 *(continued)*

Issue	Slimmer bodies	Heavier bodies	Gray/graying hair	Bald/balding
Advocate 674	11	0	1	1
Advocate 675	6	0	0	1
Advocate 676	4	1	2	0
Advocate 677	6	0	0	0
Advocate 678	7	0	0	0
Advocate 679	8	0	1	0
Advocate 680	5	0	6	1
Advocate 681	7	1	9	9
Out	11	0	1	0
10 Percent	1	0	0	0
Genre	10	0	0	0

It is not just the raw numbers in the Table 7.1 which should be of concern–there is also the context in which the photos appear. For example, furry bodies are not always presented in a positive way. In *Advocate* #681, the one image of a husky body (and two of the furry body images) is in an ad for liposuction. The husky body presented there is the "before" picture of an unacceptable body type. One of the two images of a graying man which appear in ads in that issue is in an ad for Clairol Men's Choice, a hair-coloring product. Once again, the non-young/slim/smooth attribute is something to be corrected.

The numbers in Table 7.1 indicate that there were occasional images of men with beards in advertisements. Looking at these images further reveals an interesting and possibly disturbing trend. The eight issues of the *Advocate* which were surveyed included eighteen images of bearded men. Of these, seven were in ads relating to health issues. Essentially, the bearded men who appeared in ads in the magazine were mostly men who were portrayed as facing serious health issues and, according to the ads, needed to explore health care or insurance options. Are these ads telling us that the only men who have beards are those who are sick or dying? This harkens back to the earlier discussion of television characters who only grow beards in times of great personal difficulty. Perhaps the magazine advertisers have taken up the idea that a beard indicates a failure to maintain proper personal hygiene. There are certainly no bearded faces in the ads for vacations and resorts, where apparently only clean-shaven, smooth-skinned, slim-bodied gay men frolic on beaches and in swimming pools wearing skimpy bathing suits.

One ironic note about body hair comes from an issue of *Genre* that contains an article called "The Fur Flies" (DeCaro, 1995), which ostensibly celebrates the sexiness of a hairy male body. While it does indeed have some positive things to say about hairy men, the overall tone of the article leaves the reader wondering if the whole thing is merely sarcastic or facetious. The author describes sex with a hairy man as being problematic, due to "wayward hairs," he describes a furry back as something which can be expected to make men squeamish, and he says that smooth-skinned men look better naked than hairy men, although hairy men feel better to the touch than they look.

The gay erotic magazines included in the survey were analyzed in the same way as the lifestyle magazines, as described above. The advertisements and photo spreads featuring male images were examined, and each individual image was classified according to the criteria described earlier. The results are summarized in Table 7.2.

In viewing the results of the survey of erotic magazines, it should be noted that images classified as showing furry bodies were typically only lightly furred, and the fur was only on the chest and/or abdomen, never on the back. Additionally, a number of the men who were classified as having furry torsos had obviously trimmed or shaved hair around their genitals or buttocks. Some of the models

TABLE 7.2. Content Analysis of Male Images in Gay Erotic Magazines

Issue	Clean-shaven men	Men w/ facial fur	Beard	Mustache	Other	Smooth torsos	Furry torsos
Mandate	137	8	2	5	1	100	23
Inches	122	13	6	3	4	88	36
Torso	121	9	2	4	3	99	4
Playguy	132	9	2	5	2	105	8
Honcho	100	19	11	8	0	78	30
Advocate Men	183	18	3	12	3	147	13

TABLE 7.2 *(continued)*

Issue	Slimmer bodies	Heavier bodies	Gray/graying hair	Bald/balding
Mandate	16	0	0	0
Inches	26	0	0	0
Torso	28	0	0	0
Playguy	15	0	0	0
Honcho	38	0	0	0
Advocate Men	5	0	0	0

who were classified as having smooth torsos had clearly shaved off their torso hair to achieve the smooth look. Shaving is not uncommon among models in both erotic magazines and mainstream advertising.[2] Even men who are admired for their body hair may admit to some degree of shaving. For example, furry Colt icon Steve Kelso chooses to shave his butt for his photographs (Rick and Dave, 1994).

As with the statistics for lifestyle magazines, the men in the erotic publications who were classified as "slimmer," were all on the trim/toned/muscular side of average. No men appeared who were on the heavier/softer side of average. Almost all models appeared to be young, with no older/graying men included in the photos.

The results of this analysis demonstrate that these magazines have a definite conception of male beauty which centers around trim, sleek, young bodies. Other research has found similar results about the age of models in gay erotica (Duncan, 1989). This preference for youthful, smooth-skinned men is also reflected in the fiction appearing in these magazines, in which characters are often described with words like "smooth," "solid," "hairless," "shaved," and "slim."

There *are* gay men's magazines which present alternative types of male images. It is the contention of this chapter that these magazines have arisen in response to the narrow spectrum of masculinity presented by typical lifestyle and erotic publications.

A BEAUTY MYTH FOR GAY MEN?

Looking at mainstream gay publications, it becomes apparent that there is indeed a subjective standard of male beauty which is held to be most desirable, to the exclusion of other body and appearance types. Certain kinds of images proliferate, presumably on the grounds that they are the type of images that readers want to see. But what of gay men who prefer other types of male bodies, or who *have* other types of male bodies? What effect, if any, does this deluge of sleekness and smoothness have on them?

There has been considerable research into the effects of media portrayals of the female form on the self-esteem and body image of female readers and viewers of the mass media. Much less attention has been paid to the effects male images might have on men, straight or gay. This section of the chapter, as well as the following section, will examine existing research, relating to both men and women, and see how it might apply to the particular case of gay men.

Naomi Wolf's *The Beauty Myth* provides an excellent starting point for a discussion of media effects. Ms. Wolf has done a thorough job of researching the various ways in which women are affected by female body portrayals in the media. Her research includes much that is specific to women's issues, but many of the points she makes are just as applicable to gay men. Although women are not a numerical minority in our society, their underrepresentation or misrepresentation in many circles puts them at risk for many of the same problems and concerns as minorities.

A wide body of communications and media research supports the theory that the media do have a marked effect on people although the exact breadth or depth of these effects is hotly debated. Many scholars support the belief that the main effects deal with the shaping of perceptions and attitudes (Baran and Blasko, 1984; Fishbein and Ajzen, 1975; Ajzen and Fishbein, 1980; Gerbner et al., 1986). These can range from our perceptions of crime rates and personal safety to feelings about which physical characteristics are most attractive (Strutton and Lumpkin, 1993). This is precisely why we should be concerned about them. If media images help to shape our perceptions of the world around us, then they will also shape our perceptions of how we fit into that world.

The danger is that idealized images we see in the media will distort our perceptions of ourselves, our abilities, and our self-worth. Naomi Wolf describes this situation well:

> The harm of these images is not that they exist, but that they proliferate at the expense of most other images and stories of female heroines. . . . If the icon of the anorexic fashion model were one flat image out of a full spectrum in which young girls could find a thousand wild and tantalizing visions of possible futures, that icon would not have the power to hurt them; fashion and beauty scenarios would be yet another source of the infinite pleasures and intrigues of life in the female body. (p. 2)

The same scenario is true for gay men, who often grow up with a dearth of role models to show them what it means to be gay. Young or newly-"out" gay men typically do not have a father or gay relative who can help them understand their identity as a gay man. As a result, these men may turn to the media for role models of images and behaviors. If the media presented a wide range of examples, men would then be better able to explore their gay identity. But as the earlier analyses showed, the media tend to present a narrow view, rather than a broad one, and men may feel as though they do not fit in with what the media has told them it means to be gay.

Research has shown that exposure to idealized magazine images of fashion and beauty models can lower the self-esteem of young women (e.g., Wolf, 1992, p. 6; Marquardt, 1987). The story is likely no different for gay men who are bombarded with images of male beauty to which many of them cannot, or do not want to, conform. Yet many men are trapped into striving for an ideal they cannot reach. This would explain a fifty percent jump in the incidence of male cosmetic surgery between 1989 and 1993 (*Skin Deep*, 1993), and the increase in male body image disorders and men's increasing dissatisfaction with their bodies (see Neimark, 1994, and Yager, 1988, for example).

It is not just advertising and mainstream images which cause these problems. The images in erotica and pornography play a part, as well. Some might dismiss these images as fantasy that no one would take seriously, but the truth is that they do affect their viewers. Rather than simply fantasy, pornography can "help to define the forms of the exciting and desirable available in a given society at a given time . . . it participates in the cultural construction of desire" (Dyer, 1994). Pornography and erotica can also be damaging to the self-image of viewers who see a parade of firm, fit, flesh with seemingly endless sexual drives (Senn, 1993). Naomi Wolf describes viewers' resulting feelings of inadequacy as "the ultimate anaphrodisiac: the self-critical sexual gaze" (Wolf, 1992, p. 149).

The problem of erotica and self-criticism is compounded for gay men because when they look at pornography they see images of "sexual supermen" who are simultaneously objects of desire and objects of physical comparison. When a straight man reads *Playboy*, he may be titillated by the images, but the nude women do not serve as physical ideals to which he must compare himself. Gay men are caught between desiring and eroticizing the images presented to them and at the same time feeling inadequate because they do not match the images which the media has determined are sexy and desirable.

When advertisers or magazine editors make a decision to print a particular picture in an article or photo layout, they are imbuing that photo with a power which it otherwise would not have. "Its power is not far-reaching because of anything innately special about the face. . . . Its only power is that it has been designated as 'the face'–and that hence millions and millions of women are looking at it together, and know it" (Wolf, 1992, p. 76).

Again, although most of Wolf's work relates specifically to women, the logical jump connecting her findings to gay men is easy to make. In many ways, the problem is exacerbated for gay men by their status as an invisible persecuted minority. Gay men, particularly those who are young or living in rural areas, have little or no access to positive role models. In many parts of the United States the only things they see or hear about gays may be negative stereotypes or religious condemnations. When these men do find access to gay media one might hope that they would find such media to be nurturing and supportive. But when it comes to self-esteem and body image it should be apparent that the media may end up being damaging and condemning instead.

Even articles which purport to celebrate differing body types may end up being insulting. One example was cited earlier (DeCaro, 1995), and another comes from *Advocate Classifieds* in an article titled "Jurassic Parts" (Chicklet, 1993), which is about *Chiron Rising*, a magazine for older men and their admirers. The article mentions that *Chiron Rising* readers frequently talk about being insulted or called names by other gay men because of their age. Rather than celebrating *Chiron Rising*'s presentation of alternate body types, however, the author describes the men in the magazine's photos as having "hairy, flabby breasts," "drooping, weathered genitals" and "wrinkles that could make even Penny Marshall flinch." While this article provides a service by letting viewers know about an alternative publication, the article itself is anything but supportive.

A discussion such as this raises the question of just how our current ideal male body image was constructed. In *The Beauty Myth*, Naomi Wolf discusses how the ideal female image came into being, but why do we, as a society, seem to admire smooth, slim, muscular bodies rather than larger, hairier male bodies?[3]

The male image types we see in magazines and erotica are nothing new. Through the ages the male bodies which have been painted, sculpted, and otherwise incorporated into works of art have most often been the stereotyped slim, smooth, athletic form. Michelangelo's David is probably the classic example of this type. Our society has inherited our body ideals from our ancestors, who held up the god Adonis as the ultimate in male beauty. But what of men who look more like a typical image of Zeus than they do of Adonis? What of men who are attracted to huskier, hairier men? Their images and desires have been left out of existing media, with possibly damaging consequences.

A thorough discussion of the evolution of the male body ideal is beyond the purview of this chapter, but there are a few ideas worth mentioning here. From a Darwinian viewpoint one might argue that the hard, athletic body may be seen as healthier, and that men attempt to attain such a body in order to increase health and promote longevity, and that women and gay men seek partners with that body type for those same reasons. In the age of AIDS it may be that we cling even more to the image of fit, healthy men because they seem to be the safest sexually. We may idolize men who look immune to health problems and strong enough to avoid them. This relates back to the earlier discussions of images of bearded men as representing men who have health problems and cannot care for themselves properly. Ironically, others have contended that the new popularity of magazines portraying larger men may also come from a fear of AIDS–readers may see bigger men as more robust and free from the wasting effects of disease.

BODY TYPES, SELF-ESTEEM, AND IDENTITY

This section examines research which touches on self-esteem and body image, as well as identity construction and societal evaluations of alternate body types. Using this research as a basis, the effects of the invisibility of Bearish men in traditional gay media will be discussed. The focus here is on the effects on self-esteem of men who view the media, and on societal perceptions of body types which fall outside the ideal stereotype presented by the media. Mention will also be made of the importance of group identification in building good self-esteem.

Earlier sections of this chapter have postulated a stereotypical ideal for male beauty in our society. This ideal is a man who is clean-cut, smooth-skinned, slim, and muscular. Research has shown that people tend to find other body types less attractive. One study found a protruding abdomen to be the least attractive male physical characteristic among a variety of other characteristics (Gitter, Lomranz, and Saxe, 1982). Other studies have shown general obesity to be an unattractive characteristic (Clayson and Klassen, 1989).

Judgments based on physical appearance are not limited to determinations of a person's attractiveness. Research has shown that feelings about someone's physical appearance affect judgments of their intelligence and sociability (Alicke, Smith, and Klotz, 1986) and also estimations of their personal success (Marquardt, 1987).

Almost anyone would acknowledge that there are many different physical types in the world, and that some people are more attractive than others. One might ask whether these differing levels of attractiveness have any serious consequences for people's lives. Do subjective standards of beauty have significant impact on other areas of life? Research shows that indeed they do.

On an intrapersonal level, media consumers may be directly affected by the images to which they are exposed. Viewing images of highly attractive members of the same sex has been shown to have a negative impact on self-ratings of attractiveness (Thornton and Moore, 1993). When the media chooses to set a particular standard of attractiveness, those who do not meet that standard may suffer blows to their self-esteem.

On an interpersonal level, attractiveness and physical characteristics have been shown to make a difference in job hiring and salary decisions (Frieze, Olson, and Russell, 1991; Loh, 1993). Attractiveness has been shown to have a variety of possible effects on jury judgments, the amounts of bail and fines for misdemeanor criminal charges, and the length of imposed sentences (Downs and Lyons, 1991; Stewart, 1980, 1985).

This research shows that the effects of the beauty standard set by our society are not limited to intrapersonal dimensions like self-esteem and body image. Those who do not match up to the ideal standard set by magazine ads and photo layouts are limited in many areas. In some ways we have created an elite societal class whose membership is determined by purely physical characteristics.

The effects of this beauty standard may go even further than just self-esteem. They can cut right to the very core of a person's identity. Kellner (1995) has described the importance of the media in the formation of personal identity in our society, through its powerful socialization and enculturation effects. He sees the images presented by the media as creating a culture in which identity is based more on image than substance:

> Media culture provides images of proper role models, proper gender behavior, and images of appropriate style, look and image for contemporary individuals. Media culture thus provides resources for identity and new models of identity in which look, style and image replace such things as action and commitment as constitutives of identity, of who one is. (p. 259)

In Kellner's vision of our "postmodern image culture," the figures we see in advertising and other media can give us our very identity. In his view identity is "mobile, multiple, personal, self-reflexive and subject to change and innovation" (Kellner, 1995, p. 231). Individuals can continuously make and remake their identity as a result of the life possibilities which are presented to them. The media serve an important role by being the biggest supplier of images of those possibilities. Thus when the choices presented by the media are limited, it may become harder to create an identity that is both internally satisfying and free from cognitive dissonance.

The impact this has on gay men brings us back once again to the idea that gay men already have fewer sources of identity models in our society. Gays are typically not visible in mainstream media, and as often as not are presented negatively or as restrictive stereotypes. A gay man whose only access to images of other gays is television would not have a lot of examples to draw upon. Those who have appeared–Sidney on *Love, Sidney*, Jodie on *Soap*, Luke and Steven (a bisexual) on *Dynasty*, Russell and Peter on *thirtysomething*, Matt on *Melrose Place*–have usually been restricted to a relatively narrow range of physical and behavioral types. If a gay man in the process of discovering himself looks at these TV gays and sees no one who looks like him, and no one whom he would want to look like, his self-discovery and identity formation may be stunted.

The danger of this lack of media representation is that this gay man will come to believe that his identity is superfluous or not socially validated. This may lead to what Kellner describes as, "anomie, a condition of extreme alienation in which one is no longer at home in the world" (Kellner, 1995, p. 232). That same condition could result for a Bearish man who looks at gay media outlets like the *Advocate* or *Mandate* and feels as though he does not fit in to the gay community. He is already at risk for emotional difficulties as a result of discrimination and social marginalization based on his sexual orientation, and that risk is increased if he feels he cannot be part of the community to which he would naturally turn for support.

The importance of a feeling of identification with one's minority group has been described in both sociological and psychological research. Feelings of identification with a nonethnic minority group have been correlated with positive self-esteem, which is increased by pride in one's group (Bat-Chava, 1994). Lee and Robbins (1995) feel that persons who do not have a feeling of "connectedness" will suffer from isolation, frustration, or disappointment, echoing Kellner's statements about personal identity. Other studies have shown that feelings of alignment with both a minority group and a larger culture can lead to psychological well-being and adaptability, with positive group esteem leading to positive personal self-esteem (Sue and Wagner, 1973; Martinez and Mendoza, 1984; Porter and Washington, 1993; Crocker et al., 1994). In at least one study, feelings of positive group attitudes have been correlated with positive self-esteem for gay men and lesbians, specifically (Walters and Simoni, 1993). Lack of feelings of social identity or group esteem can have potentially harmful effects, and those who are struggling to fit in may also be more prone to prejudice against other groups (Crocker and Luhtanen, 1990). This can lead to damaging intra-minority prejudice and divisiveness.

While group identification is important for developing healthy self-esteem, it is possible to take it too far. As one becomes increasingly identified with a group, it may lead to the development of an "us versus them" attitude regarding other groups, and bias toward or derogation of those groups (Branscombe and Wann, 1992). Within the gay community, which has a history of being cliquish, we can see the effects of this type of over-identification. In terms of simple physical attributes and attractiveness, those who identify with the "image elite" as presented in magazine and advertising images may deride those who do not. A survey of Bearish men would likely report that many of them had been made fun of or ridiculed, called "ogres" or "trolls," by younger, slimmer, smoother gay men. Such in-group physical biases have been reported in other minorities as well. Bias between light- and dark-skinned blacks is one example (Kroll, 1989; Freedman, 1991).

In light of this information, the Bear community must be careful not to fall into a similar trap. There is a balancing act which must be managed between celebrating certain aspects of appearance and creating cliquishness based on those very qualities. Inclusion must not be sacrificed to shallow standards of appearance or the entire community will suffer from the resulting "us versus them" divisions, as the minority group splinters into multiple smaller groups.

VOICES IN THE WOODS–THE RISE OF BEAR MEDIA

It is hoped that the preceding discussion makes clear the importance to minority groups, or subgroups, of being accurately and positively portrayed by the mass media. This feeling is not specific to any one group, be it women or gay men, and many minority groups share the same problems and concerns. All minority groups celebrate positive portrayals of group members by the media. African Americans celebrate the appearance of black characters in comic books (Rubler, 1994). Hispanic Americans celebrate the casting of an Hispanic in a major new television series (Spelling, 1995). Gays celebrate the airing of a TV movie with gay-positive characters and themes (GLAAD, 1995). At the same time, minorities keep a careful eye on portrayals which stereotype their group (e.g., Strutton and Lumpkin, 1993; GLAAD, 1995), as do researchers. Advertising's portrayals of women (e.g., Sullivan, 1988), Native Americans (Green, 1993), African Americans (Humphrey, 1984) and senior citizens (Peterson, 1992) have been studied previously.

No matter who we are, we enjoy seeing ourselves reflected in the media. When television ratings are broken down by household ethnicity, it comes as no surprise that the most popular shows in black households are not the same as those in white households (Television Ratings, 1995). The shows at the top of the list are shows such as *Roc*, *Family Matters*, *Living Single*, *Martin*, and *Fresh Prince of Bel Air*, which feature predominantly black casts. This is not just a current phenomenon; these results hold up over time (Dates, 1980). While ratings for gay and lesbian households would be hard to come by, one would imagine that the shows at the top of that list would be those that include gay and lesbian characters, such as *Roseanne*, *Melrose Place*, and *Friends*.

When media consumers look to the media and cannot see themselves reflected there, they may feel isolated or less worthy as a result. If mainstream media have rendered subgroups invisible or, even worse, presented them in a negative light, those groups may have no solution but to turn around and create their own media. In the words of noted communications researcher Larry Gross (1991):

> The ultimate expression of independence for a minority audience struggling to free itself from the dominant culture's hegemony is to become the creators and not merely the consumers of media images. (p. 41)

Naomi Wolf (1992) also recognizes the power of subgroups to create their own media outlets when the mainstream ignores their needs. Her words about women's media are just as applicable to gays or any other group.

> The marketplace is not open to consciousness raising. It is misplaced energy to attack the market's images themselves: Given recent history, they were bound to develop as they did.
>
> While we cannot directly affect the images, we can drain them of their power. We can turn away from them, look directly at one another, and find alternative images of beauty in a female subculture; seek out the plays, music, films that illuminate women in three dimensions. (p. 277)

The Bear subgroup within the gay community represents a case study of this very phenomenon. *BEAR* magazine begin in 1988 as a photocopied publication with an initial print run of forty copies (Pepper, 1993). *Bear Fax* (now defunct) followed shortly after that, and recent years have seen the birth of *American Bear* and *Daddybear*, along with other Bear-friendly publications such as *Bulk Male* and other larger-men's magazines. That the Bear subgroup within the gay minority can support the existence of multiple magazines is a testament to the power and popularity of those magazines and the enthusiasm of the community to which they are directed.

Bears have also done more than just create these magazines. Along the lines of Wolf's quote above, Bearishness is now a multimedia experience. There are videos, greeting cards, photo essays, clothing, accessories and books, like this one, which celebrate the joys of what *BEAR* magazine founder Richard Bulger has described as "nontraditional gay-identified masculine imagery" (Pepper, 1993). Bearish men can now find support and affirmation for the way they look and the men they desire.

Increased ability to identify with images in the media is associated with increased pleasure in media consumption. When viewers can see positive characters or images with whom they can identify, pleasure is increased. Laura Mulvey, in her landmark treatise, "Visual Pleasure and Narrative Cinema," describes the sources of pleasure from media viewing:

> The first, scopophilic, arises from pleasure in using another person as an object of sexual stimulation through sight. The second, developed through narcissism and the constitution of the ego, comes from identification with the image seen. (p. 202)

Bear-oriented magazines, which provide their readership with images which provide both sexual stimulation and the ability to identify with the images, are able to fulfill both of these sources of pleasure. Readers would typically be unable to find images with this much power in traditional gay or mainstream media outlets.

WHAT DOES A BEAR LOOK LIKE?

It is not the intent of this section to provide a prescription for what a Bear *should* look like. Rather, the goal is to examine the images in Bear-oriented magazines and discover, through observation, what Bears *do* look like. The core of this observation consists of a content analysis of magazine images, similar to that described earlier for more traditional gay lifestyle and erotic magazines. Bear-oriented magazines fulfill the functions of both of these types of publications. They have erotic content in the form of nude photo layouts and erotic fiction, but they are more than just that. They also include articles on legal issues, Bear club activities, music, humor and even cooking. They tread some of the same ground as magazines like *Playboy*, which contain more than just nude photos. Bear-oriented magazines also serve to galvanize a community which may be widespread and disconnected.

Other writers have attempted to describe what Bears look like. Most often the result is a narrow definition which does not come close to reflecting the diversity of men within the Bear community. The best-selling *Unofficial Gay Manual* describes a Bear as simply "a hairy and often hefty man" (DiLallo and Krumholtz, 1994, p. 215). The book, itself, contains many images of men, but there is almost no Bearish imagery. *The New Joy of Gay Sex* includes a description of Bears under its section "New Macho Images" (Silverstein and Picano, 1992, pp. 128-130). The description, while considerably more detailed than that in the Manual, nonetheless paints a stereotyped and not necessarily accurate picture:

> The Bear look is all-natural, rural, even woodsy . . . full beards are common, as are bushy moustaches. Bears are stay-at-home wild men who enjoy football, trout fishing, carpentry, plumbing, and electrical repair work. They're just regular guys–only they're gay. The clothing, generally more countrified versions of the Seventies clone's garb, says this, with its emphasis on wool workshirts, usually worn over T-shirts or thermal knits, and wide belts with big buckles holding up torn-leg shorts or standard denims. Bears wear heavy hiking boots, with Pendleton shirt-jackets.
>
> Bears are definitely hairy, often gray-haired. Their bodies are strong and masculine. They've got weight and are proud, even eager to show it. Big as their biceps and chests are, their

> stomachs are seldom washboards, their buttocks aren't discocute. Everything about Bears is several hands fuller than usual.

While there are some characteristics in this description which are common among Bears, and may represent a Bear ideal to some men, it is in no way an accurate reflection of the true appearance of all Bears. It reduces Bears to a stereotype, ignoring the true diversity of the community. There is an illustration of a Bearish man accompanying this section (p. 129), but with only a few exceptions (pp. 28, 43, 132), all of the other illustrations in the book are of clean-shaven, smooth-skinned men.

The *Advocate*, whose dearth of Bear images was detailed earlier, included an article about Bears in one issue (Pepper, 1993). Interestingly enough, while the article discussed the birth and growing popularity of Bear-oriented and larger men's magazines, no images of Bearish men accompanied the article. The only illustrations were two line drawings of bears (the animal). Apparently Bears make a good discussion topic, but are not visually appealing enough, so viewers were left to imagine on their own what Bears look like. The article focused its description of Bearishness on weight, with only passing mention of other characteristics which constitute a Bear.

The best source for images of Bears is in Bear-oriented magazines. It takes only a brief scan through a copy of *BEAR* or *American Bear* to see that the male images presented within are much different from those in the *Advocate* or *Torso*. The men are larger and furrier. They are not presented wearing bikinis on the beach. They do not look like the gay stereotypes constructed by the mass media. The earlier content analyses in this chapter examined the images in traditional gay men's magazines. The remainder of this section contains a content analysis of the images in Bear-oriented magazines.

This analysis was completed in two parts. The first examines male images in photo layouts and advertisements. The second covers images of men in photos accompanying personal advertisements. The goal of the layout/ad analysis is to both contrast the images in these magazines with those in the earlier analyses and also to be able to determine some guidelines about what constitutes the image of a Bear as presented in these magazines. To that end, there are more categories included here than in the earlier analyses.

The goal of the personal ad analysis is to compare the Bears chosen to appear in layouts and commercial ads with those Bears who place personal ads (see Tables 7.3 and 7.4).

The magazines chosen for analysis include issues #31-33 of *BEAR*, Volume 1, Issue 6 and Volume 2, Issues 1 and 2 of *American Bear*, and the 6/94, 2/95, and 4/95 issues of *Daddybear*. The images in these magazines were analyzed and classified according to physical characteristics of the men as well as other notable aspects of appearance or dress. All images in these magazines were classified, including advertisements, photo layouts, and club activity photos. As with the earlier analyses in this chapter, these classifications are based on visible characteristics in photographs. To some extent the classifications are subjective, but every attempt was made to keep the classifications as consistent as possible. If particular categories could not be determined for a particular image due to photo quality, those categories were not included.

In regard to particular categories, some general guidelines were used. Facial fur was classified as beard or moustache when possible. Other variants (goatees, Vandykes, etc.) are classified as "Other." Furry torsos included those with visible fur on the chest or stomach or back. Heavier/slimmer bodies were those which fell outside of a subjective norm. For that reason many models were not classified as being either heavier or slimmer. Gray/graying refers to graying of head hair and/or facial fur. Bald/balding refers to pronounced hair loss, not just a high forehead. Military garb includes camouflage pants or other military paraphernalia. Leather garb includes vests, jackets, armbands, wristbands or hats which would seem to indicate a sexual interest in leather. Leather belts are not included in this category because they are common among all men, and in some cases items which were probably leather were not counted because a definite determination could not be made due to photo quality. Flannel garb refers to shirts that have a definite flannel appearance. Some plaid shirts which may be flannel were not included because it could not be definitely determined if they were flannel or another material. Denim garb refers to jeans or jackets. Cop garb refers to police badges or uniforms.

TABLE 7.3. Content Analysis of Male Images in Bear-Oriented Magazines

Issue	Clean-shaven	Men w/ facial fur	Beard	Mustache	Other	Smooth torsos	Furry torsos
BEAR #31	21	117	91	20	6	14	57
BEAR #32	24	111	85	13	3	15	56
BEAR #33	17	119	90	18	11	10	66
Am. Bear 1:6	7	106	97	9	0	3	64
Am. Bear 2:1	10	141	123	16	2	0	70
Am. Bear 2:2	7	132	115	9	8	2	66
Daddybear 6/94	2	64	41	22	1	1	42
Daddybear 2/95	4	58	34	12	12	2	36
Daddybear 4/95	4	61	52	9	0	4	37

Issue	Slimmer bodies	Heavier bodies	Gray graying	Bald/ balding	Pierced ear	Pierced nipple	Pierced dick
BEAR #31	4	27	6	9	1	0	0
BEAR #32	4	23	12	21	8	10	7
BEAR #33	4	16	13	8	0	1	0
Am. Bear 1:6	3	28	3	12	0	12	0
Am. Bear 2:1	3	25	6	7	0	2	0
Am. Bear 2:2	0	23	6	9	0	12	4
Daddybear 6/94	3	23	12	10	1	3	0
Daddybear 2/95	2	21	1	7	0	9	0
Daddybear 4/95	3	25	27	35	0	1	1

Issue	Pipe	Cigar	Mili-tary	Leather	Denim	Cop	Flan-nel	Tat-too	Hat
BEAR #31	0	2	1	22	27	3	11	7	43
BEAR #32	0	2	0	28	22	2	12	9	28
BEAR #33	0	0	0	17	14	0	8	0	27
Am. Bear 1:6	0	0	1	5	10	0	3	3	26
Am. Bear 2:1	1	0	5	14	14	6	13	4	56
Am. Bear 2:2	0	0	3	70	22	1	1	1	50
Daddybear 6/94	0	0	0	3	9	0	2	1	10
Daddybear 2/95	0	0	3	30	2	0	6	16	23
Daddybear 4/95	0	0	0	7	4	0	2	0	8

TABLE 7.4. Content Analysis of Personal Ad Photos in Bear-Oriented Magazines

Issue	Clean-shaven	Men w/ facial fur	Beard	Mustache	Other	Smooth torsos	Furry torsos
BEAR #31	3	19	13	6	0	4	6
BEAR #32	0	13	6	6	1	1	6
BEAR #33	0	5	4	1	0	0	0
Am. Bear 1:6	0	26	18	7	1	3	12
Am. Bear 2:1	0	32	24	7	1	3	17
Am. Bear 2:2	1	36	28	7	1	2	16
Daddybear 6/94	1	16	8	8	0	3	5
Daddybear 2/95	0	18	11	7	0	3	6
Daddybear 4/95	1	17	9	8	0	3	5

Issue	Slimmer bodies	Heavier bodies	Gray graying	Bald/ balding	Pierced ear	Pierced nipple	Pierced dick
BEAR #31	0	2	0	2	0	1	0
BEAR #32	0	0	0	1	0	0	0
BEAR #33	0	2	0	0	0	0	0
Am. Bear 1:6	0	2	1	1	0	2	0
Am. Bear 2:1	0	4	1	3	0	3	0
Am. Bear 2:2	0	5	1	2	0	2	0
Daddybear 6/94	0	3	4	4	0	1	0
Daddybear 2/95	1	3	3	3	0	2	0
Daddybear 4/95	0	3	4	4	0	1	0

Issue	Pipe	Cigar	Military	Leather	Denim	Cop	Flannel	Tattoo	Hat
BEAR #31	0	1	0	5	3	1	0	1	7
BEAR #32	0	0	0	2	4	0	0	0	3
BEAR #33	0	1	0	3	0	0	0	0	2
Am. Bear 1:6	0	0	1	7	2	0	1	2	13
Am. Bear 2:1	0	1	1	5	4	1	2	3	11
Am. Bear 2:2	0	1	1	8	6	1	1	3	16
Daddybear 6/94	0	0	0	0	1	0	0	2	8
Daddybear 2/95	0	0	0	2	1	0	0	0	8
Daddybear 4/95	0	0	0	2	1	0	0	0	8

It takes only a cursory analysis of these tables and those earlier in the chapter to see that the men who appear in the pages of Bear-oriented magazines have a much different look than those who appear in the *Advocate* and more mainstream erotic magazines. A vast majority of the images in the Bear-oriented publications are of bearded men with furry bodies, while the earlier analyses revealed mostly images of smooth-skinned, clean-shaven men. While images of clean-shaven, smooth-skinned men do appear in Bear-oriented magazines sometimes, they are typically in paid advertisements rather than in photo layouts or reader submissions. Bear-oriented magazines present a greater number of men who are heavier, graying, and balding.

Other than facial and body fur, there are other image characteristics that seem to be common parts of the makeup of a Bear as presented in these magazines. While the tables do not reflect a high percentage of men classified as "heavier," this is a result of the way this classification was made, as described earlier. It should be noted that most of the men who appeared would definitely fall on the heavier side of average. This is not to say that they are all flabby and out of shape, many of them are just "big guys."

The Bears in these magazines also show a fondness for particular aspects of dress and appearance. Leather garb is very common, as are denim and flannel. These often appear in combination. Piercings are an occasional accessory.[4] Tattoos appear at a similar level of frequency. In doing the analysis of the photographs it became apparent that hats are the most common accessory, no matter what the Bear is wearing. This category was not part of the original plan for this analysis, but was added early on when the preponderance of hats became apparent. Baseball-type caps seemed to be the most common, but leather hats and cowboy hats also appeared frequently. Since it was often not possible to determine whether a man who was wearing a hat was graying or balding, the large numbers in the "Hat" column may mean that the results in the "Graying" and "Balding" columns are lower than they should be. The large number of hats may be the result of graying or balding men attempting to cover it up.

A comparison of the men who appear in photo layouts and ads with the men who appear in personal ads shows a high degree of similarity. There were no categories in which there seemed to be a large discrepancy. One point to note, however, is that while clean-shaven, smooth-skinned men are not typically chosen as models for photo layouts or for Bear-oriented products, there are some furless men who send in personal ad photos. They are a small minority, however, and may represent men who consider themselves "Bear lovers" rather than Bears. One must also keep in mind that the photos represent only a fraction of the total number of ads, which in turn represent only a fraction of the total readership. Further research into this topic could include an analysis of image descriptions in the ads themselves, but that is beyond the scope of this chapter.

THE "SUPERBEAR" STEREOTYPE

This chapter has postulated that the appearance and growth of Bear-oriented magazines is a response to self-esteem and other issues relating to the inundation of sleek, smooth-skinned images of men in mass media magazines. Men who do not fit the stereotypes portrayed in these images have sought alternative sources of images where they can see other men who look like themselves. Humans, as a species, seek sources of community and belonging. We like to surround ourselves with other people who are like us. This does not mean that we would be happiest in a society full of clones of ourselves, but there is something to be said for looking around oneself and feeling as though one fits in. When selecting media sources we behave in similar ways–we look for sources of media that in some way reflect who we are. Whether it be a television show with characters of a particular ethnicity, or a magazine featuring furry, heavier men, we use the media to contribute to our feelings of socialization, inclusion, and self-worth.

Bear-oriented magazines present different images than traditional media, and they also include a wider variety of men than many other media outlets. But one must remember the goal of these magazines is not just to represent the breadth and depth of the Bear community but to sell more magazines. Without sufficient circulation and revenue the magazines would not exist. To that end, the images in the magazines must be chosen to attract the greatest readership.

While this chapter continues to uphold the hypothesis that the popularity of these magazines is due to the fact that they reflect the images of the Bear community better than magazines like the *Advocate* or *Playguy*, it would be naive to think that that is the only reason. In addition, these magazines succeed because they present images which readers find sexually exciting. To that end, the editors of the magazines have the mission, to some extent at least, to choose those models who best represent the ideals of the "Bear image."

This may just seem like common sense, but in light of the earlier discussion relating to self-esteem and body image, this may actually be a dangerous fact. If Bearish men flocked to magazines like *BEAR* and *American Bear* because they felt excluded when looking at images in other magazines, what happens when they see in Bear-oriented magazines a parade of "superbears"–men of ideal Bearish beauty? What are the psychological consequences of joining the Bear community to feel included, only to turn around and feel as though one somehow does not measure up physically as a Bear? Men in this position have now been doubly wounded–they did not measure up to the ideal of male beauty represented in traditional gay media, and now they feel inferior within the Bear community.

This chapter's content analysis of Bear media images gives some idea of the similarities and differences between models (in photo layouts and advertisements) and the magazines' readers (as presented in personal ad photos). This is an imperfect comparison, however. The sample of readers who have included photos with ads is only a tiny portion of the overall readership. One would expect that those readers who submit photos would be those with high self-esteem who are secure in their appearance. What of the rest?

This same discussion is often echoed in discussions of Bear contests or pageants. While on the one hand they present an opportunity for men who have previously felt unattractive to be appreciated for their Bearish qualities, there are those who argue that these contests perpetuate a stereotype and serve to subjugate those who do not measure up to it. Each side of this argument has its merits. Bear contests can be a very affirming experience for the contestants and audience alike. The author has witnessed more than one man who definitely does not conform to any "superbear" stereotype receive sincere and enthusiastic feedback from the audience at these pageants. This cannot help but be an esteem-boosting event. On the other hand, the loudest shouts and cheers are almost always reserved for the "superbears."

In some ways this comes down to the discussion about just what it is that makes someone a "Bear." This debate is constantly being hashed out in magazines and online forums. There are those who say that a Bear is a furry man, those who say that a Bear is a larger man, and those who feel that Bearishness is more a state of mind than a set of physical characteristics. The healthiest point of view for the community would be one of inclusion, but as the community grows the divisive opinions seem to be increasing.

Bear-oriented media have the potential to both remedy and exacerbate this division. If publishers and other media producers are careful to present a diverse view of the Bear community then they may serve to, in the words of ex-*Bear Fax* publisher Ben Bruner, "promote an attitude of acceptance more than any physical attribute" (Pepper, 1993, p. 74). But if magazines and other media take sides on this issue and present a narrow view of what it means to be a Bear, they run the risk of contributing to the creation of a new image elite, and this may drive away members of the community who do not match the physical standard set by the images.

CONCLUSION AND AREAS FOR FURTHER RESEARCH

This chapter has shown that there is a bias in traditional gay media against images of men who do not fit an idealized, iconized standard of male beauty. This bias presents itself in both lifestyle and erotic magazines. The bias appears in both advertising and in the choice of models for photo layouts. Every day the average American is exposed to between 400 and 1,500 advertising messages and countless other images (Marquardt, 1987). If all of these images and messages advocate a particular body type for men, to the exclusion of all others, it is no wonder that men who do not match that particular type should suffer blows to their personal self-esteem and body image.

For men who fit or admire a different standard of male beauty there are few mass media alternatives. Bear-oriented magazines have stepped in to fill this gap for larger and/or hairier men and their admirers. These magazines celebrate an alternate view of masculinity and male bodies, and thus provide a service for men who have been overlooked by the mass media. Yet as the preceding discussion has shown, these magazines walk a fine line between serving their readers' community and continuing the cycle of oppression and stereotypes by setting new unattainable standards of Bearish beauty.

A chapter such as this one can explore only a few aspects of a much broader topic. In doing so it answers some questions and raises many others. The fact that there may be unanswered questions is not a bad thing, it merely opens the door for further research. The remainder of this final section discusses some of those areas in which further study may prove interesting and informative.

The results and discussion contained in this chapter are based on a content analysis of magazine images and on existing research. One obvious point of departure for a new study would be to take the information contained herein and extend it to a survey of men to get direct opinions and feelings about media images. Additionally, research that has been previously conducted to examine the effects of media images on women could be extended to include men or, more specifically, gay men.

The content analyses in this chapter focused on magazines which are targeted directly at the Bear community. There is Bearish content in other publications, however. Magazines like *Bulk Male*, *The Big Ad*, *Daddy*, *Husky*, *GRUF*, and *Chiron Rising* also present nonstereotypical male images and often contain images of Bearish men. The research in this chapter could easily be extended to include some of these other publications. Further research could also include an analysis of nongay-oriented media to see if the results described here would be comparable in the majority population.

There have been periods when media images of men had a greater frequency of facial and body hair, so another avenue for comparative research would include an historical analysis to determine if male body images as presented in the media have changed over time. Different countries have different standards for personal beauty–

witness Europeans' feelings about female body hair as compared to those in the United States–so a cross-cultural analysis might also prove interesting. This chapter focused on American publications, but looking through gay magazines from Japan, Germany, South Africa, and New Zealand, it appears that the images presented within are similar to those we see in American magazines.

The image analyses presented in this chapter focused on certain physical characteristics, including body size and furriness. There are other aspects of physical appearance which have not been included. One of the most significant of these is the race of men presented in the magazine images. Research into both mainstream media advertising (Few Black Models. . . , 1991) and pornographic films (Fung, 1991) has shown a marked bias toward white models. Glancing through Bear-oriented magazines also reveals a vast majority of white faces and bodies. Is this because the stereotypical Bear body type occurs more among whites, or is there something more to it?

One physical characteristic not included in this study but related to any discussion involving nude photos and self-esteem is penis size. Erotic magazines, both straight- and gay-oriented, are well-known for presenting images of extreme sexual endowment. The mainstream erotic magazines included in this study are no exception. Most of the models are very "well hung." Since penis size is such a sensitive issue for men in our society, exposure to these "sexual supermen" must have implications for self-image and self-esteem. It should be noted that Bear-oriented magazines tend to include men with a much wider variety of endowments. The relationship between images of penis size and viewers' self-esteem would make for fascinating research.

And, finally, just where does the Bear image come from? Judging from the photos in Bear-oriented publications, and also from informal discussions with Bears, many Bearish men are turned on by a hypermasculine blue-collar image. One might ask why this is. There are doubtless avenues of psychological and sociological research which could provide some explanations or theories. Research in this vein might examine how these desires are constructed and what other meanings might exist in the image. Is it a reflection of who we Bears truly are or just the enactment of a fantasy? Is it a lifestyle or a fetish? Brian Pronger has described homoerotic desire for athletes as a paradox: "it is at once a reverence for and a violation for masculinity" (Pronger, 1990, p. 135). It may be that the Bear image is caught up in that paradox as well. Or perhaps the whole Bear "look" is just an ironic take on masculinity with an element of camp included. Another possibility is that the Bear image may actually represent internalized homophobia and fear of gay stereotypes and may lead us to embrace a patriarchal, hetero-masculinist ideal. Further research is necessary to answer these and other questions.

NOTES

1. There are no page numbers in this book, but the quote cited here comes from a page located seventy pages in from the title page.
2. See Mindich, 1995, for some anecdotes about men, models, and shaving.
3. For a survey of the historical representation of male forms, see Dutton, 1995.
4. It should be noted that the piercing numbers reflect only these three issues of each magazine, and there are other issues in which piercing is more common, and some in which it is less common.

BIBLIOGRAPHY

Alicke, M., Smith, R., and Klotz, M. (1986). Judgments of Physical Attractiveness: The Role of Faces and Bodies. *Personality and Social Psychology Bulletin*, *12*(4), 381-389.

Ajzen, I. and Fishbein, M. (1980). *Understanding Attitudes and Predicting Social Behavior*. Englewood Cliffs, NJ: Prentice Hall.

Baran, S. and Blasko, V. (1984). Social Perceptions and the By-Products of Advertising. *Journal of Communication*, *34*(3), 12-20.

Basow, S. (1991). The Hairless Ideal, Women and Their Body Hair. *Psychology of Women Quarterly*, *15*(1), 83-96.

Bat-Chava, Y. (1994). Group Identification and Self-Esteem of Deaf Adults. *Personality and Social Psychology Bulletin*, *20*(5), 494-502.

Branscombe, N. and Wann, D. (1992). Role of Identification with a Group, Arousal, Categorization Processes, and Self-Esteem in Sports Spectator Aggression. *Human Relations*, *45*(10), 1013-1033.

Chicklet. Jurassic Parts. *Advocate Classifieds*, (1993, September 7), 38-39.

Clayson, D. and Klassen, M. (1989). Perception of Attractiveness by Obesity and Hair Color. *Perceptual and Motor Skills*, *68*(1), 199-202.

Crocker, J. and Luhtanen, R. (1990). Collective Self-Esteem and Ingroup Bias. *Journal of Personality and Social Psychology, 58*(1), 60-67.

Crocker, J., Luhtanen, R., Blaine, B., and Broadnax, S. (1994). Collective Self-Esteem and Psychological Well-Being Among White, Black, and Asian College Students. *Personality and Social Psychology Bulletin, 20*(5), 503-513.

Dates, J. (1980). Race, Racial Attitudes and Adolescent Perceptions of Black Television Characters. *Journal of Broadcasting, 24*(4), 549-560.

DeCaro, F. The Fur Flies. *Genre*, (1995, April), 12.

DiLallo, K. and Krumholtz, J. (1994). *The Unofficial Gay Manual*. New York: Doubleday.

Downs, A. and Lyons, P. (1991). Natural Observation of the Links Between Attractiveness and Initial Legal Judgments. *Personality and Social Psychology Bulletin, 17*(5), 541-547.

Duncan, D. (1989). Trends in Gay Pornographic Magazines: 1960 Through 1984. *Sociology & Social Research, 73*(2), 95-98.

Dutton, K. (1995). *The Perfectible Body*. New York: Continuum.

Dyer, R. (1994). Idol Thoughts: Orgasm and Self-Reflexivity in Gay Pornography. *Critical Quarterly, 36*(1), 49-62.

Few Black Models Shown in Magazine Ads: Study. *Jet*, (1991, August 12), p. 37.

Fishbein, M. and Ajzen, I. (1975). *Belief, Attitude, Intention and Behavior*. Reading, MA: Addison-Wesley.

Freedman, S. (1991). Spike Lee's Jungle Fever Reaches America's Heart of Darkness. *The New York Times*, pp. C1-C8.

Frieze, I., Olson, J., and Russell, J. (1991). Attractiveness and Income for Men and Women In Management. *Journal of Applied Social Psychology, 21*(13), 1039-1057.

Fung, R. (1991). Looking For My Penis, The Eroticized Asian in Gay Video Porn. In *How Do I Look*? (pp. 145-168). Seattle: Bay Press.

Gerbner, G., Gross, L., Morgan, M., and Signorielli, N. (1986). Living With Television: The Dynamics of the Cultivation Process. In Bryant, J. and Zillman, D. (Eds.), *Perspectives on Media Effects* (pp. 17-40). Hillsdale, NJ: Lawrence Erlbaum Assoc.

Gitter, A., Lomranz, J., and Saxe, L. (1982). Factors Affecting Perceived Attractiveness of Male Physiques By American and Israeli Students. *The Journal of Social Psychology, 118*, 167-175.

GLAAD Update (1995, March).

Green, M. (1993). Images of Native Americans in Advertising: Some Moral Issues. *Journal of Business Ethics, 12*, 323-330.

Gross, L. (1991). Out of the Mainstream: Sexual Minorities and the Mass Media. In Wolf, M. and Kielwasser, A. (Eds.), *Gay People, Sex, and the Media* (pp. 19-46). New York: Harrington Park Press.

Humphrey, R. (1984). The Portrayal of Blacks In Magazine Advertisements. *The Public Opinion Quarterly, 48*(3), 551-563.

Kellner, D. (1995). *Media Culture*. New York: Routledge.

Kroll, J. (1989, November 13). The Fuse Has Been Lit. *Newsweek*, p. 64.

Lee, R. and Robbins, S. (1995). Measuring Belongingness: The Social Connectedness and the Social Assurance Scales. *Journal of Counseling Psychology, 42*(2), 232-241.

Lob, E. (1993). The Economic Effects of Physical Appearance. *Social Science Quarterly, 74*(2), 420-138.

Marquardt, D. (1987, May). A Thinly Disguised Message. *Ms.*, p. 33.

Martinez, J. and Mendoza R. (1984). *Chicano Psychology.* New York: Academic Press.

Mindich, J. (1995, May). Cock and Bull. *Details, 13*(12), 122-125.

Moog, C. (1990). *"Are They Selling Her Lips?" Advertising and Identity.* New York: William Morrow and Company, Inc.

Mulvey, L. (1986). Visual Pleasure and Narrative Cinema. In Rosen, P. (Ed.), *Narrative, Apparatus, Ideology.* New York: Columbia University Press.

Neimark, J. (1994, November/December). The Beefcaking of America. *Psychology Today*, pp. 33-39.

Pepper, R. (1993, March 23). Bear Essentials. *Advocate*, 74-75.

Peterson, R. (1992). The Depiction of Senior Citizens in Magazine Advertisements: A Content Analysis. *Journal of Business Ethics, 11*, 701-706.

Porter, J. and Washington, R. (1993). Minority Identity and Self-Esteem. *Annual Review of Sociology, 19*, 139-161.

Pronger, B. (1990). *The Arena of Masculinity.* New York: St. Martin's Press.

Rausch, K. and Fessler, J. (1995). *Why Gay Guys Are A Girl's Best Friend.* New York: Simon & Schuster.

Rick and Dave (1994, August 4). His Father's Build & Mother's Moustache–An Interview with Steve Kelso. *Frontiers, 13*(7), 18-22.

Roush, M. (1988, October 26). More Than Ever, 'Wiseguy' Is Well Worth Uncovering. *USA Today*, p. D4.

Rubler, D. (1994, April). Black Super Heroes Teach & Inspire. *The Crisis*, p. 30.

Senn, C. (1993). Women's Multiple Perspectives and Experiences with Pornography. *Psychology of Women Quarterly, 17*(3), 319-341.

Silverstein, B., Perdue, L., Peterson, B., and Kelly, E. (1986). The Role of the Mass Media in Promoting a Thin Standard of Bodily Attractiveness for Women. *Sex Roles 14*(9/10), 519-532.

Silverstein, C. and Picano, F. (1992). *The New Joy of Gay Sex.* New York: Harper Perennial.

Skin Deep. (1993, May/June). *Psychology Today*, p. 96.

Spelling, I. (1995, April). Voyage to a New Frontier. *Hispanic*, 14-16.

Stewart, J.E. (1980). Defendant's attractiveness as a factor in the outcome of criminal trials: An observational study. *Journal of Applied Social Psychology, 10*, 348-361.

Stewart, J.E. (1985). Appearance and punishment: The attraction-leniency effect. *Journal of Social Psychology, 125*, 373-378.

Strutton, D. and Lumpkin, J. (1993). Stereotypes of Black In-Group Attractiveness In Advertising: On Possible Psychological Effects. *Psychological Reports, 73*(2), 507-511.

Sue, S. and Wagner, N. (1973). *Asian-Americans: Psychological Perspectives.* Palo Alto, CA: Science & Behavior Books.

Sullivan, G. (1988). Women's Role Portrayals in Magazine Advertising: 1958-1983. *Sex Roles*, *18*, 181-188.

Television Ratings. (1995, April 12). *USA Today*, p. D3.

Thomas, V. (1989). Body-Image Satisfaction Among Black Women. *The Journal of Social Psychology*, *129*(1), 107-112.

Thornton, B. and Moore, S. (1993). Physical Attractiveness Contrast Effect: Implications for Self-Esteem and Evaluations of the Social Self. *Personality and Social Psychology Bulletin*, *19*(4), 474-480.

Walters, K. and Simoni, J. (1993). Lesbian and Gay Male Group Identity Attitudes and Self-Esteem: Implications for Counseling. *Journal of Counseling Psychology*, *40*(1) 94-99.

Wolf, N. (1992). *The Beauty Myth*. New York: Doubleday.

Yager, J. (1988). Behaviors and Attitudes Related to Eating Disorders in Homosexual Male College Students. *The American Journal of Psychiatry*, *145*, 495-497.

Chapter 8

Beardom: The Delimited Bear as a Sign of the Recurrence in History of the Archetypal Green Man

Rychard G. Powers

Out of the ashes of illusion nature springs forth, breaking the molds of social structures we so desperately cling to. After the tragedy in the 1980s, that is, the decimation of the gay male population by AIDS, previous illusions about physical beauty were shattered by the reflection of a new form of man–the natural one. The Apollonian, structured, or artificial beauty of man began being replaced by a more Dionysian, delimited, or natural one. Gay men began to look behind the masks, and curiously enough discovered their own naturalized humanity in the form of a great grizzly who came in their dreams and growled to "come along and learn and play." This rhythmic play is the dance of nature. This rhythmic play is the resurgence of the Green Man in the form of the bear.

In art history, we are taught that Greek civilization strove for a more illusionist, or ideal image to represent people in painting and sculptures. (These were the basic staple of the gay man, offered to him by his own conditioning.) Rome, however, turned this ideal around into a form of realistic, or natural, art (akin to réal politik, only instead *réal* art, or the "art of reality"). It emphasized things as they were: worry lines, heaviness, etcetera, pushed the reflection of the human form toward an art (or artifice) more in tune with nature, more in tune with the diversity and uniqueness of individuals in general. And this is the form that bears need not strive for. They need not strive for it because they reflect it.

More recently, the "me" generation of the 1970s and the repressed sexual insecurity of the 1980s sought to remove the hair and bulk from men (both strong symbols of masculinity throughout the ages) and thereby remove their individuality and sexual power. This is why women were depicted without body hair in art up to the present day; hair represents sexual power, a trait the heterosexual European man did not want when he purchased the painting (i.e., purchased the woman in the painting).[1] And so, as marketing and profitability overtook the individual, man was commodified into a sexually inadequate product that was supposed to bring home the bacon (just as women were supposed to fry it up in a pan), and then expected to purchase products with that bacon to somehow fill the void of his immediate objectification.

Today that image of breadwinner is changing. Men are realizing their roles are not as "consumer and owner," but as individuals striking out with uniqueness in the face of a social system that glorifies compliance and sweat, but not tears. Men laugh, men cry, and men are finally realizing that it is not they who run the show, but nature. They are beginning to liberate themselves, just as women did in the liberation movements in the 1970s. Just because social codes pushed man into a position of power does not mean that he had to stay there; and now men are enjoying their own beauty without those codes that bound, gagged, and shoved them into complete submission as the ignorant white European male voicing spurious opinions through politics, religion, and academia. The stage that was once set is now being devoured by nature, in part specifically by bears. In short, we as a culture repeat lessons we so desperately need to learn. It is in this environmentally-conscious era that bears come out of the cave, and walk effortlessly through life preserving the concept of nature with their very being.

In early antiquity a myth developed that best suits our aim to discover this natural man, the Green Man.[2] Mainly depicted in ancient art with a bearded face of leaves, the Green Man danced harmoniously through nature as the bringer of spring. Foliage sprung from his heels, and rooted him deeply, preserved in the great age-old forests that symbolize the impermanence of nature, and the permanence of change. Mother Nature birthed this man, and taught him the receptive (or feminine) nature of all things. As a man balanced by art and nature, he co-creates with the universe, at one with all he perceives and reflects. He knows that what he reflects belongs to his mother, but as the child he is not concerned with the paints, nor their use. He understands the paints exist to radiate their own colors, and reflects those colors as a symbol of nature and of life. We (and I mean not only bears) absorb the colors of nature. We are the tapestry whipping in the wind and drinking up the sun. Bears are the beginning in the West of a return to innocence, to love without rules, compassion without judgment, and creativity without boundaries. The bear is the symbol of the heart returning to man. The bear is a symbol of seeing with the heart, seeing things for what they are, not for what one wants them to be. In the East this is called "awareness," if I am not mistaken.

Now, I am not saying that beardom is the road to enlightenment, but I am saying those excluded from and bound by the moral social structures of the past finally have a chance to experience "thusness," or seeing things for what they are, rather than turning themselves into something others want them to be (e.g., facelifts, chest-waxing, etc.), or for that matter playing roles others want them to play. We choose our individuality, it does not choose us. As we are social animals, this individuality can be weaseled away from us by our own unawareness and fears, and by the rigidity of systems not designed for the natural consciousness of humans, but for the paled mimetic version of a poorly-lit nickelodeon Western that is designed not only to enslave but to occlude the individual. I say occlude because the mimetic version of human consciousness that social structure provides, invented by humans, inevitably overtakes humanity and tells humanity how to behave and perceive while humanity sits, prostrate, mouth agape, at its own illusion and desire surpassing its very natural consciousness that existed before the intrusion of illusion. In short, the illusion of what humanity should be overtakes what humanity is—a self-evident reflection of and in nature—and real humanity is lost in the process. And this might be why there is such a shaky scaffolding with the definition of what a bear is: to label is to commodify and limit—even the name "bear" is a limiting label, although I would like to call it a harmless one here, harmless because it has a blurred or hazy, inaccurate, allegorical ascription to a term designated for an animal honored throughout history, and therefore, because anthropomorphized, has no accurate definition or even remotely definable limits. If you put a trademark on a bear, he is no longer a bear–he is a commodity.

And all this, specifically, is what the natural man dispels with his very nature; the stereotype that is designed to limit his will, and remove his voice. Obedience in social structure is used to keep objectors silent. I think that gay men from the beginning set out to dispel the gay stereotypes by the very nature of their uniqueness, the stereotypes perpetrated by heterosexuals, for example, that you have to be a man (not a transvestite or a transsexual), that in being a true man you have to love women (and not your own gender), and that to be loved by a "real" (read masculine or manly) man you had to somehow behave like or mimic women. I strongly believe the bear movement not only achieved but surpassed its own intent, and molted out of the images that even gay people had about gay people.

Take, for instance chicken-hawking. As a stereotype you have to be "thin, young, and lithe" (in Greek, an eromenos, or "beloved"), or a "dirty, not attractive-anymore, older man" (erastes, or "older lover") who must purchase an object he can no longer win with his heart, but can only posses through a series of lavish gifts to the boy. The boy, in turn, will accept them in return for sex, not because he truly loves the "unattractive" ("youth is beauty") older man, but because the gifts are not only part and parcel of his returning the love (we all love being purchased–it proves our worth), but also a strong symbol of his adolescence gaining ground and moving into a powerful sexual persona that can be wielded for other commodities that will prove him to be a man (or contender) who can command all that he purveys.

And so, with the inescapable net of this cycle, the boy becomes old, losing his youthful power as a man (and thus being turned back into a boy through enopause–enopause is the great humbler–it is the reification of puberty), and he is left with cash and property, and to reclaim his abandoned (or discarded) youth he pursues a young boy and lavishes his goods on the boy, only to be broken and commodified once again by a stereotype that neither nurtures, nor supports his shadowed humanity. In simpler terms, men sold their humanity for a stereotype that proved not only that they existed, but that they could connect and belong, no matter how unhealthy the dogma was that provided this service.

And this is the main reason why I think that bears refuse to define themselves. They want to remain unoccluded by their own stereotypes, remain delimited by limits of what they cannot do or be, because those social limits, differently defined, made them outcasts as gay men in the first place. Because they have become natural men (loving the beauty of their natural selves and wills), they want to remain free of the boundaries of stereotypes (a generalizing designed to imprison the individual, and then put a group of them into a box for immediate judgment) so that the individual may sing out, liberated in a crowd of unassuming, unjudging, uncategorizing participants. The bear is necessarily (but not exclusively) the liberated man, a consciously-aware loving reflector of that which bore him–Mother Nature. Nature grows the bear that must of necessity eventually return to her, both arms open. We are no better or worse than nature, because we are part of it. We are no better or worse than ourselves or each other because we are part of a greater biological system that guides us through this mortal coil together.

Now, as bears have rejected this erastes-eromenos stereotype they are freed as individuals to pursue their own desires, released from the old system of commodification, without the limiting structure of gay, man, boy, or any other delineation–older men can be bottoms, younger men can be tops. In other words, when love/sex games are played with mutual respect, two or more people can form just about any relationship that suits their desires. A bear is delimited, and so the combinations are endless.

Most bears, from what I have seen, are even breaking through those active/passive sexual relationships that stereotype and limit heterosexuals–those same relationships gay people mimicked to in some way "belong," because they had no other associations of their own. Bears are becoming versatile, able to balance themselves between masculine and feminine, active and passive, top and bottom. As a result of this power play, bears have for the most part liberated themselves from the slavery of master-and-servant. This relationship is not unlike the erastes/eromenos, but with one major difference–choice. The master chooses to become a slave to his own passions by commodifying himself to one who would succumb by assent to his desires, and the slave, mutually commodified, offers himself for sale as a product for his own self-worth. This is the game of justification. This is the game where one cannot be justified in seeking justification, as seeking justification limits the justifiability of one's own search. In other words, seek, and you will not find, because there was nothing there in the first place. And here stands the bear transformed, a foot between two polarized ideals, able to move freely from one side to the other, or stay right in between for that matter. Refusing to be objectified by being labeled, the bear is all-inclusive.

In part, breaking these stereotypes has freed bears from the seemingly necessary connection to a death-culture, and I use this word with some hesitation. When I say this, images similar to these should come to mind; jock/punk prisoners, youth as innocence raped, isolation in the guise of promiscuity, and heavy drug and alcohol abuse to hide the pain of exclusion that most gay people fear and feel. I say exclusion because the ignorance and fear reflected by mainstream society purposefully excludes a segment of society that does not fit into a moral mold they set for "appropriate" behavior.

And this is why, even in the days of yore, the Robin Hood effect was consistently being replayed. A leader of men, masculine men, Robin Hood was the paradigmatic Green Man, living with nature and reflecting nature's harmony. Essentially, he rescues Maid Marion from the "brutish heterosexual" norm of men of that age who tried to capture and enslave her; essentially, he rescues her from what he would have become were it not for his self-reflective attachment to the receptiveness of nature. The men of the Greenwood, burly hairy fellows, lived together in harmony with the (curiously) distant pining of women for their affections. I see virtually no difference between the "Merry Men" of the forest and those of today. Pockets of bears form clubs, staging Dionysian festivals for the most beautiful not (necessarily) based on looks, but on the beauty of their sexual personas. Kindness, personality, approachability turned what used to be called go-go dancing, stripping, or just plain old sex club meat-marketing into a powerful reflection of nature and a lesson for other aspiring participants to follow nature as well.

Bears have taken themselves out of the stereotype of the cities, and moved toward a more pagan (paganus–or, "rural person"–and I use this word strictly and precisely, referring to the Latin) model for self-sufficiency. This is because rural people are more in tune with nature than with the disjointed, disenfranchised, fragmented, distorted clamor of the city. And so the bears reclaim their simplicity, growing strong with bears in their "pack" or "den," and move as wide-eyed children, discovering their own natural awareness in the colorful diversity and comforting, accepting scheme of Mother Nature.

Bears are balance, bears are simplicity, bears are the movement that re-states the concept that nature is all, and everything is one with it. Those who are not one are fragmented by their own egos, and become excluded from themselves as part of a commodifying death-culture that asks them to give their very humanity away. But even this person is not excluded, because all doors to nature must be left open for those who are ready to relinquish their own unhappiness, and join in the delicately balanced timbre of planet drum. Nature, moving through life as a windy music, blows the drums toward us, and we dance the rhythmic dance, unhindered, delimited, deconstructed, and freed from our own constructs about it. Bears are the sign that the sign is the signless, and since the sign cannot be signified, it therefore cannot be objectified–a bear is the subject moving freely through a system it becomes one with, and relinquishes all forms of otherness, and so is not objectified but universally subjectified, universally aware and therefore universally subject. The curious ascription termed "Bear" transcends its own meaning, and is therefore meaningless, but the purpose of the myth named "Bear" nonetheless remains divine.

All love is unity with the One.

–Plato

NOTES

1. For an in-depth discussion on the commoditization of people (women specifically) in art and media, see John Berger's *Ways of Seeing*, England: BBC and Penguin Books, 1972.

2. A very incisive Jungian study of the Green man appears in Graham Jackson's *The Secret Lore of Gardening: Patterns of Male Intimacy*, Toronto: Inner-City Books, 1991. I cannot stress the importance of this book enough for those interested in natural self-discovery. Additionally, some good images of the Green Man can be found in William Anderson's *Green Man: The Archetype of Our Oneness with the Earth*, San Francisco: HarperCollins, 1990.

Chapter 9

The Natural Bears Classification System: A Classification System for Bears and Bearlike Men Version 1.10

Bob Donahue
Jeff Stoner

Because "bear" means so many things to different people, because bears come in all shapes and sizes and have different sexual proclivities, because classified ad prices are so expensive, we (while eating lunch at a Boulder, Colorado, Wendy's on Thanksgiving weekend, 1989) came up with this incredibly scientific system to describe bears and bearlike men.

Since we both have interests in astronomy, we are well versed in star and galaxy classification systems, which use prototypes to set the standards for describing things. Rather than just saying something is of "Type I" or "Type II" (etc.), it is better to use natural features to describe an object, in particular as a continuum of a range of features. Such is the case with bears.

THE CLASSIFICATION SCHEME

The most obvious characteristic of a bear is understandably his facial fur. So, that is the most logical place to begin. Using a capital

"B" to denote "bear," we have added a subclass characterizing "beard type" which combines a bear's beard's length, thickness, and overall "keptness," numbered from 0 to 9 and defined in the following way:

- B0– (little/no beard, or incredibly sparse) Such a beard is the absolute minimum that could ever be classified as a beard. We're talking five-o'clock shadow, here! And yes, we are of the opinion that the beardless can still find company among the ursines!
- B1– (very slight beard) This is the kind of beard that people have who want to have a beard, but can't grow one. Or someone who is constantly at the one-week phase.
- B2– (slight beard) A beard kept very short at all times, or thinned out.
- B3– (thin beard) A beard in all respects but kept thin and short.
- B4– (mostly full) A beard that is full except for a few noticeable bald spots, or kept trimmed.
- B5– (full beard) A full beard not generally trimmed, though not generally bushy. May have a few bald spots on inspection. Usually full and roundish beards fall into this category.
- B6– (very full) A full beard, not trimmed. May be slightly bushy but very full. Thick, full beards (more so than B5s) are B6s. B6s beards also generally are higher up on the cheeks than B5s.
- B7– (longish/bushy beards) A full beard or slightly thin beard with longish fur. This beard is not trimmed and does come away from the chin.
- B8– (very long beards) These beards are usually very bushy and haven't seen clippers for a very long time.
- B9– (belt-buckle-grazing long beards) The prototype is ZZ Top. Need we say more?

Okay, using this scheme, it shouldn't be hard to narrow a person down to within one subclass, although occasionally people may fall between two classes, and then the end result is left up to the person classifying, or one may use a hybrid designation (for example:

B7/4) for those who vary across time (in the given range they spend more time near the first number).

OTHER CLASSIFIERS FOR BEARS

While beards can be the most obvious trait of bears, there are other things that different people take into consideration as to "what makes a bear," and characteristics that people like in their bears. So, bearing that in mind (pun intended) there are other criteria that can or should optionally follow the "B" designation. (*Nota bene*, it is not necessary to have a "grade" for each of these traits!) For each there is a "neutral" value, which basically describes someone who is "average" or "unknown" within that trait. These "neutral" values are given below, but would not be reported. Treat them as either "default" or "assumed."

f-The Fur Factor

Some bears are particularly hairy about the rest of their bodies, others incredibly furry, yet others though rightfully bears, have little or no fur on their chests, arms, legs, back, butt, etc. So, one of the following may be added to better describe a bear's fur:

f++ *way* above average fur
f+ above average fur
f furry in a bearish sense
(none) "neutral," average fur from a sample population of both bears and nonbears
f− below average fur
f− − *way* below average fur–"Nair-smooth to the max!"

t–The Tallness Factor

To describe bears that are tall or short for their frame.

t++ a virtual giant bear
t+ taller than average

t tall but not very tall
(none) average height
t– shorter than average
t– – a bear of very small stature

w–The Weight Factor

For those who prefer their bears more or less fluffy.

w++ a round bear or *big* teddy bear
w+ a big-boned bear
w bear with a tummy
(none) average weight for frame
w– a thin bear (aka, otter)
w– – a bony bear

c–The Cub Factor

For the junior up-and-coming bears.

c++ complete daddy's boy
c+ definite cub
c cub tendencies
(none) not "cubbish"
c– looks like a cub but isn't

d–The Daddy Factor

For the cubs, etc.

d++ *daddy*, with a vengeance (even his parents call him *sir*!)
d+ definite daddy
d daddyish tendencies
(none) not a daddy
d– looks like a daddy but isn't.

Note there are now also hybrid classes "cd" and "dc"

cd a cub with "daddy tendencies"; sort of like a "grown-up cub."
dc a daddy with cub-like tendencies/features

dc – more daddy than cub
d+c *real* daddyish and also *very* cubbish

g–The Grope Factor

This is the amount one likes to be touched or pawed.

g++ loves to grope, paw, touch, etc.; will attack without warning; gives hugs to hot otherwise unknown bears on the street in open daylight.
g+ likes to be touched most of the time
g generally outgoing with ursine affection; a little more reserved about place or person
(none) average amount of receptivity to being touched
g – generally doesn't like people to invade his personal aura or lair
g – – You touch my bod, I break your face!

k–The Kinky Factor

For those who dare.

k++ likes just about *everything*, and we mean *everything*!!!
k+ picks and choose according to likes; willing to consider new ideas
k open minded; might choose *some* things on the "menu."
(none) kinky neutral
k – has definite *absolute* dislikes
k – – totally vanilla

s–The Sex (ok, Slut) Factor

In *some* people's bear codes, "s" might really mean "k" (since "k" *was* originally "s" in the earlier versions of the NBCS).

s – – strictly monogamous-relationship oriented; no outside affairs, or in some cases, sex *only* in relationships.
s – relationship oriented; prefers a formal sort of relationship over playing around; however, the scope of the word relationship is not defined here.

(none) relationship neutral
s neutral to relationships or monogamy
s+ will form relationships which are generally open-ended
s++ strictly polygamous; prefers very open relationships *only.*

***m**–The Muscle Factor*

For those who like meat on them bones.

m++ Arnold Schwarzenegger is that you?
m+ definitely works out or is a ranchhand
m some definition or blue collar
(none) muscle neutral

***e**–The Endowment Factor*

Sometimes a size queen's gotta do what a size queen's gotta do.

e++ gets complete respect even from straight men
e+ gets attention
e noteworthy
(none) endowment neutral

***h**–The Behr Factor*

For behrs (men without beards but bears). You might also put a parenthesized number for the "B" designation to give an idea of what the person would look like with a beard.

h behr (moustache no beard)
h+ definite behr (moustache no beard)
h – no beard *or* moustache! (Very rare but still cave dwelling.)

***r**–The Rugged/Outdoor Factor*

r++ "Grizzly Adams"
r+ flannel, jeans, C&W really *are* second skin

r	spends some time outdoors, camping
(none)	rugged neutral
r−	prefers indoor-type activities (techie or three-piece)
r− −	never seen in the outdoors at all

p*–*The Peculiar Factor

p	some idiosyncracies–no judgment made to whether these are "good" or "not so good"

q*–*The Q Factor (ahem)

q	for bears who are out–*way* out–and enjoy every minute it. Stereotypes be damned, get out the chiffon and anything wise, because girlfriend, as Aunt Mame says, "Life is a banquet and most poor bastards are starving to death!"

(For the stunned reading this: Yes, Virginia, *q* is a *good* thing, just as t− − and t++ are *good* things, w− − and w++ are *good* things; nothing negative should be associated with the *labels* pertaining to classification!)

ADDITIONAL PUNCTUATION

The following aren't graded; they are just flags attached to the overall classification.

v	for variable–Said trait is not very rigid, may change with time or with individual interaction, e.g., some guys who are generally *real* daddies may turn into *real* cubs occasionally, etc.
?	for traits where there is no hard information available and the value is completely guessed at, e.g., a picture of a hot bear that looks like a rugged outdoorsman [r+?], but in reality could be a three-piece suit bear.
:	for traits which are observed but uncertain, e.g., a guy who is wearing a lot of clothes, so you can't be sure he's an [f+], but his forearms really suggest that he is, hence [f+]

! for cases where the trait is as close to a prototype as possible, or an exemplary case of a specific trait, e.g., the ultimate: [f++!].

() for indicating "cross-overs" or ranges, e.g., a guy who goes from [k] to [k++] depending on the situation, e.g., a [mostly "k"] could use [k(++)]

You can make the punctuation as detailed as desired, although the best ones to read are the ones which are the most clear and simple to understand.

Note: None of the classification materials in any way suggests a ranking or value judgement, in terms of what constitutes a "better" bear. Every person has their own favorite type!

Chapter 10

John Rand, Photographer: An Interview with Les Wright

Transcription by Dale Wehrle

Les Wright: How did you get started in photography? What drew you to this medium?

John Rand: Like many students, I think. I was an art student and I began to use a camera as a Graphics Art Assistant doing graphics for the community college I attended. I began to use a 35mm camera at that time. What I was being drawn to involved a lengthier process. I was using it in a submissive way to approach painting because I was very much motivated to be an artist. (I thought being an artist meant being a painter.) But I also found that I was very excited by using a camera for street photography, because it had a kind of dynamic interaction in the real world that drawing a model in a studio didn't have, at least at that time for me.

LW: Who have been your mentors in photography? Did you draw from perspective painting?

JR: I'm not sure if I have any mentors for perspective painting. I was very inspired by Diane Arbus' photographs and Richard Avedon's work initially, I had some good teachers but I don't think they were a strong motivator for me in that way.

LW: Do you prefer to work in black-and-white or color? Why?

JR: They both have their uses. Any "fine artist," as the cliché has it, would use black-and-white because it represents art quality, and, yes, I tend to prefer using black-and-white, but mostly for the abstraction. Since I specialize in bears, and a number of bears are into leather, black-and-white and leather seem to go together pretty well most of the time. However, I like the idea of color, and I do occasionally use it. I like using it in a delicate way–I'd rather see color muted, not grossly saturated, and black-and-white with its contrast.

LW: Where do you work? What kind of equipment do you use?

JR: Primarily I work in my house–my living room is a studio. I use a Pentax 6 × 7 and I use Ilford 120 roll film, 125 ASA. I have a Speedotron strobe with umbrellas, and I tend to play with those things. In the last several years when I've gone to bear events I've been using a Contax TVS, a very high quality point-and-shoot, and it does wonderful work for that type of shooting.

LW: What do you look for in a model?

JR: I like a certain heftiness in a bear, a certain kind of look that I like. I have kind of codified that, especially in my earliest photographs. I know it's a stereotype of sorts, and I have talked in the past about my discomfort with stereotyping, but . . . there are visual elements I like to work with–a certain sense of roundness, a certain sense of bigness. Some of my best images, however, have come from the exception at times. I try to be fluid, though I have some distinct ideas that I'm excited by, and can really work well photographing them.

LW: How do you find your models? Do you "pose" them to express what you might see or do you let the camera reveal aspects of their inner selves?

JR: First, I find my models in bars, I've found some of them at parades, and of course at bear events. I definitely pose people but I also try to let them relax and let them go through their own body language, their own way of holding themselves. I think that when I can catch some of that I get very interesting images. I do not see the camera as necessarily revealing inner aspects of themselves.

Initially, I wanted my models to look angry because it reflected some of the anger I was feeling in my life at the time, my frustration with everything that was going down. But I don't see that now, and, in fact I try to have a party in front of the camera–whatever I can do to get people relaxed and less conscious that they're being photographed.

LW: Do you view yourself as a documentary photographer or a fine arts photographer? What is your purpose in making these photographs?

JR: There's been a continuing dialogue and debate between the documentary aspects of photography and fine arts. I think "documentary" is a bit of a misnomer–we've used the camera for about a century and a half now as a means of recording or at least freezing moments of events in the continuum of life. But it is really out of the sequence of our perception of the world. That may be one of the reasons it's very important to us, a way of crystallizing things in this timeless void, or vacuum.

The idea of documentary photography is incredibly manipulative. I was recently included in a show called "Veracity: Challenging the Truth and Meaning of Photography," or something like that, arranged by the County Museum of Los Angeles and displayed at California State University, Los Angeles. Basically it was saying that these photographers (including myself) were using the idea of the documentary to their own ends. I think that is *always* the case, even a "neutral" newspaper photographer who places himself in a situation, supposedly not taking a stance, is having an effect, manipulating the perceptions of anyone that reads the article or sees the images.

I am intrigued that people perceive photographs as reality or as a facsimile of such, and I like tweeking that a bit–to manipulate that both ways: to make it very obviously a lie or to very dramatically appear to be the truth. The mass audience is more aware of that than in earlier times.

I can't help but see myself as a fine arts photographer because my background is in fine art, and yet my purpose relates to that sort of propagandistic element, the documentor. My purpose is to make images that have a validity in the world.

LW: What drew you to bears professionally, as subject matter for your work?

JR: I was very excited when the first few issues of *BEAR* magazine came out. A model in the first one I got was called "Gordon," and I thought, "How wonderful! This is more like what I'm into." Then it became a stereotype, and I had my own sense of bears, perhaps somewhat bigger, somewhat older, but more varied than the direction that *BEAR* was going in at the time. I didn't see those photos as art (they weren't intended to be). I wanted to do something in a more aesthetically satisfying way, to be erotic, not pornographic. That's where I developed into my own work.

LW: What drew you to bears on a personal level?

JR: They're the kind of people I like to be around. I think they're as varied as any other group of people. But there's a visual thing, an erotic thing, a certain type of person I like to look at–and not everyone you like to look at you're comfortable being with. But, most of the friends I have are that way–I don't quite understand it, not in an intellectual way–there's an emotional thing there, a camaraderie I've never felt before.

LW: What is your connection to–or involvement with–the bear community?

JR: I've always been very much of an outsider with just about everything–art, socially, sexually, whatever. I found myself being drawn into the bear situation, and being absolutely ecstatic going to Bear Expo, and feeling part of something. I'm a part of BEARS L.A. I do some of the pictures for their newsletter, and that's where it starts.

LW: Do you have a definition of a bear?

JR: I also have a physical definition, but I think it's a state of mind, an inclusiveness, openmindedness, and acceptance of oneself as one is.

LW: Where have your works been published or exhibited?

JR: The first exhibition of my bear photography was at an OUT auction, around 1990 or so, which had a couple of my images. A show called "Photonominal '93" in Jamestown, New York, showed the first comprehensive body of my photographs. This was exciting because later that year one of them was published and favorably reviewed in *Artform* magazine, something of a lifetime goal for me. I'm real proud of that.

I've been in quite a few shows since then.

My very first show was in 1980. It was an exhibition at an art gallery at UC Riverside, of photographs of sort of a multicultural diversity I had taken while I was still rather closeted. Even though I had a sense of insecurity and fear of being honest with myself, I included bears. My street photography, which was from the seventies, also included bears. But again, I hadn't come out and wasn't really honest with myself, and *that's* what's real important about this work now. It took me many years to get to the point where I could see this is what I'm into, without having to be closeted about it.

LW: What audiences are your works drawing–other bears, the gay community, the art world, the general public?

JR: Well, it seems the art world presently, though there are lots of "art worlds." Although I don't seek them out, I'd say a few of the people typically involved in the art world which dominates a lot of the college and community venues for exhibiting have shown an interest in my work. The nice thing is that the bear community is seeing a growing interest in my work.

LW: How do you feel about the photographic art of Diane Arbus? Joel-Peter Witkin? Mark Chester?

JR: I don't know if we can put those people together! I mentioned earlier, Diane Arbus was a very early inspiration to me. Her work, the early work of Richard Avedon. When I began to do my homework more thoroughly, August Sander became inspiring to me, Timothy O'Sullivan, Weegee. Diane Arbus' work draws very heavily upon them, although she has an incredible close-ended vision and which even now has a rather timeliness for many gay people's experience.

Joel-Peter Witkin I saw, of course, in the early eighties like everybody else and the work was pretty dynamic then. There is a certain grunginess that has a turn-of-the-century perversity about it, which is kind of fun. I saw a show five or six years ago where he did Venus and he was re-doing all this art-history, art-historical stuff, and it was incredibly bad. His work doesn't do anything for me.

Mark Chester I have never seen. We've had arguments over the telephone. He's seen me but I haven't seen him, so I really can't say anything about him. But we both agreed we had a bit of a personality conflict.

LW: Are there any other photographers you have strong feelings about?

JR: Now this I become very biased about, because there's a Diane Arbus that I want to own that I still don't have the money to buy. The longer it takes, the more expensive the piece gets.

When I saw the first issue of *Bulk Male* I had an experience similar to what I've experienced once in a great while, walking into an art gallery where my jaw drops and I realize that this work is really good and I get intensely depressed because I'm angry and intensely jealous because I realize, "Here is somebody very good–I wish I was capable of doing what they have done." I literally dropped the first issue of *Bulk Male* when I opened the magazine and saw the pictures of the two guys grunging it up in the auto shop together. I believe Van Lynn Floyd was the photographer and I complimented him, I was very impressed by them.

I have gallery-directored at community college art galleries and so I have lots of contacts with artists and photographers. A couple of colleagues of mine, Gregg Segal and Nancy Floyd, did a series called "Gunsters" which I exhibited, and which I was very moved by. I have one of his photographs where he happened to do a couple of bears with their guns. ("The Gunsters" was about people with their guns which is being shown around at some of the museums right now.) Nancy's work was women with guns, so that there was kind of an edge to it, a bit off from the bear thing, but inspiring to me.

LW: What was your first professional gig?

JR: Oh god, in the late seventies I photographed weddings, and I wasn't very good at it. It was horrible, but it paid my rent. Also in the seventies, even when I was working at the community college, I got little jobs here and there, did all kinds of things. More recently I've done a cover and a centerspread for *American Bear*, one coming out in *BEAR* magazine, *Bulk Male*, and *Provocateur.*

LW: When did you know you were a photographer?

JR: I really hate that term because I think we tend to stereotype photographers as sort of "gadgety" little guys always carrying light meters around. I'm not a very technical photographer.

LW: How do you support yourself? Does your photography pay?

JR: I support myself by working several jobs. I teach, I run the art gallery. I've taught photography at the university level and would love to do that again. Photography doesn't pay very much. I make a little off my art work and my photographs, but not enough to live on, though of course I wish I could.

LW: Over the last five years there has been a proliferation of bear merchandising. How do you feel about that?

JR: This is a question that you asked me quite a while ago. As I said then, I feel very good about it. It's important, (laughs) in propagandistic terms. I have no problems with merchandising or com-

"Ron and Van" (Photo © John Rand)

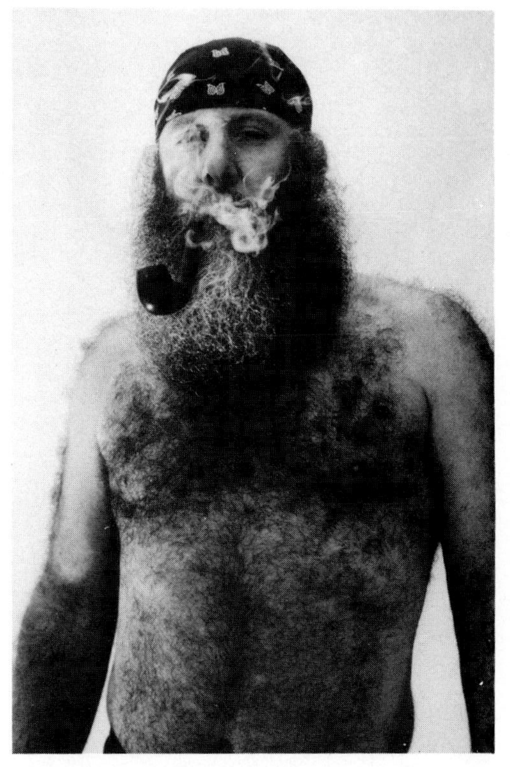

"Antonio with pipe" (Photo © John Rand)

"Ken" (Photo © John Rand)

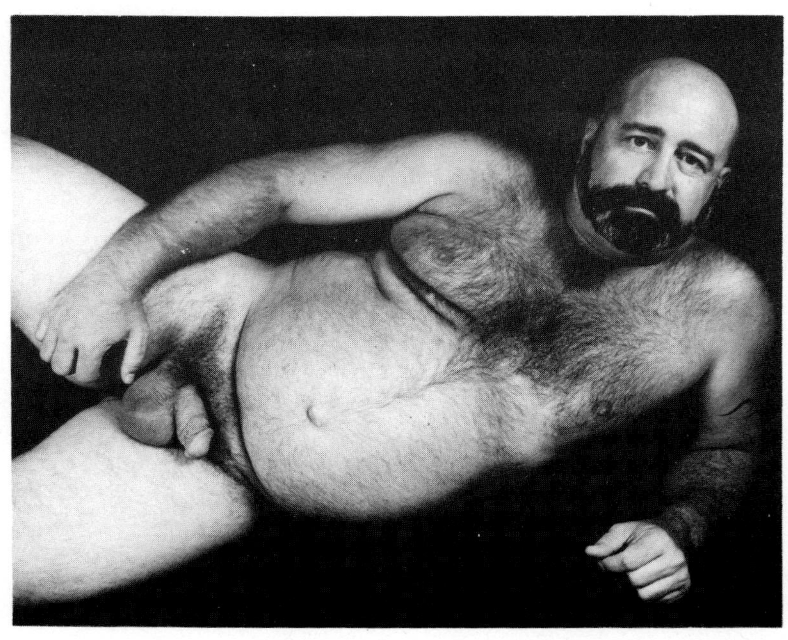

"Mike" (Photo © John Rand)

mercializing, because it says "we're here." It may affect someone having trouble coming out, the way I did, very much disliking the predominant gay culture, these skinny hairless twinkies laying around swimming pools, athletically having sex, which I was very turned off to. I could not relate to them, I could not identify with that whole scene. I think it's really important to see the bear thing. It reminds people that there are alternate ways, diverse ways that gay people are. I think that's really healthy. And if someone can make a success out of it–I doubt there are many people becoming millionaires from their bear art or bear merchandising–more power to them.

I'm not down on capitalism in that way (that's a whole other issue). It would be incredible if the bear scene became a dominant fashion for a while. Fashion's such a transient thing, but I think that would be wonderful to have our moment in the sun.

LW: What has been your relationship to the gay community? That is, are you a part of the first wave of bears who, in the mid-eighties, saw self-identification as a bear as a retort to being excluded by the then-fading "clone scene" or are you of another bear persuasion?

JR: I'm probably of the alienated art-twinkie, former-twinkie persuasion. I hate to say it, but I guess I grew into being a bear (laughs). Boy, that sounds dumb. I think having the background in art heightened whatever social alienation or personal problems I grew up with, and then rejecting the art world because of its disinterest in me helped me more in becoming a bear.

I have always liked the physical characteristics of the guys that were bears. And that blue-collar flannel quality of bear folks is almost a return to the counterculture I was part of as a high school kid.

LW: Do you see bears overlapping with other gay male subcultures?

JR: It obviously overlaps with the leather scene, although I'm not really a heavy leather person. There may be even some overlapping with the rubber scene, although rubber and fur don't go together too well usually.

LW: Have you seen the mainstream-gay press becoming more receptive to bears in general and your images in particular in recent times? Have any new doors opened for your work?

JR: Well, there was the *Frontiers* articles recently that you and Mel Baker did, and a few years back there was an article on heavier men in *Drummer* or another magazine like that. It was in fact the only one I ever bought–it had a big picture from the guy's "Beer Belly in Bondage" video, which was just an absolute wonderful classic.

I don't know if they're becoming more receptive or they're just realizing that there's a large group there that they haven't merchandised to. As time goes on an artist becomes more accepted and I'm not sure if that reflects an opening up of the culture.

Yes, new doors have opened for my work. I'm currently showing in a gallery (Rupert Goldsworthy found me) in Berlin, Germany.

LW: Do you see this gay bear iconography subliminally percolating into mainstream advertising yet?

JR: There is definitely an element of it. But I don't think that it can become a dominant thing. I think mainstream advertising sees it as surveys and marketing, and if they realize this percentage of people making up x population can be sold to they're going to do something with it. Of course, I would love to do an advertisement or something. I absolutely detest Richard Avedon's fashion photography as advertising. He is a great photographer and that's probably why I have a certain amount of jealousy. Doing a bear commercial would be soooo wonderful, but not likely.

LW: How do you define or deal with gay male masculinity in your own life and your work?

JR: That's important because initially I wanted to find a certain type of masculinity, I wanted a certain kind of machismo in my photographs. And at moments I've found that, and yet, what I think I've found is that it's the stereotypical sexual fantasies I've learned are so incredibly limited. Usually when you look for something you find something else. I wanted to find this sort of masculinist man, and I find boys. I don't mean twinkies–I see the child in every man. I said that in something I struggled to write, and it is interesting that, you know, we are what we are essentially from when we were very small children.

There is something about masculinity–I don't want to say gay masculinity, because I see ideal masculinity as being gay–something about being relaxed, being in control of one's own understanding of one's emotions, and being able to think things through rationally, I have been addressing in my work.

LW: Do you think your work has helped gay men or the gay male community to grow or change?

JR: I wish that it would or could or has. I would feel very pleased. I'm not sure I have reached enough of the gay community. I did a show last year, or the year before, at the Gay and Lesbian Center. They had these little 'plex display things outside of the HIV testing room, and when I went in there to be tested I thought it would be real wonderful to do a show because it would be very easy, a kind of irony in a way, to switch the photographs all the time as a kind of conceptual art piece. I got an incredible amount of flack from the supervising person there when I did get the show, which I got screwed around with left and right (that was very, very discouraging). I don't really know how I affected people. Friends went to see it and they were also frustrated by the way people at that particular place were handling my work.

I think I have recognized in some people what they hadn't seen in themselves. This is kind of sad, though, because I see beauty in them that they do not see themselves. I wish more people that are bears would see that, rather than chasing after a twinkie ideal or something. It's too small of a thing to have a real cultural effect. Maybe it does and I'm not aware of it.

LW: Can women be bears? Where do you stand in the inclusivity/exclusivity debacle?

JR: Oh boy, well, I guess unfortunately I'm a bit of a separatist. I have women colleagues whose company I enjoy, working with and talking to. I don't socialize with them very much, and at times I've expressed the desire to be more social, but I have very little time, and the time I do have for myself I want to spend with other bears!

LW: Do you see your work as subversive? In what ways?

JR: Oh, absolutely. I mean I wouldn't want the scenario to happen because I don't want my house to get burned down, but I think it would be just absolutely wonderful for some big burly midwestern bear and his wife and kids to discover a series of my photographs because I think these people are so unaware of the outside world, so unaware of themselves that it would shatter their notions, their presuppositions. Not that one needs to do that, but occasionally I think that could be a good thing. The danger is one would just create more hatred.

I definitely would like to subvert more of the gay twinkie world, because of their embracing of gay stereotypes, the beefcake stereotypes, not allowing themselves to be who they naturally are. I think if one can be truthful, you're being subversive, because we have so much around us that is not truth.

LW: Is there an implicit connection between your models, your work, and the AIDS epidemic?

JR: Implicit, implied–yes. I very eagerly want to photograph people. I never get tired of my photographic work with bears, there's a continuing energy which tells me it's something vital in my life. I really think it's important to get people photographed as quickly as possible because people seem to come and go so much. It's not always AIDS, but it's just that our time here is so brief and maybe for a lot of gay people it's even briefer than for most. I like the idea of their image living on past them, I think that's really wonderful.

LW: Any new projects currently taking shape or in the offing?

JR: Well, I have just published [January 1996, ed.] my first book, *10 Bear Men*, and I have the series ready I want to publish or I will publish in time. I have to find homes for a couple thousand books first. My next book will be called *Bear Pairs*.

SECTION III: BEAR SPACES

Chapter 11

The Original Bears Mailing List: An Interview with Steve Dyer

Conducted by Les Wright, May 31, 1995, Boston, MA

Les Wright: Let's start at the beginning: What's your name and what are you doing here?

Steve Dyer: My name is Steve Dyer and I live in Cambridge, Massachusetts. I've lived in Boston all my life. You could say that I am a member of the bear community and have done some things which some members of the bear community think are interesting or helpful.

LW: Have you lived other places where you've been involved with the bear community?

SD: I've always lived in Boston, although the Bears Mailing List had its start on Gay Pride Day in 1988 in San Francisco.

LW: How did the BML start? What was its inception?

SD: As you might know, there is a discussion group called soc.motss, for the discussion of gay issues by gay people and those interested in gay issues. It's been around since 1983. We had a gathering of folks there, about a hundred people, who had been talking to each other for the previous five years. This coincided with the Gay Pride Parade in San Francisco. That's where I met Brian Gollum, who was the other original editor of the Bears Mailing List. He was there with friends of friends to attend the soc.motss convention. Sometimes we call it the motss com. Anyway, Brian is also large, bearded, and bearish.

LW: And currently bald. He shaved his head.

SD: He and I were chatting, "wouldn't it be great to have a forum for men like us, for other bears?" *BEAR* magazine was in issue one, two, or three. (It was very early on.) The whole cultural awareness of this phenomenon was just beginning to get going. We thought having a mailing list on the Internet would be a fun thing to do, having no idea at the time how popular it would become. There's where it started.

LW: If we could back up for just a minute, let's talk about soc.motss. What is that? How did that come into being? What was your involvement with that?

SD: It's sort of hard to explain what soc.motss is to people who are not familiar with electronic communities. But soc.motss is part of something called Usenet, and it's like a forum or an echo. Those are terms that are used in other BBS systems, where people will write articles, and those articles are then distributed to other computers, which in turn distribute them to other computers, and so on and so on, until all of the computer users interested in receiving soc.motss receive the article. So, as a result, what you'll see are individual people's contributions engaging in several simultaneous conversations on different topics. Usenet itself is not just about gay issues. In fact, soc.motss was a forum created specifically to talk about things that gay people are interested in. But all sorts of things are discussed on there, from computer-technical issues to political rants, to just about anything you can imagine.

LW: Now, when you say discussion, there are a number of different ways this can happen over the Internet. Now, are you talking about "live chat?"

SD: That's a good point. Back when soc.motss started being able to discuss things in "real time," "live chat" as you see today wasn't available. Very few computers were physically attached to the Internet, so there was no way for me to talk to someone half way across the world. Usenet was a medium where people would compose entire essays or articles which would then be distributed, reaching the other computers over a period of a day or two, or three. So, no this wasn't in "real time" and soc.motss still isn't in "real time." You read from a selected list of things other people have written and then you may choose to respond to that or not.

LW: Every posting, every message to soc.motss, goes to all of the subscribers on the list?

SD: There's no list involved really. Let's say I wrote an article to soc.motss. It would be tagged with my name, where I'm from, and I would send that article to a neighboring computer, probably by modem. (These days it's done very frequently by the Internet directly, without the use of a modem.) Once received that other site would send that article to all of the computers participating in Usenet. (Those articles are kept on the hard disk of each one of the systems, not in people's mailboxes but in a centralized place.) And then if you, let's say on Delphi, decide to read soc.motss, you would be using a program that would essentially display the articles that were in that dedicated area.

LW: And then I would have the choice of either reading it or else downloading it to my computer ?

SD: It really depends on what the software is on the computer you're reading it on. But you could read it immediately or perhaps save it and download it later. Most of the articles that appear on the 'Net aren't worth saving.

LW: When did soc.motss come into being?

SD: There was a discussion group that predated soc.motss. Before self-identified gay people had their own forum, there was a discussion group for singles, that is, unmarried folks, generally–a lot of "hets" bantering back and forth. Out of that someone said, "Is there somewhere for gay people to chat?" Frankly, the details are lost in the mists of time. (It was a long time ago!) It may have in fact come out of a more explicit kind of prejudice, because gay people would pick up a thread of discussion and keep their own points of view. What you frequently saw back then, and still often see today, is if you're in a forum that is not explicitly for the discussion of gay issues, they'll have some troglodyte out there saying, "I don't want to hear about it!" It may have started with that. It turned out that I helped champion the formation of this group for the discussion of gay issues and was one of the people who worked to see that the group was really formed. Back then the 'Net as we know it was much, much smaller. In order to create a newsgroup you had to make a very good case for it among a select group of people. Since then it's gotten larger and newsgroup formation is more highly regimented and less personal and less politicized. Back then we really had to argue forcefully for why having a Usegroup for gay issues would not lead to the death of the 'Net. People at the time frequently would read the 'Net from their place of business. And people were frequently concerned that if their boss noticed that there was something about homosexuality there the boss would just cut the modem cable and their access on their machine would disappear. So there was a lot of politicking and persuading that had to go on.

LW: And this was roughly when?

SD: About 1983, October of '83.

LW: What were you doing at that time professionally?

SD: Professionally I was working at a company called BBN, which is a pretty well known high-tech firm in Boston, and also fairly progressive, had a fairly collegial atmosphere, much a spin-off of the MIT/Harvard educational system. I had access to the 'Net through BBN and I wasn't particularly out at the time, though not particularly not out, if you know what I mean, and I thought it was a great idea. I really fought for the group.

LW: Who did you have to present your case to?

SD: As I mentioned earlier, back then, very few computers were actually connected to the Internet, which is generally a high-speed network that often doesn't involve low-speed modems (the kind most home-users still use). So, Usenet was a conglomerate of individual computers, frequently running on a UNIX operating system, which ran software that would take articles that people would write and then distribute them to their peers, which had been set up ahead of time. There were about twelve or thirteen large computer sites, such as AT&T, informally known as The Cabal because their companies would pay for the distribution of large volumes of data to be transferred over phone wires from site to site. So, back then everybody's articles funnelled into one of these backbone sites, which would then arrange to fully distribute the articles among everybody else. So, if you couldn't convince people on the backbone that such a group should exist, then it wouldn't get propagated. Those were the people we had to convince that it was good idea. Generally, people at high-tech firms, engineers, scientists, or at educational institutions. How did we work on them? We discussed it on the 'Net in other news groups and we sent e-mail back and forth, personal e-mail, arguing for the group's creation. You might wonder why it's not called soc.gay. I should mention, first of all, that the name of a newsgroup is a top-level category, followed by a descriptor. So, S-O-C, or "soc"–sometimes pronounced "sohsh" [as in "social"] is for the discussion of social issues. But why is it called motss, M-O-T-S-S? It was a play on words, of "members of the same sex" and "motos," which was a common way to refer to your boyfriend or girlfriend at the time, as in, "I'm going to take my motos to a party tonight." We wanted to call the group soc.gay. But that was much, much, much too alarming back in 1983. It was too hard to argue for that. Plus, someone suggested motss flippantly, it was such a cute idea. And of course, it's an obscure name so that if the president of a company suddenly saw soc.motss listed they wouldn't have a clue. It was a subversive way to let the group be formed and have it widely propagated. A couple of years after that one of the members of the backbone Cabal, a guy by the name of Mark Horton, wrote and said this should be soc.gay. (This is during a time when a lot of newsgroups were being renamed anyway.) We polled the people who were participating regularly on soc.motss, and they liked the original name. So we kept it. That was probably in 1985 or so. Nowadays, I would say, it's outlived its usefulness. There are millions of people on the 'Net now, millions of gay people who don't know what resources are out there. Those are the people who aren't being served as well because they won't recognize motss as meaning "other gay people." It does have the advantage of not using the word "gay," since it sometimes refers exclusively to gay men. This gets you into the issue of how do you name a resource that is both for lesbians and gay men? Motss has the advantage of being completely obscure.

LW: Two lists that I subscribe to–one is uk.motss, the other is ne.motss–made me think it was a generic label picked up by a lot of other groups.

SD: Right. In other words, other newsgroups–uk.motss is for gay people in the United Kingdom and ne.motss for people in New England. Once someone becomes acculturated to the 'Net, becomes a part of the community, strange acronyms suddenly have meaning. Then it's easier to find things.

LW: One more question about soc.motss. Are there any other milestones in the growth of that we haven't touched upon?

SD: The group's been through a lot in the last twelve years. There are more people on there than ever. It's hard to read because there are so many people. We always thought the large number of people was a problem, but it only gets worse. Some other milestones: I think the first motss com was a transcendent experience. A hundred people who had been reading each other's material but who hadn't met in person came to San Francisco–and it was a three- or four-day lovefest. It was just great! It really changed the quality of the group's interactions too, because knowing people in person and getting the nuances you get from their being in front of you is so much different from just knowing a bunch of photons on the screen. There's been a yearly motss com ever since then. They have all been great, but they weren't . . . well you know, the first time is always the best!

Other notable issues. We had a long-time contributor, Rob Bernardo, who died in 1992 of AIDS. It happened quite suddenly. I think he learned relatively late about his condition. He sort of dropped off the net for a while, he was depressed, mourning for himself, and the next thing many of us knew he was in the hospital. I happened to be out in San Francisco when that happened. (He was based just outside of Berkeley.) A number of us visited him there and felt very lucky to do that. When he died it was really an example of collective mourning. It was a wonderful outpouring of grief and appreciation for him. People who knew Rob in person, people who had known him only through his writings–everybody–had something to say. That's an interesting phenomenon. It can only exist in an environment similar to soc.motss. I'm sure it's occurred on other electronic forums, but that was really special. It's sort of telling, too–he was one of the first people who participated regularly on soc.motss who died of AIDS. That's a long time, twelve years. In some sense, we were spared up until that point. That was really very special–very sad, but very special.

LW: I just got a letter from Bob Hay in Australia saying that Ozbears has folded, in part, because a number of key members have passed away.

SD: I had seen his note on the Bears Mailing List, that it had folded, but I didn't hear what the reason was.

LW: Well, he actually gave quite a long analysis. We've been talking about it for a while, and he is doing a chapter for *The Bear Book* about bears in Australia. One of the things I want to focus in on, tying all this together, is that the Ozbears were a very special group when they started out, there was actual camaraderie–Bob talks about the Australian sense of "mateship"–but over time the group just got too big.

SD: This is a real, live group of people, right?

LW: Oh yeah. It's a social group. The same thing was my experience in San Francisco. My original understanding of beardom was that it was basically a sociosexual environment, a place to meet people and be sexual. The original calling together was a group of people who got together for private sex parties, in a very warm and supportive kind of atmosphere. Friendships grew out of it, and the group just grew bigger and bigger and bigger and bigger. It also went through a transformation, from that sense of a special community to a dissipation because it had gotten so large.

I didn't go on-line for several years and I used to raise the question, "Is it possible to be a bear if you're not computerized?" because so much communication among what I call the bear community now was happening both face to face in San Francisco and, at the same time, people were connecting through cyberspace in an international community of like-minded bears.

SD: I think there are a couple of things going on there. I think that the bear community is much larger than the "cyberbear" community. I read a comment just today from someone who had just come back from the Bear Pride gathering in Chicago, who said, "I didn't realize there were so many bears that had never heard of the Bears Mailing List–or of computers!" We have such a large community that is on computers that it's easy to forget that there is a much larger bear community that has grown up and out of individual bear clubs in different cities, who are not at all computer-literate and have not plugged into that. There are more people to be recruited!

LW: This was one of the dynamics early on–that people were communicating "by word of mouth" through computers. That was a separate path from *BEAR* magazine, or the Bear Hugs.

SD: I think you're quite right. The Bears Mailing List started at the same time, at almost exactly the same time, as the original Bear Hugs in San Francisco. And, in fact, the first issues of the Bears Mailing List contained trip reports of the first Bear Hugs–how great the orgies were, who was there, and what great sex was there. I think you're really right in that.

LW: Do you have any dish to share with us?

SD: Nope, not me! I think that a lot of the seeding and spreading via the 'Net at that time got a lot of people, who otherwise would not have been plugged into the initial growth of this phenomenon, to feel like they were a part of it.

LW: What was the group atmosphere, initially, of the people who connected through the Bears Mailing List? Was there a particular sense of connectedness?

SD: This is what we did: Brian and I talked about it in the summer of 1988. I had a computer of my own, that I could use as the distribution point for his mailing list. Essentially, people would send in their e-mail addresses. They would submit articles. Those would be compiled into a longer document, a digest if you will, and then I would run a program that would say: send this digest to everybody on this list. We called it a mailing list. It's very similar to a U.S.-mail mailing list, except that it's with all these computers. When it started there were very few people on it, mainly the people we thought would be interested already, other bears we knew who happened to be connected by computer. We also mentioned this on soc.motss, and I think that was about it. It grew very slowly. I wish I had a graph of the growth of the group. There were probably no more than two hundred people the first several years of its existence, by 1990 maybe 200 or 300. We can get a sense of that if you look back in the old issues, because every now and then when we'd hit some sort of double-zero milestone, I would remark on that to others on the mailing list. It had a real exponential growth once it got past a certain point. More and more, people would hear about it through different means. There was an article in *Drummer* magazine. I think you wrote it, didn't you?

LW: Oh, yeah, that was in 1990.

SD: Yeah, the summer of 1990. Brian Gollum was able to mention the Bears Mailing List and its e-mail address in *Drummer*.

LW: Yes, that's right.

SD: I was away that summer in the Soviet Union, the then-Soviet Union, and I came back and there was an issue of *Drummer* here. Brian had pointed it out to me, and here was my e-mail address in *Drummer*! Things were still very regimented and government-oriented network back then. So I had a lot of concerns, well, it flashed through my head for about a millisecond, but I was a little concerned when I saw that. I stopped moderating the Bears Mailing List in October of 1994. By the time I stopped we had almost sixteen hundred people. That's a lot of people!

LW: And that's literally from all over the world?

SD: Yes, Thailand, Poland, Mexico, Columbia, France, the UK, everywhere you can imagine. And since the list has started up again under Henry Mensch's editorial role, I'm sure it's even more varied. Finding out that there is this common archetype, this sexual attraction and desire, that is cross-cultural is amazing.

I've often been struck by the number of men from Asian countries (many Asian men are not hairy. There are some hairy Asian men, but many aren't) who just crave bears. And I've certainly heard that often enough when they hear about the list and they write to me and say please give me more information about it.

LW: That's another discussion, too: what is a bear? It seems to me that, depending on the person, it might be body hair, it might be beards, it might be bellies–the "three B's." For some people it has to be all three. I still find that confusing, what each person means by a bear. It's certainly not univocal.

SD: It's a perennial discussion, and one that is hard to discuss on an electronic forum with many people with different opinions. What I mean is, the discussion doesn't go anywhere. It can't. It's like discussing flavors of Christianity, everybody has his own preference.

LW: The BML has a categorizing system.

SD: You're talking about the, oh what is the name of it? I'm completely blanking out. And I've been living with this for the past so many years. . .

LW: . . . the bear code.

SD: Yeah, the bear code. It was really a joke.

LW: Did you have . . . ?

SD: No, I had nothing to do with it. Two members of the Bears Mailing List were at either a Wendy's or a Denny's the Thanksgiving of 1989, and they were both astronomers, so they were very much given to categorization. How do you describe a star? Well, it's this string of attributes and those attributes are generally abbreviated. They thought it might be fun to try this on men who think of themselves, or who other people think of, as bears. So, they invented a classification scheme based on the astronomical classification of stars. It's cryptic–if you were to see this without knowing the bear code it would look like gibberish. In fact, it's just a series of letters, potentially with little pluses or minuses after the letter, where a letter is a particular quality. . . . Anyway, it was completely a lark, but people picked up on it and took it very seriously. Perhaps too seriously, because when people would introduce themselves on the Bears Mailing List they would say, "I don't know what the bear code is so I apologize I have to use English." This is of course the preferred language to begin with! It was never intended as a serious classification scheme. But it can be useful as a kind of shorthand. Say you love guys with long beards, if someone has a description of himself as a B8, that might catch someone's eye.

LW: This is another perennial topic that gets bantered back and forth on the BML, discussions about the validity and appropriateness of the bear code, how accurate it is. You know, there's a very subjective aspect to it.

SD: It's a very subjective aspect. I mean, that's part of the joke, of course. You know, astronomical classifications are based on objective and quantitative criteria. Everybody can describe the length of their beard by using a B and a number, but not everybody will agree on what those numbers are. The bear code was a parody of that, but now it's getting used semiseriously, or seriously. You'll get people who are librarians, or "libearians," as they're sometimes called, these are male librarians who are bears . . .

LW: . . . some of my best friends are libearians.

SD: . . . who argue for a much finer-grained classification system.

LW: This has been a thread in recent months, of further refining the classification system.

SD: My own opinion is I'm not very interested in that–it's too anal for my taste. It's a lark, so why bother? But it's important to some people. It's hard to supplant something that's already out there, too. People are already using whatever the current one is. Unless someone is interested in rewriting it seriously, and making sure it's disseminated, there's not much chance of it getting adopted.

LW: We've been talking about the BML. What is in the BML? What actually gets discussed?

SD: Well, it's sort of funny. You might ask, how much can you say about hairy men? And the answer, as we have found out, is "quite a bit." You essentially say the same thing over and over again.

But it might be useful to give some background. "What is a bear?" A bear might be a large, hairy man, but maybe not. Maybe just a bearded man, or maybe a bearded man with a lot of hair. It's some sort of approach around an archetype, and this archetype–maybe not so much in the 1970s but in recent years–has been a devalued archetype. That is to say, if you buy most gay magazines these days, you tend to find thin, young, hairless men, sort of the Ganymede archetype. Men who don't look that way have always felt excluded, and frustrated, because very often these men, or men who like men like that, can't find cultural manifestations of the archetypes they like. Everyone looks like a twenty-three-year-old who looks seventeen. The Bears Mailing List is for men who want to discuss what they like with others who like the same things. That's a universal human desire.

What's on the Bears Mailing List? Frequently you have introductions. People may have just joined, or may have been reading for several months, and want to "come out" electronically and say, "Here I am, this is who I am, what I'm interested in. This is what I look like. Write to me, if you're interested." These introductions really aren't personal ads, they've never been intended on our part to be personal ads, although they might have the effect of a personal ad. In fact, they're much richer than personal ads. You have as much space to write about yourself as you like. You don't have to write in four-letter abbreviations. You have a chance to say more about yourself to people. It doesn't necessarily have to have a sexual animus to it, though some people are obviously looking for life-mates or sex partners, or both. That's one class of things that is discussed.

Another one is, "Hey, did you see the bear in 'movie X' or 'TV show Y?' Isn't he hot? Woof, woof!" And other people will offer their own comments. What else is discussed on there? Life stories, people's experiences growing up gay, perhaps gay and heavy. And then there's being gay and being married, which doesn't seem like such a bear topic, but there was a period several years ago when several of these incredibly hot-looking, hairy, bearded men, who happened to be married, would discover the Bears Mailing List by accident, join, and their participation would be the catalyst toward their coming out more fully, perhaps, opening up to their wives, perhaps the marriage would break up or disintegrate, or perhaps it wouldn't. There are all sorts of flavors, issues of being married, how to deal with being gay in the context of marriage. For a while I thought we should call it the MBL instead of the BML–the Married Bears List. You'd be surprised how many married men there are, people who are still married, who participate. A lot of bisexual men who may be married but are still interested. So, we have gone off on topics like that, the experience of growing up heavy and the experience of isolation, or feeling devalued, as a result of that. A lot of it is a forum for self-esteem (Oh, I hate the term; I certainly appreciate the concept) a forum for validation. It's nice to hang around with other people who like what you like and who reinforce that. So, yeah, I don't know how many issues we had published when I stopped last year, maybe about six hundred, maybe more, in the space of about seven years.

LW: I don't remember exactly the numbering, since now it is BML 2, the numbering has started over, and we are now approaching 350.

SD: Anyone who sees [this interview] should realize that BML Number 2 started about four months after I gave it up and started off with a completely new subscriber base. They sent messages out to the old list, saying that if you want to resubscribe this is how you do it.

LW: There were a lot of people talking back and forth, saying, "Oh my God, is this the end of the BML?" There was a lot of serious concern that it wouldn't be revived.

SD: It was simply a matter of someone having the right resources, like Roger Klorese, who runs a machine called QueerNet out of his own pocket, and someone like Henry Mensch who had the interest and time (he was an old BML subscriber) who manages the group. In the first six months we have already logged in two-thirds of the total number of articles of the entire first volume, so things have gone way, way up. This is not necessarily a good thing.

LW: Have you been following along now that you have "retired?"

SD: Yes. I subscribe to the new BML. You have to understand, when I was editing the previous incarnation of the BML I would get people's articles or submissions as they sent them and then, every few days or so, I would go through them and do some editing. Because I was involved in the production of it, every article that came in was of interest to me. I cared about it. It might have been a lot of work sometimes, but I had a level of interest in what was being produced that really sustained me. Now I'm just another subscriber and I finally appreciate what I heard a lot from other people who were subscribers when I was editing the list, which was, "There's just so much there! I don't have the time to read it all," "I haven't read a Bears Mailing List in six months. Maybe you should take me off the list now because I find that I won't have a chance to go back to it." I know where they're coming from. I actually still try to keep up, but if you get three 30k issues a day, and you're working or you have other things to attend to when you get home from work, I can appreciate that there can be such a thing as too much of a good thing.

The list got more and more popular and, as more and more people were on the list, when you have 1,500, 1,600 members on the list, you'd have more and more people who felt they had something to say, and legitimately so. It was really a sort of Dutchboy-with-a-finger-in-the-dike–you'll pardon the expression–because managing the volume is an issue. I don't know what the answer is.

LW: How does Henry manage editing the list at this point? I am constantly amazed, I say to myself, "Henry Mensch must not have a day job; this editing must occupy him full-time."

SD: When the new Bears Mailing List started out they made a deliberate decision not to edit anything. People would submit articles, which would get cued up to be sent once an appropriate number of articles had come in, then software would automatically send out that collection of articles.

That lasted for about six weeks, and then someone said something hurtful and nasty, which caused other people to take issue, which caused a big argument in cyberspace that appeared in subsequent issues of the mailing list. A lot of people were taken aback. They'd never seen this before. And the reason they hadn't is because when I sent the list out not everything that was submitted would be printed. If I found something that had a poor signal-to-noise ratio–more flaming there than content–I would send it back to the person and say, "Not a good idea." Now, in fact, I almost never did that. I could probably count on one hand the number of times that I had to do that in the six years that I managed it. But it just takes a spark–and we got a spark–in February. We went through a month of all sorts of nasty things being said back and forth, and people were taken aback. They said, "Well, I'm unsubscribing. I don't remember the Bears Mailing List being like this. Bears are supposed to be warm, fuzzy people who are very tolerant and don't say bad things to each other." Maybe that was sort of a Potemkin village, fostered by my–with a minimum of effort–invisibly filtering out stuff. Since that time, Henry has started doing some degree of manual moderation similar to what I was doing. As a result, things suddenly got peaceful again. It's all invisible to anyone who would be receiving the digest. This was a period where you saw a much livelier group, but also a much less interesting group, because when things degenerate into personal squabbles it brings out the worst in anybody, including people who are identified as bears.

Overall, they put a lot of work into it, and I'm glad I don't have to do it. It feels very nice to just be on the receiving end of the digest.

LW: I do see occasionally where Henry will have a bracketed comment, saying, "This is an old thread, this is something that's been discussed at great length. Go to the archives it you want to see what people had to say," or "This is not appropriate, it's too far afield from the topics for the bear list. Please take it to another list." Another comment I see is, "Please direct your reply directly to the sender of the posting of this message, not to this (public) list."

SD: And that is the kind of input that is frequently necessary. I had to do that more and more, especially toward the last few months, because it was very easy for the list to veer off away from something that might be interesting to the majority of subscribers, to things that weren't bear-related. One reason I stopped was because it finally got to me, after six years of doing this. People were discussing underwear and whether you liked boxers or briefs. Someone in the meantime had submitted a long essay on boxers and briefs and the wonderfulness of one or the other (I don't remember which). After a couple of weeks of discussing this I said "this is it" and I put a parenthetical remark in the digest. And I got back a note from the author of this magnum opus who said, "Well, I put a lot of effort into my essay, and who are you to say it shouldn't be published?!" [Steve groans to himself.] And it's funny, normally, this sort of thing rolls right off my back, but I was in a mental space where I was tired from personal issues I had encountered that year, tired from grappling and trying to know what to do with the whole problem of volume, how to direct a herd of bears. It was like herding cats. How do you keep four hundred people, who were submitting articles, on some semblance of a mainstream topic, which is very broad? I mean, it's hard to say what should be on topic for the Bears Mailing List. But you sort of know what isn't. You know, political discussions aren't. Three weeks of discussing underwear is beginning to get off topic. You try to have a rather loose leash, but I yanked on the leash and got bitten. And that was the straw that broke the camel's back, and I said, "Well, I'm not getting out of this what I am putting into it." It's not a personal issue with that guy who made that comment; it was one of many comments. I had just reached a point where I was ready for a break. And it did start up again and, if anything, it's more popular now than it was before.

LW: There is also the dynamic with volunteer, grassroots, community things, where you reach a point where you have to pass the torch. I've seen this over and over, you just reach the point where you think, it's a good idea, but somebody else needs to do it now.

SD: I think that's quite true. I had originally thought that we would just take a break for just a month or so, but I guess I really enjoyed not having to worry about that. The size of my mailbox shrank amazingly. I was no longer as popular as I thought I was. It was nice not to have that!

There were times when I was working in Europe and I was also still working to get the digest out. I would go through a couple of Internet hops, to get across trans-Atlantic, and send it out. I really felt I had a duty to do that. I also thought the only way to handle [my departure from editing this list] was some sort of shock therapy. The list had gotten too big, too unmanageable, and people needed to see the consequences of that. Again, there is no personal responsibility there; you're talking about the collective effect of 1,500 individual participants. You can't point to anybody in particular. It's a mass action. It's getting there again. But Henry is a fresh face and he hasn't burned out. He's doing a good job.

LW: I have one more question to ask you, and that is about the archives. What's in there? And why?

SD: I own my own machine, which has a lot of disk space. This is where we keep the back issues of the digest for people to refer back. Everything that's ever been published on the BML is there for later perusal. It's larger than the Bible right now; it's probably larger than all of Shakespeare's works. That has some archival quality in itself. It's really valuable that that's around. And I know that you [i.e., the Bear History Project] have a copy of it.

This archive is available electronically so people who are on the Internet can copy the material that's there to their own computers. One thing is back issues, in addition to that we have digital pictures, or digitized pictures of one sort or another. The most important ones are pictures of other members of the Bears Mailing List. People send pictures to me to be scanned in on the archive in digital form, then someone else can access that archive, bring the picture over to their computer, and see what the person whose writing they've been admiring looks like. That's a normal human curiosity and it's great that resource is there.

We also have a collection of miscellaneous erotica. Well, that's probably the wrong word–pictures that might be interesting to men who like bears, really good-looking bears who appeared in advertisements or newspapers, as well as nudes of bears or of almost-bears. There's also a collection of erotic stories written by people who belong to the BML, erotic stories that are in some sense bear-related. There is a directory solely of Tony Dias' pictures, for people who are interested in Tony Dias, Tony being a nice example of one variant of the species–a swarthy Portuguese, a very hairy, bearded man!

Fun stuff. It's there for a lark, to supplement the main Bears Mailing List. Hopefully it enriches people's appreciation of the list. It's fun to go out to an archive and see what's in there and bring something over and get pleasure out of whatever you might come across. We're still adding stuff to that. Even though I'm no longer moderating the list itself, I still maintain that archive, and I still add material to it on a regular basis. [Note: In 1996 the photo archives were withdrawn from Internet access due to increasing and repeated misuse of the materials. LW]

LW: Thank you, Steve.

Chapter 12

Front Range Bears: A History

Van Lynn Floyd

The Front Range Bears are from Colorado. They were so named because the area east of the Rocky Mountains is called the "Front Range." The name gives a sense of region without limiting the focus to Denver or even Colorado. The club was officially organized in June of 1992 and incorporated as a nonprofit corporation in March of 1993. The unofficial group is much older than that.

The real origins probably started with Van and Ron's Bear Trek parties. Bear Trek was a group of bears gathering at the home of Van Floyd and Ron Triplett to watch *Star Trek: The Next Generation*. Jeff "Boulder Bear" Stoner came down to do laundry at Van and Ron's and to watch *ST:TNG* on Saturday nights. More and more bear types were invited or were guests of other bears until many Saturday nights there would be thirty bears in a pile in front of the television. The timing was perfect for a weekend party. *ST:TNG* started at 6 p.m. You could "do trek," go out to eat, and still have time to go out to the bars and dance the night away. The reputation of the Bear Trek parties grew. Van and Ron's home included a hot tub and sometimes after *Trek* they would make "Bear Soup" in the tub. Everyone who was anyone came to Bear Trek when they were in town. Bears in other towns started doing similar parties. In fact, some were disappointed that other hosts were not able to make "Bear Soup" as if it were essential at any "Bear Trek" party.

One of those bears, Rich Reynolds, started organizing other adventures. For an out-of-town guest, Rich organized a bear dinner at the Parlour Restaurant. There were eight bears attending. We were seated at a large table upstairs along with the rest of the restaurant patrons. Everyone got a big laugh when a man from another table interrupted to say, "We noticed you all have beards. Is that significant?"

Rich started a database and planned more dinners. He would mail postcards to those on the list and soon we had regulars attending dinners and other functions. It soon became evident that we were going to have to form an organization if only to manage dues and pay postage for notices. Rich put his corporate skills to work and collected a group of guys to organize the club. The first board members were Rich Reynolds, Van Floyd, John Griffin, Steve Heyl, and Walt Pedigo. They drafted the bylaws and filed the papers with the state to become official. Van did a rough draft of the bylaws and the rest of the group refined them. They have become a model for many other clubs around the United States and Canada.

One reason for becoming an official organization was to be able to sign contracts. Some members wanted to hold a weekend party that would attract bears from all over the world. To make arrangements, buy food, and rent halls it was necessary to be a nonprofit corporation. October is a great time to see the mountains of Colorado. The group took the name from a Saturday night party planned by Van and Ron as the name for the weekend party the following year. Front Range Bears held the first OctoBearFest in 1992. The real force behind OctoBearFest was Steve Heyl. The First OctoBearFest was hosted at the Comfort Inn (now the Ramada Inn) on Colfax. The weekend included a drive through the mountains, a German dinner at the hotel, and a Bear Hug party at one of the member's homes. In subsequent years the idea of a host hotel was discarded because not many people stayed at the hotel. OctoBearFest has become a party designed around its friendly members. Out of town bears are paired with locals for accommodations. Our own chef bear, Ira "Chef-from-Hell" Meyer, does all the catering in a rented church hall. The Bear Hug party has been moved to the Community Country Club, a gay bathhouse in Denver.

During the early years of the organized club, the club voted on a name for a formal newsletter. The name that won was the *Grizzzette*. The trick is to remember that there are three Zs in Grizzzette. The first editor was John Griffin. John set the form and style for the newsletter. Ron Triplett took over as editor and continued the standard adding interesting graphics and refining the look. Ron also was the driving force in the creation of the Front Range Bear's photo calendar in 1994 and 1995. The calendar featured photos of member bears.

In October of 1993, Van Floyd was elected president of FRB. He remains an active member.

Chapter 13

The Bear Essentials of Country Music

Lars Rains

I grew up in a small town on the Canadian prairies. One of the strongest memories I have from that period in my life is the sound of country music. You couldn't escape from it because it was everywhere. CKLQ were the call letters of the local country radio station back home. Its offices were located in the east end of town, as opposed to the much more urbane KX96 situated in the relatively affluent west end. Radio waves, however, know no boundaries other than signal output and CKLQ broadcasted for all listeners in "Q-country" who shared a common set of values and principles reflected in the music played by the station.

Of course, it wasn't very cool back then to admit that you liked country music. Especially when you were gay and all you desperately wanted to do was just fit in and be accepted by your friends—even if they were a little narrow-minded in their musical tastes. Well, you can imagine my surprise when I finally made the big move to Toronto several years later and discovered that there were in fact gay men like myself who enjoyed country music and the complexities of line dancing!

Now, the casual reader might be wondering what all this stuff about country music has to do with bears. The astute reader may actually be quite worried that I am going to describe, in excruciating detail, the entire story of my coming out as a bear and country music enthusiast! In the following pages, I hope to address both readers by demonstrating my understanding of the similarities between the development of bear communities across North America and the current interest in country music and line dancing within gay circles. These comparisons will focus primarily upon issues of identity construction and social interaction.

I believe that bear groups and gay country bars arose out of the same need to belong that I felt growing up in the middle of nowhere. After losing so many friends and loved ones to AIDS, gay men in the late 1980s and early 1990s wanted to reinforce a sense of community in environments which offered activities that were more social and inclusive than furtive cruising in leather bars or anonymous sex at bathhouses or parks. Bear organizations and line-dancing clubs provided a welcome alternative to the impersonal, often sexual aspects of bar culture. Sharing a common interest in fur or country music allowed gay men to socialize and to participate within a larger group dynamic than those previously available to them.

Unfortunately, the question of who is and who isn't allowed into these groups inevitably arises when dealing with nascent structures, as the debate over strategic essentialism clearly demonstrates. It is not enough merely to critique the membership criteria of these organizations; it is also important to determine who has the authority to make the decisions concerning who is granted or denied admission to these clubs. Issues of exclusion and inclusion, as they relate to bear communities, have already been discussed by other authors in this collection. But has anyone ever stopped and thought about how intimidating line-dancing can be to the uninitiated?

A favorite activity at country bars everywhere, line dancing incorporates intricate steps and confusing turns with popular country music. Most of the line dances take their name from the particular song to which they are danced, such as the "Achy Breaky [Heart]" or the "Boot Scootin' Boogie." Others have generic titles such as "The Line Waltz" or the "Tush Push." All involve memorizing an average of thirty-two or thirty-six distinct dance steps in order and repeating them until the song is over. The majority are danced individually; that is, no partner is required as all participants form parallel lines across the dance floor. Other dances require a partner and involve complicated weavings that could rival those found in world-class figure skating programs. The most popular of these couple dances is the relatively simple "Texas Two-Step." Yet another type of line dance necessitates the constant exchange of partners in a large, communal celebration. The most popular of these group dances are the "Barn Dance" and the provocatively entitled "Circle Jerk."

In order to be accepted out on the dance floor, you have to know the particular requirements of each dance. Most of the time, more experienced dancers are quite willing to help novices learn the requisite steps; after all, the more the merrier! But if a fast two-step is on the jukebox, it is probably best to stay out of the way until you have had a bit more practice. In addition to open dancing on the weekend, many establishments offer various levels of instruction during the week. These lessons provide yet another alternative to the regular bar routine.

Of course, when dealing with any gay male phenomenon, sooner or later one has to discuss issues of image and representation. The sudden appearance of gay male country music fans, known derogatively as "cowboy queens," merits closer examination in this regard. The cowboy is one of the archetypal role models boys look up to when they are growing up. A "real" man, the cowboy is one of numerous mechanisms society has in place to reinforce gender stereotypes. I know that when I was younger, I oscillated wildly between desire and identification; that is, I couldn't decide whether I wanted to sleep with a cowboy or be one when I was older. Country line dancing thus provided me with the opportunity to live out one of my childhood fantasies. I would put on my cowboy boots and my big ol' Stetson and go to town! By meeting other people who were dressed in a similar manner, I felt that I truly belonged to a distinct subgroup within the gay community.

I think the same sort of thing is happening among bear organizations worldwide. Hairy-chested guys with facial hair and big, furry bellies are also considered by society to be "real" men. Gay men have always had to confront the stereotype of the nelly, effeminate queen with the high voice and the limp wrist. The bear phenomenon allows gay men to identify with a more masculine ideal while continuing to celebrate their sexual attraction to other men. The main difference between the two representations is that the image of the cowboy is constructed from images or stories handed down from the past, whereas large, hairy men have always existed within the gay community.

One of the joys of being a gay man in the 1990s is the inheritance of various traditions from our elders. Of these traditions, drag is perhaps one of the most important to the development of a gay sensibility. Our rich history of female impersonation endows every young boy that comes out of the closet with an almost innate sense of camp. It is this tongue-in-cheek approach to the world that makes gay life in the 1990s unique and special. Gender roles have always been up for negotiation within the gay community because the prevailing standards adopted by the heterosexual mainstream have not, by and large, been acceptable to the vast majority of gay men and lesbians. In a country bar, this gender-bending can often lead to hilarious results.

Country music and line dancing became popular in gay establishments at roughly the same time that karaoke reared its ugly head. First developed in Japan, karaoke–for those of you fortunate enough to have been spared the assault on your eardrums–involves a member of the audience singing the words to a favorite song as the accompaniment plays in the background. Professionalism is not a prerequisite for performing; in fact, it is usually more enjoyable for all involved if the performer can hardly carry a tune. Many a friend has embarrassed himself or herself while holding a microphone.

Of course, it wasn't long before country music began to appear at karaoke establishments. These country songs, generally speaking, are easier to sing because of their straightforward rhythmic structure, their narrow range, and their reliance on repetition. The most popular song by far among gay male country music fans is Tammy Wynette's "Stand By Your Man," with its ironic opening line: "Sometimes it's hard to be a woman." This playful approach to gender may actually be a response to some of the misogyny inherent in both country music and certain gay male circles. I believe that gay white men (including, unfortunately, the bear community) can be just as hypocritical in terms of race and gender as the country music industry in Nashville.

For example, a recent discussion on the Bears Mailing List centered on the appearance of a (gasp!) woman on the List. Some bears could have cared less about the female presence in their midst;

others, however, felt strongly that no women should be allowed to participate in, what to them was, an exclusively male domain. Likewise, the patriarchal network operating within country music circles has, in the past, attempted to limit the access of female performers to financial and commercial success. Many early country songs offered very few acceptable roles to women: wife, mother, homemaker. However, the emergence of strong, independent female country performers marks a challenge to this antiquated view of gender equality.

Reba McEntire, Mary Chapin Carpenter, and Wynonna Judd are all examples of this new breed of country artist. These women defiantly refuse to be subjugated by men or restricted by the limited opportunities that they provide. Both gay male and lesbian country music fans can identify very closely with these performers and their fight against social injustice. One of the most popular songs by Garth Brooks proclaims that "We Shall Be Free" when we are free to love whomever we choose. Adopted by some as an anthem demanding equal rights for lesbians and gay men, this song reflects the growing awareness among country music performers of the need to engage critically some of the racist, sexist, and homophobic attitudes prevalent within society today.

Most Nashville insiders consider it surprising that the gay community would attach itself to a genre that has long been identified as redneck, almost backward. I, too, find it ironic, even a little frightening, that gay men and lesbians could appreciate country music, with its traditional espousal of family values at the expense of alterative lifestyles. However, many country singers also address themes and topics that are universal, ranging from the end of a relationship in Collin Raye's "Someone Else's Moon" to the pursuit of pleasure after a long week on the job in Brooks and Dunn's "Hard Workin' Man."

Of course, the attraction of country music for some gay listeners does not stop at the level of assimilationist politics. For many fans, the portrayal or marketing of male performers adds greatly to the genre's appeal. Favorite artists among gay men include Billy Ray Cyrus, Alan Jackson, Aaron Tippin, Travis Tritt, and Hank Williams, Jr. This appreciation is due in no small part to the performer's appearance as an attractive, butch, and masculine man. The connection between these artists and bears should now be quite obvious. Many of these performers are bears themselves!

At this point, I must confess that I once purchased a Dan Seals CD based on the cover photo alone. His eyes, his smile, his beard—all contributed to an image that bordered on ideal for me. Here was a bear that not only looked great, but also sang with a passion and an intensity that has rarely been matched by any other performer. This juxtaposition of desire and identification with country artists is by no means limited to my own experience. I have several friends who drool all over the television set whenever a music video by the all-bear group Confederate Railroad appears on the screen. The band members portray themselves as a close-knit group of drinking buddies who ride Harley-Davidson motorcycles and who back each other up in barroom brawls. Normally excluded from such nonconformist groups, my lustful friends yearn for the type of male bonding displayed by these and other country "outlaws."

Bears have often been pushed to the margins, excluded from the straight world and mainstream gay culture alike. The notion that body hair and extra body weight are undesirable qualities has been continually reinforced by a gay community that emphasizes appearance above all else. By reversing, or perhaps only modifying this aesthetic, bears have learned that true acceptance comes from within. Associating with others who share this belief creates a sense of community among bears which celebrates their status as a group of outsiders.

Similarly, gay male country music fans are somehow marked as different from the gay community-at-large. The appeal of new country music, with its attention to contemporary political issues and universal themes, is irresistible to these queer listeners. In addition, the opportunities for interaction and participation offered by line dancing establishments are quite attractive to gay men who have felt isolated as a consequence of losing so many friends to AIDS. More important, gay male country music fans experience a similar feeling of belonging, as each member shares a common interest in country music and line dancing.

Personally, I feel fortunate to consider myself to be a member of both subcultures. I have forged life-long friendships with bears and country music fans alike who have accepted me for who I am and with whom I can identify and relate on a wide range of topics. Many of these friendships began with nothing more than an understanding and a commitment to a shared set of values and principles, much like those reflected in the music played by CKLQ back home.

SECTION IV: BEAR SPACES: SAN FRANCISCO

Chapter 14

The Bear Hug Group: An Interview with Sam Ganczaruk

Les Wright: What is the Bear Hug group?

Sam Ganczaruk: The Bear Hug group was founded for the sake of providing a safe, social, and sexual meeting ground for men who are bears and who like bears. The name came from a time in mid-1987 when "bear" was just beginning to assume its current meaning. The early Bear Hug meetings were called, "Bear hug/Bare hug." We wanted to encourage an erotic feeling and safe sex practices. Remember, the mid-eighties were a time of fear and paranoia about AIDS. The "playgrounds" were being forced to close. We wanted to provide private places for fun.

LW: Why "bears?" Why "bear hugs?"

SG: Bears, well those of us who founded the group either were bears or liked bears. We saw "bears" as guys who had facial and body hair. Bear is not "chubby" or "fatso"! While "bear" may include men who are of "full figure" we didn't mean to make this into a chubby club. We welcomed all kinds of men, young, old, small, tall, short, and husky. Bear hug? Bears (*Ursus*) are famous for their hugs and we capitalized on that image to encourage the erotic and romantic atmosphere we wanted to have at the parties.

LW: When was it started? Who founded it?

SG: Bear Hug was started in June 1987. The idea started when we were at Jim's home discussing what we would like to do for a fun party. Sam mentioned his fantasy of a bare bear party. Jim said he did something like that in February 1987. After that, it was an easy step to plan the first Bear Hug party. The founders were Jim Burch, Darrell Hill, Sam Ganczaruk, and a fourth man whose name I can't remember. That man now lives in Denver as last I heard.

LW: How did you all come together originally?

SG: The first gathering or "Bear hug/Bare hug" was in July, 1987 at Jim Burch's home in Berkeley. We combed through our respective address books and invited who we thought would like this kind of activity. After that, word of mouth took hold and by the third party, the mailing list was over one hundred guys. I remember typing labels and sticking postage stamps on all those envelopes. We asked for contributions at the door at the time of each party to cover the cost of postage and party supplies. We did not intend to make this into a "commercial" enterprise. When Frank and George started attending the parties, they added their mailing list to the group. Some of the parties in 1988 were held at their home on Church Street in San Francisco. The last party at Jim Burch's home in Berkeley was just after the earthquake of 1989. By then, Ben Bruner was in the group. He offered his services to the group. We gladly let him take over the by-then backbreaking job of doing the mailings. He found the space on 14th Street and started *Bear Fax* in January 1990. Ben has been the leader of the group ever since January 1990.

LW: Anything else attract you to the "bear thing?"

SG: What attracts me to "Bears" is the welcome that men over the age of thirty-nine extend to each other. There is almost no "attitude" problem. Guess that "bears" are mature and more at ease with themselves. Of course, each one of us has a "type." Mine is a husky guy with a beard and body hair who is affectionate, intelligent, and sure of himself. I find most of these kinds of men think that "beardom" is where they fit in best.

LW: What is a bear, in your way of thinking?

SG: Other than the physical thing, i.e., beards, body hair, and huskiness, I think a "bear" is a mature, stable man, at peace with himself. He has the courage and ability to show affection and receive it. Some guys have to wait until they are mature in years while some can be a bear at a very young age. That's why we have polar, grizzly, and cubs. A bear is very sure of himself, has the confidence to accept others as he wishes others to accept him.

LW: When and how did you know you were a bear?

SG: I guess it was in 1987. I always felt that I was a minority or "different" from most gay men. For one thing, I always had body bulk . . . not FAT!!! I never could wear a size 28-inch pair of pants! When "bear" came along in 1987, I knew that I would fit in!

LW: What has it meant to be a bear?

SG: It meant that I, at last, had a place where I "belonged," in a sense, it meant that I had a community. I found other guys who appreciated the same looks and feelings I had. Being a bear has brought a lot of erotic fun, good companionship, new friends, and excitement into my life.

LW: What were the first play parties like?

SG: The first play parties were similar to what the latter day ones are like. I do remember a sense of "shyness" at the first party. Probably we emphasized the "bare" too much! Some people thought they had to get naked and were shy about that! We didn't require nudity . . . ever! At the first party, one guy came up to Darrell and said, "I've been here over an hour and all I've seen is a bunch of guys over there talking computers . . . ." Well, the party did get started and after that, nobody was shy . . . ever. Jim's house had a secluded backyard and some of the guys liked their fun outdoors. That was nice, if it wasn't drizzling or foggy.

LW: When the group got too large for private gatherings then what happened?

SG: The November 1989 party was the last in a private home. The mailing list got to be too much to handle and postage was killing us. By then, the list was approaching three hundred names all in the Bay Area. That was when Ben Bruner offered his services. In January 1990 he was running the show and found the space on 14th Street in San Francisco. Talk with Ben about that.

LW: What were the Leather Bears about?

SG: Ask Ben Bruner about Leather Bears.

LW: What was a typical Bear Hugs party like in its heyday?

SG: Bear Hug parties "heyday" I suppose was between 1988 and 1992. They were uninhibited and erotic. Since we were building a sense of community, and there was a sense of novelty there wasn't any of the "been there, done that" feeling. The early parties were not as frequent as the ones today are. We only had four parties in 1988, maybe as few as three. Those were the days when there was a sense of anticipation, a "special, don't miss" feeling. Attendance was better then since the parties were at irregular intervals. There was more sense of spontaneity then. There were more reports of people meeting that "special" someone at a bear party. I doubt if that happens today.

LW: How were they run?

SG: It was all done by volunteers. First we had to find a place to have the party. Somebody–usually Darrell and Sam–had to do the mailing. I remember doing all those envelopes and licking all those stamps!!! We "corralled" somebody to be at the door to greet people. The "greeter" job got to be very popular as I suppose the greeter could "inspect" the arrivals and then pick out who he wanted to meet later. There were volunteers at later parties to clean up. Jim had to do that all by himself at the first few parties at his place.

LW: What kinds of guys participated?

SG: Kinds of guys? How many "kinds" of bears can you imagine! We had every kind imaginable, including some guys from Germany. As long as you felt at home with fellow bears and didn't drink/smoke to excess or were a physical threat–violence–we had them all!

LW: What generally happened at these parties?

SG: Sex–eroticism–making dates–talking. Just like any other kind of party. Some guys said they were like the baths in the "good old days" . . . whatever that was!

LW: How did Bear Expo come about?

SG: Ben Bruner started the idea of Bear Expo in mid-1991. He proposed the idea to Sam, Darrell, and a few others. It seemed like the time was right and the idea would "fly." The first Bear Expo was in February 1992. Speak to Ben about the "hows" and "whys."

LW: What was the purpose of the Bear Expos?

SG: The purpose of Bear Expo was to extend the Bear Hug party concept to a national scale. By 1990-1991 parties at 14th Street, we were attracting guys from all over the country. I guess that we wanted to have a special event once a year to bring all the guys from other than the Bay Area to meet each other. I felt the motivation of the Bear Expo was one great big social event where you could meet new people and extend your circle of friends. We succeeded with that beyond my wildest anticipation.

LW: Wasn't calling them "international" a bit overreaching?

SG: NO!!! "International" is not overreaching. The mailing list alone by 1991 had many guys from all over. By then we had many guys from Canada, Europe, and even as far away as Australia! "International" might be a little of an understatement, I felt that "universal" might be more like it!

LW: Is there a "bear lifestyle?"

SG: Not in so many words. There isn't a "if you live like this, you are a bear." I suppose the lifestyle depends on the individual.

LW: Has the vastly expanding world of "beardom" impacted the original spirit of the Bear Hugs?

SG: Yes and no. Since the Bear Hug parties are monthly now, the "special event" feeling has gone. Many of the old-time attenders are gone for one reason or another. Many new people have arrived. Of course, time will make changes. Those of us who have been with it since the early days feel the changes the most. As the group(s) got larger, there tended to be some fragmentation as differences of opinion were bound to happen. "Beardom" is so big that most likely some specialized groups would develop.

LW: Would you agree that Bear Hugs were "safe spaces" for bears to come together?

SG: Yes, that's why we started the Bear Hug parties back in 1987. The need still exists today and probably will continue well into the future.

LW: Anything else you'd like to add?

SG: You must speak to Darrell Hill and Ben Bruner. They have much to add to my comments.

Chapter 15

BEAR Magazine

Luke Mauerman

If you're reading this, you probably already know what it's like to sleep next to a big furry fella–preferably one who snores just a little bit. Myself, I've never been much for the feminine curve. It's how I know I'm gay. The way a man's hunky, hairy thigh resolves itself into a full-sized torso; the way the smell of a man's chest is amplified by a thick growth of hair–for me, these are the things of which Sensuality is made. And get on with your sorry self if you've never felt a bearded face rub in betwixt your legs.

Most of gay culture, when it isn't trying to find the perfect, buff surfer boy, has worked to distill the ultimate masculine icon–to either make oneself into, or to have sex with. The 1970s were all about exaggerated masculinity: Tom of Finland, leathersex, hyper-butch tough dudes and men dressed as "clones." Gay erotica, the lasting validation and record of gay culture, has usually been in the hands of big publication houses, looking to maximize their bang with mainstream drivel: Pretty boy Twinkies–soft, tan, and creamy, with an indeterminate shelf-life. Until recently, mainstream gay media have ignored the fireman that lived down the street when we were kids. The one who drove a pick-up truck, had just a bit of a belly (with hair on it), a beard, and maybe smoked a cigar. That's a true masculine image. It's the way real men are. It's a departure from what we, as gay men, have been taught to accept as a sexual icon.

That is, until the mid-1980s, when, among other things, a magazine called *BEAR* started up in San Francisco.

I saw my first copy of *BEAR* magazine (it was issue 10) in a now-defunct Seattle magazine store. This was the spring of 1990.

The magazine was black-and-white, and featured bearded, hairy, masculine men. Real men. But the magazine was sleazy. It had a real open, trashy, in-your-face sexuality. For me, back in 1990, that was a little hard to swallow. So I put *BEAR* 10 back on the shelf and left Magazine City empty-handed.

But hormones are wonderful stuff. I kept thinking about that magazine. I went back two days later in my suit and tie and bought *BEAR* 10 anyway.

Six months later I became *BEAR* magazine's Associate Publisher. Through a long and perverse journey, I've wound up in the proximity of *BEAR* for the past six years, and spent a year and a half as *BEAR*'s editor. I came a long way from feeling scared of a magazine in a bookstore. Indeed, I've fallen into a life of eternal sin and damnation, and I've loved every minute of it.

When I first saw *BEAR*, I felt a rush of excitement that many have felt when seeing the magazine for the first time. Finally! I wanted to capture that masculinity–to have sex with men like that, maybe even to marry one. I didn't think such real, masculine men could be gay. No one's ever showed it to us before.

In the spring of 1990 I left Seattle ready to see the world and live in a bigger city. I'd only been around the block a little, as a gay man. I'd had precisely two relationships back in the Northwest, neither of them good, and in those days I still felt that you had to love a guy before you tried to get into his pants. And I didn't have much enthusiasm for what I understood gay culture to be. Although I had decided on San Francisco as my new home, I vowed that I'd never descend into the gay lifestyle: The Castro, 24-Hour Nautilus, Boy London designer fashion, Falcon Video, and that turn-of-the-decade icon of gay culture, Enigma's first album.

Still, I knew what I was craving. I stopped by the *BEAR* shop on my first day in San Francisco. It was in a 1907-surplussed firehouse in San Francisco's Mission District. A creaky, wooden building with the ghosts of firemen-past soaking the place with a strange smell–definitely augmented by beer from the punkish straight bar on the main floor. The *BEAR* office was upstairs. You had to go in from the back, up a long, groaning staircase.

Nervous as hell, I went in to buy a dirty video for myself. And I wanted to see the place from which came *BEAR* magazine and all those nasty ideas. I don't know exactly what I expected, but I was sure it would be evil and powerful. Some long-haired guy named Killer working there was friendly and we chatted. I looked around the small retail area, eyeing the dirty videos, T-shirts, magazines, and dildos. The place was full of stuff: boxes, files, video equipment, and old computers. It wasn't quite so evil-looking as I'd suspected. I was starting to feel less nervous, and, on a lark, told Killer I'd need supplementary income while I was getting settled in San Francisco. "Do you guys need a towel boy or anything?"

Surprisingly, Killer didn't laugh at me. He recommended I get my résumé together and make an appointment with the boss.

I left feeling excited and triumphant . . . like I'd done something scary and lived to tell about it. The thought that I could possibly wind up working there was too ridiculous. But it put a smirk on my face that lasted several days.

A week later I wound up in an interview with some guy named Richard. At the appointed time I headed back up those creaky stairs, résumé in hand, feeling ridiculous and out of place. That sense of evil was back, hanging in the air. I decided not to take any of it seriously.

Richard Bulger is a good-sized guy with an incredible beard. He has a charismatic personality, verbal style, and a rugged nature. He smoked cigarettes at his cluttered desk. He asked some surprisingly probing questions about my work background, philosophies about sex, and why I'd be interested in something like *BEAR* Magazine. A Siamese cat named Ann made herself at home on my lap and I was hired to be a file clerk.

The whole thing was like a freak accident. At first, I had serious issues with being in a smut-filled environment. I was scared; I was ashamed; I was thrilled to the core of my being. Everything was new, each sexual image was an affront. I was sure I didn't fit the style, either emotionally or physically. Although I'd had a beard for a while, I'm kind of skinny. And since I hadn't been to wild sex orgies, dated dozens of men, or even been to the Castro or the Lone Star Saloon, I felt like a rube. Sometimes, one of the models would come in and Richard would keep him spellbound for hours in his office with his intriguing talk. I'd try to fuss and organize check-stubs in there so I could check the guy out.

Despite my shyness and occasional discomfort, my work duties expanded–so many piles of uncashed checks, unpaid bills, uncompleted mail orders. My administration training kicked in and I started doing what I could to create a little safe spot around me. I worked hard to situate my desk where I wouldn't have to look at the video monitor and the pissing/dildo scenes being duplicated.

In fact, any time the atmosphere got a little too heavy, I'd just dive into my work and keep my head down.

Richard Bulger was pretty amused with my reticence. We spent a lot of time talking, getting into each others' heads. An anthropology major from Maine, Richard has quite a way with people, and a disconcerting ability to get a man to share his deepest inhibitions. To best understand his personality, read up on the astrological sign of Scorpio, which he is, and multiply it by ten. Then add too much coffee, nicotine, Orange Crush, and Hostess Ding-Dongs for a good sugar balance. That's Richard. He acts as chief confessor to most men he meets, and never seeks the approval of others. He'd grab me when I was halfway through paying a UPS bill and we'd go out for drinks at eleven a.m. and then go shopping for equipment, art supplies, CDs or antiques. Richard leaves cigarette ashes wherever he goes.

One day, right at the beginning of my career at *BEAR*, a gorgeous hunk of a man had come into the office and Richard took him to the adjacent apartment to shoot some video footage. I guess it wasn't going well. The guy wasn't getting a boner. Richard came out and told me the man (JJ Montana, not his real name) thought I was cute and wanted to see me. I went in to the old men's shower room of the stationhouse and there he was, naked, sitting on a stool with a beer in his hand. I could smell his sweat. But for all the world he looked like a kid being potty trained, sitting there, head down, fingering his dong, waiting. Richard left us alone, yet I just stood there. We talked, and . . . I left. Flustered. Ms. Manners hadn't covered how to handle this type of situation.

Also very early on–I think my second week there–I was working late and Richard was shooting video of a guy named Jim from Vancouver, BC. He asked me to come on in, and, on the floor of his office, was Jim, jockstrap around his ankles. Richard handed me the video camera and kept on talking dirty to Jim, working his purely verbal magic. Later, Richard told me he'd never let anyone else hold his camera before, but that I did a very good job with it. To this day I don't know if he was just feeding me a line or not. But that night he took me out for Thai food and showed me the Castro for the first time. I definitely felt my personal boundaries shifting.

Some nights I'd stay until nine or ten in Richard's office, alone, with Ann asleep on my lap, a single lamp burning and Bonnie Raitt on the CD player. The firehouse atmosphere, potent during the day, became palpably magic at night. Shadows, pictures of the hottest men on the walls, and the undying thought, "How in hell did I wind up here?"

I taught myself the computer programs the best I could, did a little bit of writing. My first published "piece" was a favorable review of the magazine *MONK* in *BEAR* 14. (Don't look at it–it was awful!)

I feel honored that I've gotten a good look inside the head that made *BEAR* magazine. Richard himself will be quick to tell you that his ideas for the magazine and how things settled out as "bear culture" are not the same thing. He understood what had always been missing from gay publications. He put into *BEAR* all the natural masculinity and kink he knew men weren't getting, and added free personal ads so they could find each other.

It was a concept so simple and necessary–but no one had ever done it quite that way before.

BEAR started in San Francisco in 1987. Richard had been running a model/talent agency, scoping out men for video companies and magazines. His lover, Chris Nelson, was a burgeoning erotic photographer. Together they got to know a lot of guys, having a strong affinity for skinny, dangerous street trash. I suspect it's in this role that Richard really found satisfaction in his "getting to know" the kinks and twists of disenfranchised San Francisco gay men. He practiced his own videography while Chris Nelson brushed up his photography. A friend, David Grant Smith, apparently coined the phrase "daddy bear," suggesting to Richard that a magazine geared to natural, rugged men would be a revelation. Since all manner of models, photographs, and true-to-life trashy stories were already lying around, Richard didn't have far to go to put a few pieces together.

BEAR 1 started as just forty copies of a digest-sized, underground 'zine printed on a xerox machine. A line-classified in the *Advocate* and a few local San Francisco bookstores were the sum of *BEAR*'s original exposure.

As of this writing, *BEAR*'s press run is well over 20,000, with a color cover and distribution all across the planet. It's considered the largest gay-niche publication in the country. It's a brilliant example of how desktop publishing and niche marketing came of age in the late 1980s.

The early issues have little to do with today's publication, some of which is a good thing. Early *BEAR* grew from a biker, scooter-trash, ZZ-Top culture. That's sort of where Richard and Chris were coming from, along with their buddies TC, Lang, and Rick Redewill. Extra body weight and hairy bodies were part of it, but it was based on the off-hand attitude, independent spirit, and humor of Harley biker culture. Obviously the word "bear" conjures up certain images of weight, dense hair, a man affable (until provoked), curious, and sexual. So things started to swirl together. Word got out; an identification began, and the tone of *BEAR* started to swing to a little more logger, trucker, leather-daddy-without-leather tone.

People always ask, "What's it like to work around all those gorgeous men?" You never completely get used to it. Just when you think you can't stand the sight of another naked body, someone would stop by the shop who'd be so good-looking your palms start to sweat. I'm convinced God knew what she was doing when she made the male form, and getting to look at nude men while at work is way high on the job-satisfaction meter. But you do get desensitized. Erotica and sexuality occupy a different place in my life than they did six years ago, which, given my ridiculous shyness, isn't necessarily a bad thing. Except for the occasional overwhelming hunk, I've lost most of the thrill and adrenaline I used to feel in the old days. I can't look at a dirty magazine or video and not see the technology, rushed choices, wrong lighting, or bad color trapping.

Models were selected by consensus between Richard and the editor. We'd meet people through the mail, out around town, or just in the shop. Some guys would come in and want to get naked in *BEAR*. They'd say so, drop their drawers right next to a stack of invoices, and we'd pretty much believe them at that point. Richard would usher them into his office and, whether they were an actual candidate or not, at least a good forty-five minutes would be spent, the guy would wind up spilling his deepest, darkest kinky secrets to Richard, willingly, and cathartically. Everyone liked the arrangement.

Sometimes a guy would walk into the shop and we'd try to hit him up. Often they'd say no and walk away. . . only to come back into the store a few hours later, just browsing. "Um . . . that offer still good?"

It's strange to watch how men face their discomfort around all the nudity. Some swagger, get bigger. Others joke, make it all cheap. But you can tell they can't even process the information they're seeing until after they've left the shop.

Other than that, working in the hole mines isn't appreciably different from any other kind of work. It's just that we have all these dicks and buttholes hanging around. It's easy to forget how the lady at the bank maybe doesn't want to see the drippy-dick notepad paper stapled to the back of our deposit. Jack-off calls were a regular office feature. Guys at home with a lot on their mind would call and try to get it on with us over the phone–as if we'd want to talk about cheesy foreskin with IRS forms all over the desk. There's work to be done.

One subscriber to *BEAR* is a seventy-four-year-old woman living in a Virginia nursing home. Women call and order *BEAR* hats and dildos for their husbands. San Francisco Public Schools wanted to sign us up for their eleventh-grade after school work programs so we could train eager young minds (we quietly declined). Two Jehovah's Witness women stopped by the shop to give us their publication, *The Watchtower*. (We made sure we gave them our publication as well.)

And just you pick up the phone and try to order thirty-five rectal butt spreaders without a physician's reference number. . . .

Employees came and went from *BEAR* at a high rate, for several reasons. Richard Bulger set what could best be described as a dynamic work environment. Those who weren't willing to hang on and go for the ride didn't last long. Still others came in expecting the place to be little more than a sustained orgy–and were in for quite a disappointment when there was actually work to be done. Once in a while we'd hear word of an employee or two trying to run their own personal little casting couch, which always created unusual social quagmires.

As we expanded it became harder to spend time forming impressions and relations with the men in *BEAR*. We lost something there, but we tried to make sure the model was–and is–a VIP, all fan mail forwarded and occasional signing parties, invites, and special projects.

BEAR magazine never came out on time. Lots of reasons for it, some legitimate and some not. Most of the time we were just these guys at the shop, doing what we could when we could. Unlike a lot of gay erotica businesses, money was never a problem. Richard knew what he was doing and cashflow was always good. But delays came from all corners. Having to take the affable, off-hand voice of *BEAR* and churn it out on time somehow seemed to go against the whole grain of the thing. We'd get bumped off the presses, clerical and administrative problems would crop up, or there'd be problems with our distributor in New York. Shit happens.

People got upset, of course. The phone would ring off the hook starting a week before *BEAR* was due out–and then, many subscribers were signed up for third-class mailing. This meant that half the subscribers got their magazines while the other half still had a three-week wait. The phone lines and Internet chat lines were abuzz with, "Did you get it yet," "Is it out," "How come you got yours and I didn't get mine?"

Much to my disappointment, we moved offices out of the Firehouse to a nondescript location on Ninth Street in San Francisco in 1992. The new location had easier access to the Lone Star Saloon, the ultimate hangout for the clan. It was also roomier–we had space for a bigger retail store and many more colonies of field mice. But the place was without character, and had no good places to fetch a decent lunch.

Killer, the guy who originally encouraged me to apply for work there in the first place, became *BEAR*'s editor in late 1990, taking Richard off the duty that had been his from the beginning. Now there were employees and a growing business to take care of. Frank Strona took over the job in 1991 and, at the same time, Richard started a new–and aggressively kinky–magazine called *POWERPLAY.* Local artist Steve Stafford was on retainer as art director for *POWERPLAY.* Stephen Stafford was later hired as managing editor of both magazines in the spring of 1992, right when we moved offices, while Frank Strona moved over to administration and sales.

I wound up doing increasingly more editorial work for *BEAR*. Mostly, I inherited the flood of personal ads that went into each issue. At one point we were publishing over 750 personals each time. I also responded to letters to the editor, did the events calendar, and helped out with various projects in both *BEAR* and *POWERPLAY.*

Working with Steve had me concerned at first. He cut such a drastic figure: reed thin, prior Lone Star Manager, biker image. He was funky, creative, brilliant, and temperamental. Lots of skeleton tattoos on his arms and skulls on his desk–you know, the real upbeat type. But despite our differences we forged a respectable working relationship, and a friendship. He taught me to communicate when things weren't right, and to be okay about having differences.

He died of AIDS in May 1994. He'd worked until ten days before his death, occasionally needing help to get through the door and to his desk. We let him keep going–the reality of getting his thoughts onto a page was the only thing keeping him alive. As his health deteriorated, his sense of humor became more acute. When things got frustrating, he'd laugh it off, "Just call me God's last Diva."

When the phone call came, and they told me he was dead, I was at Stephen's desk, working on *BEAR* 29. I was just about to call him to find out what he wanted done with page fifty-six.

There's no really accurate way to describe having a close coworker die. It creates a hole, obviously, but the cessation of ideas, cut off midstream, is a shock. He was just gone, with his notes all over his desk, half of *BEAR* 29 still in his head, and the number pad of his computer keyboard still stuck where he spilled hot cider on it the week before.

It was at the time of Stephen's death that Richard Bulger knew he wanted out of the smut business and out of this city. He sold *BEAR*, *POWERPLAY,* and Brush Creek Media to its current owner, Bear-Dog Hoffman, and retired up in the Sierras. I stayed on as editor for another year, until December 1995. Now I just do a column. I spent a little over five years working in the smut factory–from September 1990 to December 1995.

And lasted longer than anyone else.

What is a bear? Am I a bear? Are you a bear? She's not a bear; she's just a bitch with a beard.

And so it goes. . . .

As an employee and writer of *BEAR*, it was incumbent upon me to blow smoke up everyone's ass and keep a positive attitude. But what started out as an escape from roles and labels, has become just another form of gay drag. It's a natural progression, I think, as more and more men get interested and try to distill an image or identity. People like to belong. Nothing wrong with that. And now, with clubs in every city and conventions every other month, people are all set. Go for it. Have fun and for gawd's sake, get some sex while you're at it.

But *BEAR* was originally about being your own man. "Here's what I'm not producing: a big men's magazine, an older men's magazine, a trucker's magazine, a biker's magazine, a hairy guy's magazine. I *am* producing a men's magazine." So said Richard Bulger in the Write To Papa section of *BEAR* 15, 1991.

We didn't use the word "bear" in *BEAR* to describe a man. And surprisingly, few people noticed. Richard didn't want that stereotype reinforced. We tried to steer the tone of the magazine in a certain direction, even when readers asked us not to. We only grudgingly began to add club listings in 1992; event highlights in 1994; and finally, under Bear-Dog Hoffman, wound up putting a contest winner on the cover.

Along with *BEAR* magazine, Hoffman acquired at least seven other publications, and now runs a substantial publishing venture from the Ninth Street offices. Both he and his managing editor, Joseph Bean, are steeped in the rah-rah contest/club/regulatory tradition of the leather community. They seem to see the world in terms of status, roles, contests, organizations. This, by its very nature, is contrary to what *BEAR* originally wanted to be. But business is business. It'll work. *BEAR* magazine will become even more popular. It will satisfy a huge demand, have a higher budget, it'll come out on time, and will reach a broader audience.

But the original *BEAR* magazine, such as it was, began to die a long time ago. It's an age-old dilemma: you can't mass-market individuality.

Just to give myself a little thrill, I'm going to define what a bear is, in public, for the first time in my life: "A bear is a furry, smelly, four-legged, omnivorous creature of considerable mass. They've been known to eat their young, to kill their mates, and to shit all over the woods." You can be one if you want, but I bet no one would sit next to you on the bus.

And this is where you're supposed to imagine a good-looking, bearded, hairy biker riding off into the sunset. Alone.

Chapter 16

Bear Mecca: The Lone Star Saloon Revisited

Ron Suresha

The Lone Star Saloon in San Francisco is one of those places whose reputation precedes it, whose myth carries various images of being the birthplace of Beardom, a wild and freewheeling cruise joint, an accepting and nurturing environment, a place to score drugs, an intellectual salon, a biker/leather/Levi's bar, and many other things to different kinds of people. This is evidenced by the slogans and nicknames it has accumulated over the years: "Bears, Bikers, and Mayhem," "Bear Mecca," "Cow Palace," and "Heifer Hideaway," to name a few. It's also apparent in the way that Bears around the world speak of this place with such reverence and awe as if to denote a holy site. Indeed, for Bears everywhere, especially those who are connected somehow to the urban Bear scene, the Lone Star Saloon seems as sacred ground.

The Lone Star began as the entrepreneurial brainchild of Rick Redewill, a somewhat ordinary gay Bear with rather extraordinary business ambition. It was his combination of business and marketing savvy, his personal connections in the San Francisco bear/biker community, his friendship with Richard Bulger, the owner of *BEAR* magazine, and his sheer luck in timing, that made the Lone Star the right bar in the right place at the right time.

Following the demise of the Ambush bar circa 1988, the San Francisco leather/biker communities were hungry to create a space that would serve their prurient interests. Rick was aware of this need and, after several years without success, finally in August 1989 collected the resources and found a suitable location.

The old Lone Star, on the corner of 6th and Howard Streets in the leather community's South of Market (SOMA) area, was in a nondescript building with no sign and a double door that opened onto a short landing and several steps down to the barroom floor. Whenever some hapless person would enter the bar in late afternoon with the sun directly behind him, holding the door open so that the direct sunlight streamed into the small bar, it would blind the bartender and patrons, causing everyone to yell out in unison, "Close the fuckin' door!" It was, in fact, this slogan that graced the back of the first Lone Star T-shirts.

Rick's choice of barroom decor–a mix of rustic and industrial elements–and bartenders enhanced the image he wanted to create and attracted a small, select crowd to the bar. Word of a new SOMA sleaze bar seemed to shoot through the San Francisco Bear community, partly due to Rick's friendship with Richard Bulger, then publisher of *BEAR* magazine, who featured notices of bar events and ads in the publication. This alliance between the two businesses continues to this day.

On the afternoon of October 17, 1989, the Loma Prieta earthquake ripped through the Bay area, severely damaging the building in which the first Lone Star was housed. It is said that the toilet collapsed through the floor onto Rick's desk in the small basement office. Although the risk was acute, later that night Rick locked the doors for all who wanted to stay and held one last all-night party at that location.

For nearly a year, Rick searched for a new site in which to house the Lone Star. Finally, he secured a lease on a two-story building with a patio, on Harrison near 10th Street, and began renovations. Even before the building was complete, however, Rick held several "private" parties to promote the bar, where members of the SOMA community packed in for the first of the weekly "Bear Busts." Booze, drugs, rock 'n' roll, laughter, cruising, and bathroom sex abounded, and set the atmosphere for the bar for the next two years.

Once open, the bar began rather intensive promotion and programming. Rick and the staff worked with amazing dedication and creativity to create a space where Bears could be themselves. He had T-shirts, caps, posters, and belts designed and opened a small shop where these items, as well as the latest issues of *BEAR*, were sold to patrons. Every holiday became a reason for a party, and these became lavish affairs, with amazing decorations constructed by Steve Stafford (who later became *BEAR*'s art director and managing editor) and Bonsai Pete. For one New Year's Eve party, Dali-esque clocks were placed around the walls, several of which had hands that began spinning wildly backward at the stroke of midnight. Halloween, Christmas, Father's Day, Independence Day, Easter, Pride March Day, and especially the Earthquake Anniversary parties, all received grand treatment. In addition, the bar sponsored benefit beer busts for local gay and AIDS organizations, annual Mr. Chubby contests, and a softball team.

During its first year on Harrison Street, the bar flourished and Rick prospered, reveling in the notoriety and wealth of his most popular bar. His ambitious desire to have another SOMA bar, this time a multilevel mainstream club, led him to open Cocktails in the winter of 1992. This proved to be not as successful a venture as hoped: two weeks after it opened, Rick had to lay off over half of the hired staff. In the meantime, Rick neglected the further development of the Lone Star and the maintenance of his health. Seen increasingly as a girth-and-mirth rather than a leather/biker bar, and straining with staff and community conflicts, business fell off. As Rick's health deteriorated, he spent more time in the hospital undergoing treatments and at home recuperating, and less time tending to bar affairs. The bar manager Lyn Light was also becoming increasingly ill and unable to work, and was eventually replaced by Art Kelley.

Shortly before he died in April 1993, Rick signed a deal to sell the bar to three men from LA, who declared their intention to keep the bar just as Rick had intended, but to improve service and maintenance. After the deal was finalized, however, certain changes in the style and atmosphere became noticeable, as well as staffing changes: the bar seemed to become slicker and more LA-like than before. Its identification as a Bear bar was weakened also by the eventual sale of *BEAR* magazine by Richard Bulger; although the new management of both businesses are affiliated and their relationship continues, it has never quite been the same as the friendship between Rick and Richard. Sadly, due to the death of dozens of its early staff and patrons who were at the forefront of the SF Bear movement, and although it continues as of this writing to attract a steady Bear and biker clientele, the bar is not the same institution it used to be.

SECTION V: BEARS ABROAD

Chapter 17

Bears in the Land Down Under

Bob Hay

While bears are big in America and increasingly popular in Europe, the movement is losing momentum in Australia. This is for many reasons, not least of which is the relative insignificance of the word "bear" in this part of the world. Put simply, there are no bears in the Land Down Under.

Geographically, the closest true bear is *Helarctos malayanus*, the Malaysian sun bear. However, as far as we big, hairy men of Australia are concerned, *Helarctos* is totemically no more significant than are the great brown, black, or white bears of Europe and North America.

If we seek a native species for our totem the most obvious choice is *Phascolarctos cinereus*. Originally named koolahs (from the Aboriginal, or Koori, *kulla*) by the European invaders in 1788, the Australian native bear or koala with its long grey fur and cuddly appearance is now well established as an icon of Australia. Long part of Koori legend, koalas have also entered our nursery stories and folklore. Of all these anthropomorphic characters, Blinky Bill is surely the most famous. He is also probably our oldest Living National Treasure Bear, having seen service in several wars as well as in the kindergartens of the nation.

However, although now much loved at home and well known abroad, the koala is not a true bear but an arboreal marsupial. For some of us, a more fitting totemic native animal would be the wombat. There are currently three species of these large, burrowing marsupials of the family Vombatidae, the most common of which is *Vombatus ursinus* which lives in temperate regions of southeastern

Australia. About the size of a small pig, these "common wombats" are furry and heavily built, with short legs and a rudimentary tail. Curiously, in the male, the testicles are above the penis. Although normally nocturnal and solitary, these wombats are reputedly the most intelligent of all marsupials, and, when they do congregate they are playful and like to frolic. Above all else, wombats are stubborn: millions die each year on our roads because engineers build highways across their traditional pathways and wombats will not detour!

Neither of these animals, however, has the charisma and power of the bears of Northern legend. If we who call ourselves bears Down Under identify with any totemic animal, it would be most probably with the teddy bear which, at least for those of us of British descent in this most multicultural of all countries, are more psychologically important than are members of the species Ursus and certainly more charismatic than the koala and wombat. Although named after Teddy Roosevelt and inherited through our English nursery traditions, the teddy in our view is an estimable animal which stands for the cuddly lovability we claim for ourselves.

BEAR CLUBS IN OZ

So far, only six bears clubs have been founded in Australia and of these, two are now defunct and one, the most recent, exists only in cyberspace. The first was *Ozbears Australia.* This was started by a charismatic big and bearded man, David Hill, after his return in 1990 from a holiday in San Francisco. Sydney is one of the great, gay cities of the world and it is normal for foreign gay movements, fads, and fashions to take root here first before they spread, if at all, to other states and the smaller cities. It is also usual for Sydney organizations to presume that they represent the whole of the country and so the first bears club called itself Ozbears Australia without thinking twice about the implications. Only later did the ambiguity of the name become a nuisance by not identifying its location and consequently its catchment area.

In the same year–1990–a smaller Melbourne Ozbears was founded. The two clubs combined forces and marched together in the 1991 Sydney Gay & Lesbian Mardi Gras behind a banner which read "Ozbears–club for hairy men." This began a tradition which continues still, by which bears from all over the world are invited to join with the Sydney club in the annual Parade.

Melbourne Ozbears, however, collapsed within the year. News filtering up to Sydney suggested that the founding president had withdrawn because too few members would help with the work of the club. It was also suggested that meeting as it did in the city's most popular gay hotel meant that bears who did not like gay bars would not attend, and it soon became just another night out for the same bar crowd.

Two years later two other bears clubs were formed. *Ozbears of South Australia* was founded on April 3, 1993. This is a small unincorporated club centered on Adelaide and surrounding districts where the bulk of the sparse South Australian population lives. The founding president, Karl Newman, had joined Ozbears Australia during a visit to Sydney some months earlier. The founding secretary and treasurer are a well-known gay couple retired to the arid Malee (a kind of small eucalypt tree) country near Swan Reach, about an hour and a half drive from Adelaide, where they keep virtually open house for gay men. Their property is called "Wombat Flat" because on their land is one of the largest and most thriving colonies of the more gregarious but now seriously endangered southern hairy-nosed wombat. Club activities are mostly of a social kind and venues are generally in members' private homes, of course including Wombat Flat. OOSA seems to have no particular club logo. Their occasional publication features photocopies of hairy men suggesting that the principal focus is upon body hair

In September, 1993 Ken Beer from Perth visited Ozbears Australia while in Sydney. After many discussions about many things, including those of logos and totems, he invented the acronym WOMBATS (*West Australian Marsupial Bears and Their Supporters*) and not long afterward, the Perth-based bears club of that name came into existence. WOMBATS was really born of two men, Ken (its founding president) and Kevin Knighton, who was the first secretary-treasurer. Kevin's personal taste for beards has lent the club a strong bias in the direction of a "bearded men's club" while Ken has connections into the leather community of our westernmost capital. Events include dinners and parties in members' homes, picnics on local beaches and at a popular BBQ place in a local pine forest, train rides, zoo visits (WOMBATS officially adopted a baby wombat at the Perth zoo) as well as bar and den nights. WOMBATS is fortunate that the proprietor of the local bathhouse has lent them a basement for their den and after their Sunday night meetings, allows the members free access to the bathhouse upstairs. A monthly newsletter is sent to all members. WOMBATS, which is still an informal (i.e., not an incorporated association), accepts as members men who not only live in Western Australia but further afield and has several foreign members on its books.

The youngest of the face-to-face Australian clubs is *Brisbears* based in Brisbane, Queensland. Brisbears held its first meeting at a local gay hotel on October 16, 1993. The moving force behind its inception is Andrew Dyason who continues to be the main contact and organizer. Supporting Andrew there is a group of men who meet socially and who organize a variety of club events, including outings to popular islands in the Moreton Bay, car rallies, and even a safari to a legal nude beach on the north coast of neighboring state, New South Wales. But by far the best known of Brisbears events is their monthly beer bust at the Sportsman's Hotel where the hotelier lets them use a downstairs, unfrequented bar. Here, although of course it is a public place because it is a public house, there is also provision for on-site sexual activities. More than a hundred men commonly attend on those evenings. The logo of Brisbears is a brown bear ambulant. A monthly newsletter is (desktop) published and not infrequently, in color.

The newest Australia-based bears club is called *Bears Down Under* and is an e-mail address book or "virtual club" on the Internet. It had its origins in the two pilot editions of a national newsletter of that name published by Ozbears Australia on behalf of all clubs in the country. Reasons for publishing such a conjoint newsletter significantly included the aims of facilitating contact nation wide by bears and their admirers and of fostering a wider sense of bear brotherhood. The reincarnated BDU requires much less effort yet still achieves these national objectives of its paper-based predecessor. Essentially it lists the e-mail addresses of clubs and of individual bears living in Australia who wish to be in contact with other bears. Gay men who are bear-admirers are, of course, also included.

To receive this list, men must first volunteer to be on it. Provision is also made for a separate address list of members offering to host foreign visitors to Australia.

THE DEMISE OF OZBEARS

Ozbears Australia, the first bears club in Australia, shut down a month short of its official fifth birthday. Many factors contributed to this club's demise. However, before examining some of those reasons, to keep things in proper perspective we should first look at Ozbears as we ex-members like best to remember it.

Ozbears in Its Golden Age

In the early years of Ozbears, the "den" was a two-storied office building of a disused bitumen factory. The old office was comfortable, well lit, furnished with plenty of soft chairs and sofas, and had basic kitchen facilities. The disused lot provided off-street parking and privacy. Next door to the den was the actual factory building, a rambling multilevel construction which in the moonlight of a hot Sydney summer night, provided an exciting backroom of Gothic proportions.

Although there were parties and other functions, the strength of the club rested on its regular Sunday evening get-togethers. We met every Sunday at 6 p.m. for two to three hours. When members and guests arrived, they were greeted (often with the Great Aussie One-Handed Bear Hug–one arm around the neck, the other hand on the lunch; see Hay, 1994) at the door; money changed hands to cover the rent and evening's food; newcomers were introduced around; a light meal was served and men ate in little groups all over the den; later they drank their tea or coffee (not many brought alcohol to these functions) cuddled up together on the sofas or benches and later drifted off singly or in pairs to the backroom. "Going down the back" or–because of the historic nature of the old factory–"taking the heritage walk" was comfortably regarded as part of the evening and no one felt embarrassed by going there. Indeed, the club provided free condoms and lube, affectionately known as "the after dinner mints."

Five or six times a year we held a party. Ozbears parties became famous for their friendly and raunchy ambience. Usually about 250 men, including foreign and interstate visitors, and men from all over the local gay community, as well as our own sixty-plus paid-up members attended. The best known were the "Dare to Bare" parties, held usually at the beginning of the Sydney Gay & Lesbian Mardi Gras festival. Of these, the most famous featured a body painting "art" competition. On another occasion, we staged a Christmas Pantomime which, with apologies to *Into the Woods* for some of the plot, was called *Goldie Showers and the Three Ozbears*.

In this Golden Age, we had a constant stream of foreign–mostly American and German–visitors who consistently remarked on the immensely caring attitude among our members. Some of what our guests saw was the Australian institution of "mateship" in operation, but it was true, we did care for each other and expressed this in manifold ways.

This Golden Age lasted only while we occupied the old bitumen factory. Although after the site was sold and the factory demolished, we tried several other venues and meeting formats, we were never able to bring all those ingredients–most particularly sex, food, and male bonding–together so serendipitously.

However, while there were many marvelously good things about Ozbears and certainly, to outsiders, all seemed to be working well, behind the scenes there were serious problems right from the start.

Reasons Ozbears Failed

There was of course no single reason Ozbears eventually failed. In one view, it simply lived out its allotted span. But there was a complex interaction of several other factors, one of the most notable being the impact of HIV/AIDS. Ozbears suffered proportionately more HIV/AIDS-related deaths than any other men's club in Australia, and most significantly, it lost those members (including the founding president and several other office bearers) in its early stages. Such profound, cumulative loss meant that the opportunity was missed and little was done to publicize the ideals and features of the Bears Movement in Sydney and indeed, in Australia, as might otherwise have been expected by this, the first such club in our continent.

There was a serious problem too, obvious to many members right from the inception of the club, in that too much depended upon the energy and leadership of the founding president, David Hill, a born leader who ran the club more or less as his own fife. He not only contributed the driving force but did most of the work himself and only with difficulty delegated chores to others. The club never really recovered from his AIDS-related death.

Later another similarly charismatic and energetic leader eventually emerged. He was afraid of public speaking and would never stand for election as president, but in many ways for three years he was the de facto president of the club. He too took on most of the organizing and was the main driving force behind everything that happened, including parties and our annual participation in the Sydney Gay & Lesbian Mardi Gras.

Meanwhile, for almost two years another man was officially president. Although kind and popular, he was not a leader strong enough to countermand the often opposing directions given by the principal organizer whom the committee backed, not only because he had the ideas but also because he did so much of the work. The result was that there was constant tension, the president contradicting the organiser and undermining his efforts, the organizer playing the martyr and blaming the president when things went wrong.

Worst of all, however, was the fact that the president very publicly gave his first allegiance to another club—a leather club—and that at a time when leather had become a cause of division within Ozbears. This one-sided conflict of loyalties was only resolved when the president's partiality so outraged the Ozbears members and committee that he was hounded from the position and from the club.

Like many clubs in other parts of the world, Ozbears in its middle years experienced an uncomfortable division among members who were pro- and anti-leather. Like the Bears Movement in general, Ozbears had its origins partly in the leather community and consequently many early members and guests wore leather to club events. For the most part, members did not mind what anyone wore but some felt that leather, particularly full leather, was as much a barrier to communication as ultra-fem drag. As one disgruntled bear put it: "You never feel like you're talking to a guy, just to a lot of dead cow's cast-offs." This points up a basic difference: just as drag queens maintain their dress is "them," so too leather men feel that their leathers are part of their identity. However, to those of us not into such things, both drag and leather are fancy dress costumes the semiotics of which can make many men uncomfortable. The problem was exacerbated by the fact that from the beginning we rented our den space from Sydney's premier leather club with the result that in the gay community many men came to believe Ozbears too was a Leather and S&M club and stayed away. Eventually we had to advertize in the local gay newspaper that while leather men were welcome, Ozbears was not a leather club and had no dress code. At one stage too, we seemed to attract a number of leather men whose "attitude" most bears found ill mannered and therefore disruptive to the club as a whole. Much of this "attitude" had to do with the S&M power games and hyper-masculine fantasies favored by the men in question.

Although almost until the end, superficially things appeared to be going well, behind the scenes at Ozbears from its very inception there was a serious problem getting members to share the workload. Indeed, before the end of the first year, the founding secretary had resigned because he received too little help. Although this applied to other chores, it came to a head most frequently over the weekly catering. From its earliest days, Ozbears had provided a light meal—often just soup and a bun or a pasta dish—at the Sunday evening meeting. The members and guests all appreciated the opportunity to eat together and did not object to paying a little extra to cover the costs. However, it became increasingly difficult to find men to do the cooking. Many of those who had done it for a year or more now refused; newcomers claimed to be unable to cook or to be too busy or more often than not, unable to do anything because their families would demand to know why. They also refused to help with other chores—the same few men Sunday after Sunday washed the dishes and cleaned up after the meetings and did all the other simple, necessary chores. Eventually this "I've paid my subscription, now feed and entertain me" attitude drove all but the most dedicated members away, while those who were committed to the ideals of the club increasingly complained of "Bear Burn-Out" and began to replace their previously welcoming attitude to other members with resentment and anger at their lack of consideration and mutual support.

"Bear Burn-Out" is a term often heard in bears clubs and it certainly was one of the major causes of the demise of Ozbears. With the benefit of hindsight, there were many reasons so many new members showed so little of the mutual care and commitment expected by their more dedicated brothers, but one of the most important (albeit least understood at the time) was the fact that Ozbears attracted too many gay men who were, at the time of their joining, still in the early and fearful stages of "coming out" (stages III and IV in the Cass, 1979 model). Not only were such men not yet ready to commit themselves wholeheartedly to gay life and other gay men, but we were also virtually hamstrung because so many of our members were afraid to be seen publicly to be gay. For example, at one stage we could barely get enough members to man our float in the Sydney Gay & Lesbian Mardi Gras Parade. In a city as gay-friendly as Sydney there is little rational reason, just fear itself, for not taking part in that great social event: there are even hundreds of straight men who pretend to be gay for the night just so they can be in it!

Another reason the club failed stemmed directly from its incorporation. In Australia it is essential that clubs become "incorporated associations" because legally in an "unincorporated association" the members are "jointly and severally" responsible for any debts and damages. The process of incorporation was begun very early in the club's existence but faltered when the first Public Officer became too ill and eventually died. And so it was not until September, 1992 that Ozbears Australia Incorporated was actually achieved. However, although legally necessary, incorporation was a mixed blessing. Many of the older and more committed members were unfamiliar and often uncomfortable with the formalities now required in meetings and procedures. Some saw this as a bureaucratization of their erstwhile free and informal club. Some feared government supervision even though this was minimal and very much at arm's length. Whether these fears were justified or not, incorporation certainly contributed to the club's decline. It is not just that there is some truth in the observation that bears are often anarchistic: the real loss was the diminution of spontaneity and spirit of improvization.

The announcement of the closure of Ozbears shocked the other Australian clubs. "Rome has Fallen–Ozbears Folds!!!" was the headline in the WOMBATS' Newsletter for June, 1995. "The unthinkable has happened!," wrote Ken Beer in his front-page editorial. "Ozbears, the parent club of all the Bears clubs in Australia, has been disbanded a month short of its fifth birthday."

Reasons why the closure of Ozbears was felt so strongly, even on the other side of the continent, were twofold: first, as Ken said, to some extent Ozbears had been the stimulus to the formation of the other clubs. Sydney is not only the largest and "gayest" city in Australia, it is also the major destination of around eighty percent of all foreign visitors to the country and so is the trend-setter and leader in most matters. If a bears club could not make it in Sydney, then chances are it can't elsewhere in the country. Second, the other clubs in Australia–like many others around the world–also suffer from many of the ills which caused the demise of Ozbears. Ken Beer expressed his empathy for the points enumerated in "Post Mortem of a Defunct Bears Club" (Hay, 1995), thusly:

> We are at present in crisis. The Bear ethos is taking second place to self interest. If it is too much trouble to be part of our movement, then we don't want you. If you just want a place to meet potential sex partners, then join the plastic twinkies at the local gay bars and venues. If you are afraid of being seen in the company of demonstratively affectionate bearded men, then retire back into your closets. (WOMBATS, 1995)

These are strong words which reflect not only Ken's own deep personal commitment to the Bear ethos but also the insecurity most of us feel for the future of the Bears Movement in this country.

THE FUTURE OF BEARS IN AUSTRALIA

Of all the remaining clubs in Australia, Brisbears is, by all appearances, the most secure and successful. This is for several reasons. One–albeit a cynical one–is that it is still young and the energy and enthusiasm of the founding leader and other core members is not yet diminished. Another is that Brisbane is a rapidly expanding subtropical city which by the end of this century will be an urban agglomeration second only in size to Sydney. It is not only from Brisbane itself that Brisbears attracts members: they come also from the satellite cities on the Gold Coast to the immediate south and from the Sunshine Coast to the north, and from even further away, from neighboring regions to the west and even from the Tweed Valley in northern New South Wales. These places are all within commuting distance for the thousands of gay men who have immigrated there from other parts of the country and who find a bears' night out a good way to meet and make new friendships in their new home.

Another reason is that Brisbears has been fortunate in acquiring access to a meeting place in a well-known gay hotel in a bar which, although public, offers reasonable privacy, enough at least for Brisbears–like Ozbears before it–to offer on-site sex. It is not simply that the prospect of sex is a draw-card: gay men bond through sex and incidentally, thereby cement their relationship to the club.

But Brisbears also offers more than a transient, if satisfying, experience of a gay bar with an emphasis upon sex with fur. Men who seek more than a once-a-month social and maybe sexual contact also have the opportunity to enjoy other social activities. Brisbears has a sociable core of mostly young men aware of the Bears ethos. This, in its turn, generates and preserves the energy to keep the club going with the momentum it has demonstrated these past couple of years. The problem for Brisbears is to find a way in which the charismatic leadership and energy of its founder can be delegated to others who can then succeed him if (and when) he tires.

WOMBATS, although much the same age as Brisbears, is not as secure and confident as its Northeastern brother. This is partly because Perth, which lies a long way from anywhere else in Australia, is a small city in a sparsely populated state the size of India. Although there has been immigration to Perth in recent decades, it has not been on the scale of the northward movement of the Australian population bringing the boom to Queensland. In other words, WOMBATS has fewer bears to draw upon and those who are available, tend to be longer established and more set in their ways. Significantly WOMBATS, while able to attract members to functions other than those in its den beneath the bathhouse, has suffered a noticeable attrition in membership and is having difficulties recruiting new men to its ranks. Significantly too, several of the long-term core members are beginning to complain of Bear burn-out and there has been talk of regrouping and continuing principally as a more or less private friendship club, one of the main aims of which would be to welcome foreign and interstate bears who visit Perth.

OOSA is much more difficult to characterize: there is only a handful of members, few of whom appear to be hirsute while most know little or nothing of the Bears Movement as such; activities are held mostly in the homes of members and are primarily friendly, social occasions with much talk of gay sex but little action. The dominant theme, if there is one, is an awareness of isolation. Indeed, for OOSA, bears seems less of an ethos and more of an excuse for men to band together in the face of almost unbearable isolation. South Australia, while not as distant as Perth from the big, gay cities of the East Coast, tends to be more often overlooked and forgotten even if this was our first state to legalize gay sex.

In short, although represented in Australia, the Bears Movement is not strong here and its future is uncertain. It is unlikely that it will experience the popularity it is currently enjoying in North America, not least among the reasons being the more accepting, tolerant attitude toward gay men in this country. In the United States, where the political climate grows more homophobic by the day, bears clubs appear to be offering gay men, whether dedicated bears or not, a safe haven in a hostile world, particularly in those states between the coasts where gay communities are still small and vulnerable. If a sense of external threat promotes attendance at bears clubs in Australia, it is more likely in the smaller cities such as Perth or Adelaide. The strength and visibility of the gay communities in our larger East Coast cities as well as the plethora of social, recreational, and welfare services catering to gay men in those places means not only that there is less need for sanctuary but rather, that bears clubs must survive in a highly competitive market.

Unless Brisbane in the next few years steals the crown from Sydney as the Gay Capital of the South Pacific, in all probability a resurgence of the Bears Movement in Australia would require a new club to arise here from the still warm ashes of Ozbears. Furthermore, it would be essential that any such club establish itself very much as the trendsetter by conducting a very vigorous publicity campaign to build on the slowly emerging fashion–if trends in our gay magazines are to be believed–for body hair. This is probably what Ozbears should have done but it didn't and, with the loss of the opportunity, it is now most likely that our example of failure will live on after us to inhibit any new venture for some time to come. Even if it were to happen, it is unlikely that a club requiring more commitment than attendance at a "bear bar" would eventuate. To a large extent, whatever vacuum Ozbears left is already on its way to being filled: one of the leather clubs is holding periodic theme parties called "Bears, Bikers, and Big Men" while one of the gay bars has established itself as a bar for bears as well as other "masculine men."

Finally, it is unlikely there will be a resurgence of the Bears Movement in Australia because, as I said at the beginning, there are no bears Down Under. There are hairy men and big men here, but fewer men of the kind epitomized by the bearded lumberjacks of the Pacific Northwest who rightly can be called "bears." Our genetic pool is still too British–and increasingly Asian–to provide otherwise.

More important, there are no heavily-built, thick-furred, plantigrade quadrupeds of the genus Ursus (as the Australian-English *Macquarie Dictionary* defines a bear) in Australia which gay men might easily adopt as their totem. These are strongly nationalistic times in Oz: we are currently seeking to remove the last vestige of our European colonial past by becoming a republic in the year 2001; moreover, after 200 years in this wide brown land, those of us most likely to join bears clubs no longer think of ourselves as Europeans displaced into the Antipodes. Now, like the Kooris who have been here for more than 40,000 years, we too identify as Australian and no matter what we take as our totem, it must be one of our own.

REFERENCES

Beer, K. Front page, *WOMBATS News* 21 (June 1995).

Cass, V.C. Homosexual Identity Formation: A Theoretical Model, *Journal of Homosexuality* 4(3) (1979):219-235. A "Plain English" simplified version of this paper was published as Appendix 3 in "*Gay Counselling 80–Report on the Proceedings of Three Workshops*," Bob Hay and Terry Goulden, eds. CAMP NSW Sydney 1980. Appendix 2, compiled by the editors, is also an abstract of the Cass paper but oriented to gay counselling strategies.

Hay, B. Letter to the Editor, *Brisbears News* 12 (September 1994). This account of the invention of the *Great Aussie One-Handed Bear Hug* has also been published on *Bears Mailing List* (volume 2) and is in Bear History Project Archives.

Hay, B. Post Mortem of a Defunct Bears Club, *Bears Mailing List*, Vol. II, 29 May 1995.

Chapter 18

Kiwi Bears

John Webster

This is probably the first attempt to bring together a history of the Bear movement in New Zealand. Existing evidence of Bears in New Zealand reveal two organizations.[1] Although they were formed some years apart, and the first is defunct, they grew from similar social aims, flourished with almost equal membership numbers, were entirely male, and generally based in the same main city with a small spread of members throughout the rest of the country. Although the first group had certain Bear attributes, only the second has continued a positive ongoing promotion of Bear qualities by the production of frequent newsletters and a variety of social occasions.

The term "Down Under," while applied mainly to the continent of Australia also includes New Zealand. Both countries are autonomous and physically separated by sea. However, the governments and citizens of each country have shared fraternal feelings for decades.

For a number of reasons New Zealand gays and lesbians have perceived Australia as the place to flee to when coming to terms with their lifestyle. The city of Sydney particularly has been portrayed as more accepting than the hometown left behind. In the last twelve, or more, years this has lessened with a nationwide move toward an increased outward appearance, and acceptance, of gay behavior. One of the significant advances toward this tolerance was the passing, in 1993, by the New Zealand government, of a Human Rights Act, which made it unlawful to discriminate against a person on the grounds of sexual orientation. From early 1994 there has also been an antidiscrimination law relating to sufferers of HIV and AIDS.

New Zealand consists of three islands. The North Island and the South Island are roughly equal in size, while the third, Stewart Island, is hardly a quarter of one. The entire population is 3.7 million with three-quarters living in and around the city of Auckland in the northern part of the North Island. There are two major cities in each island with one of them, Wellington, on the southern end of the North Island, the capital and seat of government.

While people in Auckland may look to Sydney for gay affirmation, residents of New Zealand look to Auckland as their first mecca, and sometimes, temporary refuge, before embarking on their great overseas experience.

If New Zealand gays have considered Australia a gay mecca they have also been attracted to the seemingly freer shores of gay America. Over many years a variety of media has been available that have expounded the ideals and influences which have filtered through with role models being established on what was read, seen, or heard. It is not surprising then that the two Bear groups had their genesis in the observations made by their respective founders while visiting America.

Despite having no indigenous bears, or bearlike animals,[2] an affinity to these creatures, along with the toy teddy bear, exists among men in these New Zealand groups, as among men in other countries. The first established group did not have a name which included the word "bear," however the second does, prefacing it with the word "Kiwi"–hence Kiwi Bears.[3] The kiwi is a national symbol of New Zealand derived from the flightless native bird kiwi (Apterygidae) and is used for identification on flags, banners, signs, coins, and banknotes, plus a wide variety of other goods and services. The name kiwi is also used to denote a New Zealander.

The two New Zealand Bear groups are, first, Des Hirsutes, subtitled The Hairies, and the second with a joint title, Kiwi Bears K.U.B.S. Des Hirsutes was inaugurated by Peter in 1985. Interviewed in mid-1995, he recalled his youthful experiences growing up during the 1920s and 1930s in a large rural town devoid of any visibly gay individual who may have provided a reference for him to explain his feelings of being "different."

An attraction for him after school was to observe the shirtless and sweaty workmen at the local foundry, or the stokers in the local railway yards.

At puberty he was introduced to adult sex by one of the workers who was about eighteen years of age. Peter willingly went with him and engaged in mutual fondling and masturbation to full orgasm for the first time.[4] Naturally this made quite an impression and he related that a significant arousing element of this first encounter was that the man was extremely hirsute. Not only did this episode confirm his attraction to men, but initiated his lifelong desire for hairy men, though he is not excessively hairy.

Later he married and fathered children, but continued to be drawn to men and his subsequent career as a seaman on merchant ships provided opportunities for sexual adventures afloat and ashore all over the world. During these years he found it easy to connect with other men who shared his hirsute affections.

In 1985 he left the sea, living in early retirement in Auckland. Having lived in Canada and visited the United States he had encountered, but never joined, groups of similarly minded men and found a complete lack of them back home. Believing that there must be others in New Zealand interested in hairy men led him to place the following advertisement in a gay magazine, published in September 1985.

> Auckland/Anywhere: hairy men or men interested in hairy men and interested in forming a group similar to "Hirsute Club" of USA, for social contact or correspondence, write in strict confidence. Write PT 29/85.[5]

He advertised again before the end of the year, and once again in 1986. The response was immediate. Interest was expressed by letter only with him replying to each as they arrived.

His initial idea was to publish a newsletter containing a small amount of news followed by a classified listing of members. Each new member had previously filled in a form that gave name, address, body type, interests, and what sort of man they were seeking. They were encouraged to be "as frank and explicit as you wish," so there were allowable differences in replies. For instance some advertized almost every body part and function, while others wrote hardly anything concerning these aspects.

There were no set subscriptions save for the request that each new member provide stamps for a year's postage.

It was left to members to write, or telephone, each other. Apparently on only two occasions was there a social function at a member's home for others to attend. Although Peter had vague memories of this, two ex-members recalled the parties with some interest. Also, in the second newsletter issued, Peter did write that, "I have been fortunate enough to meet one or two of the guys on a social basis and there are some really nice guys around, I assure you."

Newsletters and lists started in October 1985, continuing to early 1987. By this time Peter believed the group, as such, was no longer necessary. In his final letter he wrote, ". . . interest has been on the wane for a period of time now which only leads me to believe we have reached saturation, at least for the moment, of those sharing our common interest. I have therefore decided to put the group into temporary recess. I hope you all got what you wanted from the organization. I enjoyed operating it."

Peter recalled that sometimes he mailed out up to 150 newsletters. However, surviving copies indicate a stable total of forty-two members for the whole country. Twenty of these were in Auckland, with seven in Wellington, and the remaining spread fairly evenly over the country. Of the forty-two, six were in their twenties; ten in their thirties; ten in their forties; and five in their fifties. The lowest age was twenty-two and the highest fifty-eight.

From the newsletters an analysis can be made of "hairiness." Eight declared themselves as "quite hairy"; twelve were medium; thirteen were light; while nine stated smooth, or none. Some also stipulated what they preferred hairy–chest, legs, buttocks, or back, being usual, with moustaches and beards generally favored. Having or wanting hirsute genitalia was seen as an advantage by at least a quarter of the members. Sexual acts were not directly referred to, being hidden in expressions such as "unafraid of nudity and spontaneous activity," "have no hang-ups," or the old standard, "flexible." Circumcised or uncircumcised penises ("cut or uncut") also had their share of admirers.

So, was Des Hirsutes/The Hairies a Bear group as we know them today? This question was asked and responded to with an affirmative answer by the founder. Certainly hair was the admitted main concern, but along with this came the components of bulk and nonconformity to accepted body types. Attraction was to manly, butch, woodsman, leather, bikers, and uniforms.

Identification now, by Peter and his partner, is to Bearism and both avidly read Bear magazines from the United States, have Bear videos and host Bears from around New Zealand and overseas. Both have belonged to the "Nude Exchange" while the partner recently joined "Chestmen of America" because of his predilection for large and pierced nipples. Both are admirable examples of gay men in their seventies.

Obviously in thought, word, and deed Des Hirsute's founder was, and remains, a Bear, but what of the members?

No attempt has been made to locate the members from the existing lists. Contact with the founder, Peter, came about when an advertisement was placed in the Kiwi Bears' newsletter[6] as to the origins and remembrance of Des Hirsute. Of the two ex-members previously mentioned, only one identifies with and belongs to Kiwi Bears.[7] The other had drifted into other commitments and professes no great desire to join in bear life again.

As with any other country there are probably more Bears outside clubs than within. Classified advertisements in New Zealand gay publications testify to this with frequent requests, or offers, of Bear and hairy company.

Attitudes to sexual practices and the impact on members by the revelation of AIDS cannot be ascertained from the newsletters.

Des Hirsutes was never formally set up as a registered society and therefore when Peter believed it was at an end it was his prerogative–no committees, no legislative requirements, and apparently no backlash from any disgruntled members!

A slightly amusing aspect to the origin of the name Des Hirsutes points up the social mores of the time and the real, or imagined, need to be covert even when simply addressing an envelope. Peter stated that the name was never meant to be true French. He hoped that mail carriers and others who might by chance see the letter would believe it was addressed to a Desmond Hirsute, known as Des, and that no one would really understand the word hirsute.

K.U.B.S. Kiwi Bears was started by Mel, in Auckland, in early 1992. As a result of numerous visits to the United States and his observations of the gay scene there Mel found that the Bear attitude and appearance was the one to which he was attracted. Coupled to this was his belief that body type should not be the principal condition of acceptance by others. Auckland had a few gay venues which promoted the drag scene or the blond boy image, or a clone encounter. The videos and magazines were dominated by such images, with little in the way of hairy men being seen.

As with Peter, Mel believed that there must be others of the same persuasion, being endorsed by his friends. To gauge the interest he prepared a handwritten A4 poster, copied it off, and placed them in gay venues. With a small sketch of a bearded man wearing a Bear cap, it read

> Yeah! It's a K.U.B.S. Meeting
> Let's get together and chat.
> Meet each other over a quiet drink.
> What do you want to see happen
> with our group?
> So come on up to "The Bar" on Sunday
> the 1st March at 2.30 pm!
> Let's get K.U.B.S. Up & Running.

The result of this endeavor was encouraging and a newsletter was started to maintain contact with the interested men. On March 1, five met at the gay bar. During the course of the afternoon they talked at length of the next proposed meeting and the most practical way of keeping in touch, giving consideration to those outside the Auckland city area.

Five days later a barbeque meeting was held in a local park. The admission fee for this was donated to a local bowling group to assist them with travel expenses to Dallas.

There have been over thirty newsletters produced since the first, with production evolving from handwriting to typing, and then onto word processor. From the start they were produced by Mel; however, from the tenth, Phil C. has been responsible. Save for the odd one or two, newsletters have been drafted jointly by Mel and Phil C.

Apart from an oblique reference to "cubs" in the group's name, the meaning of the acronym was queried by members. The answer was Kiwi United Bear Social. With the publication of the newsletter for January 1993 the letterhead had changed to Kiwi Bears K.U.B.S. This letter also announced that a subscription would now have to be levied. To quote,

> It had to happen! The time has finally arrived for some sort of charge to cover our expenses . . . for the great amount of $10 a year you will get–Wow! a newsletter sent to your own personal address, giving you invites to our social events, and a badge. The Kiwi Bears badge is crafted by our willing band of expert bear enthusiasts . . . I have opened an account in the name of "Kiwi Bears" so that cheques are entirely acceptable.

Later a charge of $15 was introduced for couples.

Successive newsletters have given reports of previous functions and detailed forthcoming attractions, frequently up to four, based roughly on two per month. Newsletters usually have illustrations culled from news clippings, postcards, and magazines. Travel notes, puzzles, and crosswords have also appeared–all Bear-orientated of course! Voluntary work on the newsletter and other arrangements by Mel and Phil C. is quite significant, as there is no committee to assist in the work.

Over the years social gatherings have been held at homes of members. Held in the evenings they have been great excuses for bringing along food for a shared meal, watching videos, or just sitting and standing around for a good gossip! Variations of this have included a musical evening with members entertaining others on an assortment of instruments, the odd night out to a local restaurant, visits out of the city for much the same reason, and also an attempt to encourage members distant from the city to join in for the night.

As Kiwi Bears are listed in overseas publications they do get requests for tourist information on New Zealand and Bears. Fortunately, many visitors during their time of touring the country have attended a function. This has been an enriching experience for the local Bears as it heightens their awareness (and probably the visitors') of Bear life elsewhere in the universe.

Other happenings have included visiting bars, a cruise club, and one of the local saunas ("tubs"), along with attendance at films and musical events. There was even an introductory visit to "Jacks and Jocks," a j/o party held every Sunday afternoon at a city cruise club.[8] It should also be mentioned that there have been "sex evenings," when porn videos and magazines have assisted the mutual enjoyment of members present.

Perhaps a uniform characteristic of Kiwi Bears is the inhibition, or reserve, of many members when attending a group function. While affection is observed between the established couples, there is little in the way of physical contact between other members. There may be a welcoming hug, or a departing kiss, but usually no other physical touching at a member's home, or in a public place such as a bar. Obvious exceptions to this would occur at the "sex evenings" and the sauna and j/o club visit. That some contact does take place is shyly acknowledged, without any excessive boasting.

It is hard to define the origin of this conservative attitude. When members have traveled overseas and visited Bear groups they have nearly always mentioned the intimacy they've experienced and enjoyed. For instance, Ozbears, of Sydney, appeared to have one member whose job it was to give a ritual greeting to new members or visitors consisting of a combined hug and grope![9]

The reserve may have its roots in the attitude to man-to-man sex and male physiology in past and present New Zealand social mores.

A member of the New Zealand AIDS Foundation prevention team has made remarks which could be applied to this situation.

> Men in New Zealand, whatever their sexual orientation, have never been encouraged to explore our bodies, or discuss sexual matters with others. We are usually too embarrassed to acknowledge that we are sexual beings who have needs of intimacy, tenderness and sharing. Mostly we are too embarrassed to go to a bookshop or a library and request books about male sex–in the unlikely event that such a range is available. As a result of the lack of information, many of us have concerns about what is "normal sex" for men.[10]

When preparing this essay the author consulted Phil C. on the make-up of membership in the same manner as used to analize the Des Hirsutes newsletter lists. As the detail required by Des Hirsutes does not occur with the membership mailing lists for Kiwi Bears K.U.B.S. we could only rely on information acquired at gatherings.

At the time of discussion there were forty-seven members overall, with thirty-nine in Auckland, two in Wellington, with the others throughout the country, including five overseas members. An age range could only be estimated at about two in their twenties, sixteen in their thirties, seventeen in their forties, seven in their fifties, and unknown for at least five. The lowest age is probably twenty with the highest thought to be fifty-two.

"Hairiness" was believed unknown for about twelve, smooth or very light hair at nine, twenty-one for other light, three for medium, with only two definitely very hirsute. Moustaches and beards were generally de rigeur. There is some bulk among members, but also a leanness, an attribute which has caused on the very odd occasion the remarks–what is a Bear? What is a Bear admirer? Are you a Bear, or a cub? Cubs, apparently, are thought by some to be admirers without the hair, bulk, and other attributes considered necessary to qualify as a Bear. This analytical reasoning has raised a question posed here and overseas, namely, by insisting on certain criteria are we not establishing the very same restrictions imposed by other gay septs that we have rebelled against?

Is Kiwi Bears K.U.B.S. a Bear group as we know them today? Of the two groups, Kiwi Bears is undoubtedly a true member of the international norm and spirit.

The ready availability of Bear literature from overseas and being on other groups' mailing lists help Kiwi Bears to remain up to date and to incorporate ideas from what has been read or seen and experienced. Unfortunately, Des Hirsutes did not have this advantage.

Currently Kiwi Bears appears to be sound financially, even though the bank balance is not what would be regarded as major holdings, and appears to be maintaining interest, with a few new members joining each year. Members, in fact, are encouraged to bring along friends to most meetings, not necessarily with the intention that the guest become a member, although many have.

Because Kiwi Bears is centered in Auckland, there is a tendency for members in the rest of the country to feel slightly frustrated that they cannot partake in meetings or meet the other members. As the population is largely in the Auckland area, this appears to be without a solution, unless groups can be set up within other cities and towns on the initiative of a Bear or Bear-friendly individual. Kiwi Bears are not dictatorial, and could take no legal recourse against anyone setting up another group. In fact, they would probably welcome such a move. At present there is no other Bear group in New Zealand, or at least not one that does advertises itself in the gay publications, as does Kiwi Bears.

Kiwi Bears can enjoy a fairly good social life in New Zealand's four main cities as gay venues are to be found in each, again, something that was not available in the days of Des Hirsutes.

Three of the four major cities have saunas ("tubs") and other venues such as bars, nightclubs, cruise places, cafes, and occasional dances. All these are run and patronized by all types within the gay community, with none specifically for Bears. However, some are Bear-friendly, or as much as they can be, given that some cater to the men and women of the leather brigade, or drag queens, to name two.

Once again, because Kiwi Bears are centered in Auckland, some venues have given them recognition by encouraging, or agreeing to allow, Bear parties entering as a group, with a concession on entrance fees. Auckland males have the opportunity of visiting four saunas, one cruise club (with the Sunday j/o session) each day if they wish (or have the energy). There are two annual street parades to join in, one being a "Coming Out Day" during an afternoon, the other a night-time event known as the "Hero Parade," which terminates in a large dance party until dawn, when the participants somehow find their way home. The party is usually held in a large showgrounds building, or in a disused railway shed. Kiwi Bears have not yet taken a stand in any of these public events, though some individuals do attend along with friends or lovers.

Discussions current elsewhere in the Bear world: Can a woman be a Bear? Can straight and married men be Bears without the sexual component?[11] and other such queries have not yet arrested the attention of Kiwi Bears, though it would be unfair to say that they had not been broached in conversations during the last three years.

To conclude this history of Bears in New Zealand I can do no better than to finish with a quote from a recent newsletter written by Phil C. in answer to a member inquiring about the aims and objectives of the group

> [T]here is some difficulty in knowing what exactly is expected. It would be pointless to have a group which was apparently formed to appreciate Bears and then to feature blond skinny guys . . . . Obviously our attention is on Bearishness . . . . As a group we don't insist that our members have to conform to a certain physical type but we do try and concentrate on a certain rather neglected, yet appealing profile of a gay man . . . . I think that bearded, hairy, and/or chunky guys are, in fact, better looking. That's what I like to think, that's what most of the guys in the group like . . . Bears are sexier, more interesting, better looking, more down-to-earth, hotter, sexier, more fascinating, more intriguing, more honest, sexier, more real, more fun, trustworthy, better lovers, sexier . . . . I mean I'd buy a brand of coffee a Bear advertised, or believe a news reader just a tad bit more, because you can trust Bears, can't you?[12]

REFERENCE NOTES

1. *Des Hirsutes/The Hairies Newsletter*, 1985-1987. G. Underhill collection, Lesbian and Gay Archives, Alexander Turnbull Library, Wellington, New Zealand. Also copies held by author. *K.U.B.S. Newsletter*, 1992-to present. Author's collection.

2. Apart from zoo or circus exhibits no bear has been introduced to the country. A sighting of a "Greenland bear" was reported by a sailor in 1791 as being seen on shore. The report was regarded as improbable even then. MS Edward Bell, *Journal of a Voyage by HMS Chatham*, Alexander Turnbull Library, Wellington, New Zealand.

3. For a short time there was a real Kiwibear! the Australian possum which was liberated in New Zealand during the mid-nineteenth century has become a pest and is branded as a noxious animal. There are programs for eradication throughout the country. An enterprising business some six years ago proposed farming them and exporting the meat to Asian markets for human consumption under the generic label "Kiwibears."

4. Peter was not entirely naive. He had experienced the normal process of bodily change including erections, fondling, and masturbation, but his efforts at

the latter never resulted in ejaculation. He had seen others climax, but this reported instance was genuinely the first time he had experienced a full conclusion to the act.

5. *Pink Triangle* 55 (September/October 1985) 19.

6. *Rumblings: Newsletter of Kiwi Bears* 26 (February/March 1995) 6.

7. Both contacted in 1995 by author, after they had identified themselves as ex-Des Hirsutes.

8. "Jacks and Jocks" is held at the venue "Lateshift" which is open every night, but on Sunday afternoons opens for this j/o session from 2 to 5 p.m., with entrance only between 2 p.m. and 2:30 p.m. This is a normal gay happening and attracts between 30 and 80 each Sunday, and is run on much the same lines as overseas j/o parties. Bears are present, even if they do not belong to Kiwi Bears. (This observation by author and other members who have visited the venue.)

9. Mentioned and observed and experienced by the author in June, 1995.

10. New Zealand AIDS Foundation newsletter *Red Ribbon* 14 (June 1995) 1. Remarks by Dave Hookway, Project Development Officer, and, incidentally, "Mr. Gay New Zealand 1995!"

11. Several members of Kiwi Bears are ex-married, with children, which gives them another point of bonding within the Bear cave. Some other members are ex-leather-scene and possibly some in the bikers/leather groupie scene–which all makes for a wonderful variety.

12. *Rumblings* newsletter of Kiwi Bears 30 (July 1995) 3.

Chapter 19

Atlantic Crossing: The Development of the Eurobear

Tommy McCann

BEAR MARK I–THE AMERICAN MODEL

> The parallel problem that confronts homosexuals is that they set out to win the love of a "real" man. . . . If you ask a homosexual what his newest true love is like, you will never get the answer, "He is wise or kind or brave." He will only say, "It's enormous." (Crisp 1968)

The central theme of this quote by Quentin Crisp, and by much gay male pornography and erotica, is the search for the quintessential real man. A "real man" must, by definition, be a man who is "real." But what does this entail? How is it expressed? And, more important, does it stand up to any kind of scrutiny?

Following Stonewall and the birth of a mainstream gay liberation movement there was the gradual evolution of a uniform, something to set the male homosexual apart from the rest of society–a badge of honor, defiance, strength. In the 1970s the first major flirtation with stereotypical male imagery began–with that which was seen as butch and somehow bigger than ourselves. It had to be so, in order to confront a disapproving society which considered gay male behavior as something sissified. The clone look epitomized in the late 1970s was, perhaps, the most successful of these many experimentations. Its widespread acceptance and the ease with which those adopting the look could pass in a sometimes hostile straight world was certainly part of its success.

Over time, however, the clone look became just another gay male uniform–no more radical than any other, and perhaps ridiculed more than is justified. Behind the uniform of the clone, however, was the idea of what a "real" man was. And from the look it was obvious what the conclusion was: Real men are tough, stand up straight and tall, have gym-trained bodies, big pecs, flat abs, and are generally GI Joes, presumably with the personality to match.

The initial flowering of freedom in the 1970s, with its correspondent openness, was effectively closed off by the adoption of a constraining uniform intended to disseminate a message of "normality" and, above all, "masculinity." Since this time gay men have been effectively constrained regarding the expressive possibilities of masculinity. Thus, the range of what is truly masculine is somehow denied to us–largely by ourselves–simply because we do not allow ourselves to be fully open to the richness of the masculine experience.

Furthermore, while masculinity and its associated form of male sexuality is socially acclaimed and admired in America (Cary Grant, Bruce Willis), male homosexuality was and is severely castigated as a sign of weakness (Edwards, 1994). The development of the Bear Movement in the 1980s was, perhaps, a reaction against both the constraints of previous gay male imagery and a synthesis of maleness in a broader form with homosexuality–in some respects, the ultimate nightmare.

Initially there was much talk about bears being comfortable with themselves, being in touch with their maleness, with their homosexuality, and moving away from the body fascism which defined the disco era of the late 1970s. That the acceptance of less streamlined body shapes should coincide with the onset of AIDS as a serious disease with its well-documented wasting syndrome was, perhaps, more than coincidence. Furthermore, the development of a new gay male iconography based on blue-collar attributes seemed to be a further desire to remove bears from the interior designer/flower arranger sphere. Of greatest importance, perhaps, was the idea of male bonding–a form beyond sex–which would lead to the establishment of a group of men, comfortable both with their masculinity and their sexuality, who could be torch-bearers for new models of gay male behavior.

So, what went wrong?

BEAR MARK II–EUROBEAR: THE GENERAL MODEL

> North America's position as the "superpower" of western society and as the epitome of consumer capitalism, individualism and freedom of expression invoking imagery of the 1950s American dream, glamor, fame, California and Hollywood, created a connection of America at the level of individual fantasy and social ideology with particular forms of sexuality, including gay sexuality. The sheer size and diversity of the United States, geographically and culturally, temporally and spatially, presented particular problems for the maintenance of social, economic and political order. (Edwards, 1994)

In the 1980s the first stirring of a Bear Movement began in the United States. Initially confined to the West and East coasts, it rapidly found favor with gay men everywhere in the United States and has subsequently spread across the entire country. At the time of writing it would be difficult to name a state without some sort of bear group or club, and the numbers of bear-related magazines, shops, mail-order companies, T-shirt manufacturers, etc., has continued to grow, almost exponentially it would seem.

As with all things gay and American–all roads of communication lead to Europe. European gay men tend to look to the United States for information and culture, San Francisco and the Castro, New York and Christopher Street are the "universal homeland" of every gay Euro-male. European gay men, as well as their American counterparts, had managed to weather the rough seas of the late 1970s and early 1980s with just Colt Men and Videos, Al Parker, Bruno, "Kansas City Truckin'," and not much else to remind them that there was more to gay imagery and iconography than what was generally being offered. It was, therefore, not at all surprising that when the first rustlings of bears in the undergrowth became evident the whole package eventually found its way across the Atlantic to Europe.

My initial exposure to the world of bears came in Dublin in the early 1990s. It was there that I answered a small advertisement in a local gay newspaper placed by a man seeking contacts with other men interested in hairy men and men with beards. Having always been attracted to such men and not really knowing that there were lots of other men out there like me, a kind of a second coming out led me to reply. When I heard back from this man he told me about *BEAR* magazine, and about his philosophy of what it all meant. His own filtered meanings were based on his travels, what he had read, and his vast life experience. While we never met, we did keep up an active correspondence, and I learned much about the early Bear Movement from him.

When I relocated to Berlin, Germany, a couple of years later I found that there was a bear group already in existence, and after less than a fortnight in the city I had already made contact with the small group of men who comprised the Berlin Bears (*Berliner Bären-Bartmänner*). The group had come into existence following the opening of the Berlin Wall when a bear from former East Berlin paying a visit to Cologne met up with a nascent bear group there. He returned to Berlin and placed an advertisement in one of the gay newspapers giving an address and telephone number to contact.

The first meetings were relatively small affairs and the Berlin Bears today are still a relatively small group—certainly smaller than many of the clubs in large or equivalent-sized American cities. The group has grown over time, without the need for any real formal structure. This lack of organization—while not very German—does preserve a very informal atmosphere within the group. There is no process for joining, apart from turning up, no forms to be filled out, no money to be paid. There is little in the way of club paraphernalia—occasional T-shirts, but certainly no hats, badges, or other items which seem to be very prevalent in the United States.

One of the two regular monthly meetings acts as a forum for all interested members to make suggestions regarding group activities, outings, etc. These can then be organized and run by the proposing members. Thus, there is a certain dynamic at play—the group functions largely because the members wish to have participatory activities, the onus then being on the members to ensure that they take place and that the ongoing dynamic is maintained. The problem encountered by many other groups, where members wait for everything to be organized for them by an elected committee, is therefore avoided. The Berlin Bears are then truly dependent on the interest of the members, and the further existence of the club and the interests of its members are closely intertwined.

The above approach has led to the evolution of an easy, informal, and relaxed bear group, and while the method does have its drawbacks, the positive aspects are very great. The belief in individual responsibility, which is prevalent within the group, leads to a feeling that each member has something valuable to contribute. As previously mentioned there was already a bear group in existence in Cologne and, over the last couple of years, there has been a significant growth in the number of groups elsewhere in Germany. Hamburg, Frankfurt, Oldenburg, Bremen, and Munich can all now claim bear groups, though many are still very informal, consisting of just a regular bar night maybe once a month.

In many ways these are still the very early days of the Bear Movement in Germany, and would probably compare with the situation in the United States in the early 1990s. The main difference now, however, is the considerable number of gay men traveling from Europe to gay centers in the United States (particularly New York, San Francisco, and Florida) and the vast amount of information which is readily available either via bear-oriented magazines, contact with bear groups in the United States, and over the Internet.

Outside of Germany there are large and established groups only in England (Bear Hug and Bear Club UK), in Amsterdam (*Nederbears*), and in Switzerland (*Bartmänner Schweiz*). Of these, Bear Hug, the group based in London, would be the closest Euro-equivalent of an American bear club. They are less leather-oriented than in Germany, tending to the jeans-and-flannel look as favored by American bears. In addition to the European bear clubs there are many affiliated groups, mostly catering to bigger men, in the European Association of Big Men's Clubs. These exist either in parallel with bear groups (e.g., Heavy Teddies in Berlin, Bulk in London) or take precedence (e.g., Orsi Italiani, Girth & Mirth).

BEAR MARK III–EUROBEAR: THE GERMAN MODEL

Having discussed the emergence of bear groups in Germany in the late 1980s and early 1990s, it would, perhaps, be useful to examine whether or not there are any differences between the model here and the original in the United States. An initial observation might suggest that German bears are very leather-oriented. This is certainly true. Leather is much more noticeable at bear meetings in Germany (particularly Cologne and Berlin) than in the United States, or even Britain. The preponderance of leather has much to do with Germans themselves. Leather is very visible in German society, indeed leather trousers, jackets, and vests are frequently worn by straight men. Germans are somehow predisposed to leather, it being as ingrained as their insisting on coffee and cake at four o'clock in the afternoon. Combine a predisposition to leather with being gay and most will go running to their local leather shop to get kitted out to a greater or lesser degree.

Admittedly the leather look favored by gay men differs somewhat from that of the straight community, but still falls within fairly stringent guidelines derived from the iconography of the outlaw biker, too many viewings of *The Wild Ones*, and a general Euro-tendency to "be chic." Other trappings of the leather community per se, for example, cockrings worn as indicators of sexual role, colored handkerchiefs, etc., have all been adopted by many German bears, leading to the phenomenon of the "leather bear." This is not to say, however, that all German bears are leather wearers. As mentioned earlier, leather is part of a general German predilection, and so many bears might wear just a jacket or vest (this is particularly favored) rather than go for the complete black cowhide look. Thus you will find lots of guys wearing denim and checked shirts, looking very much like any other group of bear-identified gay men one would encounter anywhere in the Western hemisphere.

German bears, in my experience, tend to fall within a narrower age range than in the United States, with most being in their thirties and forties. This is unlike San Francisco, for example, where rumor has it that bears tend to be older, or some New England cities where younger bears are to be found. Indeed a casual perusal of the Bears Mailing List postings reveals large numbers of young (early 20s) bear-identified gay men. This is something that has not really been seen in Germany. German bears tend to congregate in leather bars. Institutions such as western bars or denim/blue-collar bars (i.e., "leather & levi") do not exist in Germany, and so the links between the bears and the leather community (e.g., MSC [Motorsport & Contacte]) tend to be strong.

One example of this is the annual leather meeting held in Berlin every Easter. The Berlin Bears usually organize a buffet evening or sauna party during the leather meeting to provide an opportunity for leather guys with a bear bent or bears with a leather bent to come together for what bears do. And this is where things, while initially different, are gradually coming together.

Bear club listings in the United States are usually full of beer busts, video evenings, and the like. In Berlin the Bears, apart from the regular meetings, tend to go on hikes, eat together, or attend cultural events, such as the opera, theater, or concerts, as a group. These pursuits would be largely at odds with the "blue-collar" ethic, as espoused by many bear clubs in the United States. But, again, this has more to do with the nature of the Eurobear. The arts are not seen as something removed from the everyday citizen. They are heavily subsidized and so affordable to all. As a result, there is a significant amount of interest in attending such events–and little of the inverted snobbery encountered in bears from the United States, where the picture of accountants and doctors playing at being blue-collar is too frequently encountered.

Many of the differences between Eurobears (at least in Germany) and American bears are simply based on the differences between the two societies. Germany is a relatively peaceful, tolerant, largely middle-class country in contrast to the United States, which has great gaps in wealth distribution, high crime rates, and a low tolerance for difference. In Berlin, for example, gay men can live relatively open and free lives, untroubled by fears of societal disapproval, something that, in the United States, is really only encountered in San Francisco, Provincetown, Greenwich Village, or Key West.

The relative openness of German society and its acceptance or tolerance of homosexuals is something that many Americans can only dream of, or experience on vacation. Similarly, the fact that German society is largely middle class means that there is little to be gained from pretending to be something that you are not. There is little in terms of class politics as seen in England or the United States. A middle-class identity is something which is largely a given for most, whether it is always true or not. Thus, many activities, such as attending the opera, are not seen as the prerogative of some narrow band within society. Instead, they are something for everyone, the only criterion being whether it is to one's taste or not.

German and American bears, then, would appear to be largely the same, apart from certain minor differences, and these largely resulting from the societies themselves. Any differences in the fine-tuning of the bear paradigm, however, are rapidly being eroded by the increasing similarity between the two scenes. This is most clearly demonstrated by the increasing success of the bear beauty competition begun in Cologne a number of years ago, which has grown to American-size proportions. In recent years the winners have gone on to participate in the largest bear beauty competition in San Francisco. What price difference?

BEAR MARK IV–WHITHER EUROBEAR?

"Masculinity without the trappings"

The above quote would appear to encapsulate something which is simple and not quite definable. Far removed from this is the bear as often encountered in the United States and, increasingly, in Europe. The ideals of what a bear is, does, and looks like have been rapidly, some would say too rapidly, encoded and reproduced for mass-market consumption. What began, perhaps, as a reaction against prevalent gay behavioral and visual models has led to something that is just as rigid and just as reactionary as what went before. The increasing number of bear beauty competitions has led to a narrow definition of what a bear should look like. The subdivision of these competitions into Mr. Bear, Mr. Bear Cub, Mr. Moustache, or whatever, are in no way an attempt to address what is fundamentally wrong with the way this whole movement is developing or has been allowed to develop. That more and more bear groups are being founded has little to do with increasing numbers of men getting in touch with their masculinity, or expressing it with simplicity, love, or affection for other men. It is now largely a matter of belonging to another exclusive group, another clan–of the cave bear, this time round.

> Homosexuality has existed throughout history, in all types of society, among all social classes and peoples . . . but what have

> varied enormously are the ways in which various societies have regarded homosexuals, the meaning they have attached to it, and how those who were engaged in homosexual activities viewed themselves. (Weeks, 1977)

In Europe the number of bear clubs are on the rise. So too, however, is the narrow classification of what bears are, how they look, and what they do. It would appear that anyone can now don a flannel shirt and jeans, grow a beard and, hey presto–*bear*! What is somehow lacking, however, is any radical appraisal of what it means to be a gay man and how we relate to one another. Such thinking cannot be achieved by the establishment of increasing numbers of beauty competitions, which, however entertaining, can only have a profoundly negative influence on us as gay men. Rather than focusing on ever more restrictive modes of behavior it is perhaps time to stand back and reappraise what being a man is, accepting ourselves and our masculinity in its widest form, accepting our need to love and be loved, our need to be affectionate with other men, to enjoy their company, and to be wrapped up in the support, comfort, and love of our fellow man. Literally.

We love another man, his body, his passions, and desires. We love another man's loving ourselves, our bodies, passions, and desires. That love is more than sex. It is the creation and maintenance of relationships of significance (Dowsett, 1987).

REFERENCES

Crisp, Quentin. *The Naked Civil Servant*. Glasgow: Collins, 1968.

Dowsett, G. Queer fears and gay examples, *New Internationalist*, 175:10-12, 1987.

Edwards, T. E*rotics and Politics–Gay Male Sexuality, Masculinity and Feminism*. London: Routledge, 1994.

Weeks, Jeffrey. *Coming Out: Homosexual Politics in Britain from the Nineteenth Century to the Present*. London: Quartet, 1977.

Chapter 20

A French Bear Asks: Are Bears an American Thing?

Pierre De Mey

The second I met my lover Richard, I knew without hesitation that he had everything I liked in a man. That was in 1988, in a small town in southwestern France. At that time, I had never heard about "bears," but I knew I wanted bears, and I knew he was one. My quest could be expressed with a single, coherent idea, although I had no word to communicate that idea. The best I could do was to list features: beard, huskiness, manliness, body hair, pride, simplicity, good nature.

Back in the early 1980s, I had just managed to drag myself out of a comfortable straight life that was not made for me. I was ripe for a continuation of my inner voyage. In 1983, I managed to get a postdoctoral position at Harvard. In retrospect, my American experience gave me much more than a nice working environment and some proficiency with English. It gave me the opportunity to reincarnate in a new, more mature man and to see the world with new eyes. My sexual tastes became very clear. Back in Europe, I started to cruise bearish men on the gay services of the new French Minitel system. Years before Internet became common, the Minitel was a perfect means of communication for us at that time. Its ubiquitous, yet private and anonymous character did a lot for many an isolated gay man. Its forums, personal ads, and live talk helped to sharpen the expression of desires, and to bring people together on the sole basis of these desires. I met many men thanks to the Minitel. Some were bears, some were not. Some of them, for example, married men with children, or isolated farmers, could not have been cruised at a bar. I made good local bear friends at that time. Some of the opinions I will express below are the result of discussions we had over the years.

Later, the "Bear Movement" was to appear on the scene, mostly in North America. Somehow I managed to keep in touch with it with the help of visits to the United States, bear magazines, and the Internet. Our local bear group here expected the bear wave to progressively outgrow North America and take over the Old Continent's gay scene. And indeed we have witnessed the appearance of a few bear titles and bars in the largest European cities, but nowhere near the level of popularity it has now reached in North America. Of course there are differences from one country to the next. From the number of personal ads in the bear press, the United Kingdom seems to be the most favored country, Germany being second and the others somewhere behind. However, as of today, critical mass has not yet been reached.

My friends and I are surprised that most French gay men have never heard about bears. Bear topics are almost never discussed in the gay press. The Minitel did not help make the idea popular either. Minitel personal ads finishing with the words "No beards, fats, glasses" are still very common. I hear that similar rejection practices are experienced to various degrees by bears in other European countries. Not only are bears not popular with the mainstream gay community here, but most bear types do not identify themselves as bears, and have a very negative image of themselves. This is true of all the Latin countries of southern Europe (France included). Richard, for instance, had a very bad image of his own body when I met him. He would not go to public swimming pools. Over the years, he finally became interested in the bear magazines to which I subscribe. Those magazines and my attentions paid to him have managed to change the way he sees himself. I can see that he is now at ease with his body from the way he uses it.

The Bear Movement is seen by some as an important advance in gay history for reasons discussed elsewhere in this book. From that perspective, we should wonder what prevents the bear community from going global. Let me speak for Europe, which I know best. Are we just, as usual, lagging behind? Or is there some other reason, or a mix of reasons? Are bears an American thing?

First of all, there is a critical mass problem. There is no strong Bear Movement in Europe because there are not enough interested men, and one of the main reasons why there are few interested men is that bearish men, gay or hetero, are not visible enough here. Just walk in the streets of a major city here and see for yourself. This is a perfect vicious circle. It is important to understand the forces that keep us locked in this circle.

The way I see bears in general is as a male type (our "totem"), not as a gay type, in contrast to, say, leathermen. There are many straight men I would definitely call bears, and who may one day identify themselves as such if the wind blows long enough. In the same way that Baudelaire depicted his natural women, I would depict bears as natural men, i.e., men who exist and make their own basic choices in life completely independent of women. This does not preclude them from living with a woman. A bear, gay or hetero, does not hate women (he has no reason to), but he does not feel the need to look pretty. In particular, he does not feel the need to shave. He is not permanently driven to seduce and to be aggressive with competitors as a consequence. In a word, he lives in a man's paradise. These characteristics make the bear–the natural, strong, proud, self-defined man–attractive to us bear-lovers in our quest of the quintessential man free of all female influence.

The problem for us here is that Latin societies such as France and southern Europe are chiefly matriarchal. The really critical powers at the family level and thus at the personal level are held by women. In my family, women are feared. They control matters such as religion, marriage, festivities, and even the family's heritage, because they live to an older age. More to the point, beards are not desirable. This may be a surprise to the outsider who has been impressed by Mediterranean men's macho stance and alleged sense of honor. The reality is that women here divide and rule, mostly by using our pride against us. It is a permanent fight for influence. Women know how to keep their men in their orbit, of course. Straight men get all sorts of compensation. Singles and gays don't. Society itself acts as a relay in applying our mothers' pressure. I can feel it almost physically each time I land here on my way back from the United States, for instance in the way I have to be nice to any woman clerk in order to have anything done.

In Anglo-Saxon countries, things are less integrated. Men and women live more separate lives. They tend to ignore each other's world more than in Latin countries. The men have more privacy in their own culture, such as the pubs and men's clubs in the United Kingdom, where no female is supposed to tread (at least that's how it used to be). Here the "cafés" are open places where men and women go, and to frequent a men's club you either have to be gay or a Freemason. This is closer to the "man's paradise" I described above. Therefore it is easier for bears and natural men to be happily themselves in Anglo-Saxon countries.

Let us stay a bit longer on male/female roles and Latin/Anglo-Saxon differences. Here bearded men are not very common. Beards are almost taboo–you don't mention them–just like genitalia. Both are seen as subversive and sacred at the same time. Therefore growing a beard is not neutral here. My mother didn't like it when I grew a beard, just as it disgusted her when she noticed the hair growing on my legs when I was a teenager. I think that beyond the attraction/repulsion complex women often have for body hair, she felt that the mothering times were over. Soon I would betray her for another woman. When I grew my beard later, she understood it as another mark of independence, and my first girlfriend convinced me to shave it off. Similarly, in those few northern European countries where individualism is seen with suspicion, such as in Germany, thick beards are very uncommon. In addition, while a beard is historically viewed everywhere as a mark of power (just like boots and cigars, incidentally), it is often ridiculed as such in Latin countries. In France, bearded members of Parliament have to be pre-World War II socialists. These are the kind of political men whom you expect to speak with ample gestures but do little.

A few reasons for the short supply of bears here are more typically French. First of all, we are not bearish people. We Gauls tend to be average in height and in girth, and we sport a moustache more often than a beard. But to be fair, most of us are uncut and we tend to be on the hairy side. Second, the gay community here is structured in two groups of unequal size: the mainstream, and the leather/uniform/SM group. The former, by far the largest and most influential, is totally mesmerized by an ideal of young, sleek, perfect, clean-shaven, Mapplethorpe bodybuilders with no body hair.

Bears are just not what most gay men are seeking here. This does not mean that they won't. They will, if it's more fun than drag queens, and if the bear "look" becomes fashionable (bear in mind that the French fashion industry is mostly controlled by gays). Of course bears cannot be reduced to jeans, flannel shirts, and baseball caps, but if "bear fashion" (gasp) is an entry point, and if straight bears join in and flock the streets, let it be!

What is nice with rules is that you have exceptions, especially if you leave the cities. There are many bears out there in the country. One of my friends is a rugby player. A few years ago, his team was to play in a small town not far from here, against a team from a neighboring small town. I asked him if he could get me tickets, since the area is famous for its rugby (the local team here beat the All Blacks in 1995). The field was muddy and soon the players, some of them bears, were in a pretty messy state. The game was gripping. To be honest, I do not remember who won (my eyes were not too focused on the ball). After the game, to my surprise, I was invited by my friend to join the "third half-time" as they call it, and I was surrounded with big bears all over the pub. Well, we drank beer, had fun telling stories and laughing and patting each other's backs and hugging each other. Of course, I couldn't have them, but I was happy to see some French bears coming out of their dens here.

Let us try to go a bit further. What is our image of a bear made of? With what fantasies are bears associated on both sides of the Atlantic? The bear community strikes me as being characterized by the very fuzzy definition of its totem. None of us agrees on the definition of a bear. However, when chatting over the Internet, for instance, we usually have a pretty good idea of what the other is talking about, even when their viewpoint is different. In my opinion, this is because we have some archetypes in common. Those archetypes, or images, have been acquired early in our learning process. They are shared among us, but their relative importance varies according to each individual and to his cultural background. I have tried to list a few of them (my own bear archetypes, I guess) and see whether or not their importance could vary geographically.

The first building block I can think of is the image of the woodsman. The lumberjack, mountain man, and maybe the drifter, fall in the same category. The man lives by himself, but he enjoys company from time to time. He wears a beard that is never groomed, a flannel shirt, corduroy pants, perhaps smokes a pipe. He lives in a log cabin by a lake. Now this is stereotypical American frontier life. Elaborating on this image a bit further, the man is a loner, a bachelor; he never sees any women, and prefers the company of men. He cuts wood, and fishes, and cooks, and cleans. He is both man and woman. He is son of Gaia, who cuddles him on her hairy belly, the biggest of all, Earth. We have such types in Europe (we call them bears, incidentally), but in small numbers, because we have lost direct contact with wilderness and nature, with Gaia. This is mostly a North American type.

A second archetype is the blue-collar man. Workers often form groups which are inclusive and mutually nurturing in a way akin to early bear communities. In a hostile environment, everybody is accepted. It does not matter if you are short, tall, fat, bald, a bully, silent, black, or white, as long as you're honest with the group. This type does not appear to be linked to any particular country. It is valid worldwide. Blue-collar looks do vary though. In France, the image of the typical working-class man is that of a short, gaunt man with brown hair and a short moustache. In North America, one might imagine instead a big, burly man with a baseball cap. In both countries, truckers are often bearded.

A third archetype is the patriarch. He is found in Europe, mostly in the rural South, and again in scenes of the frontier life in North America. He is often a religious man with a big beard, in the image of an Old Testament figure. He is a strong, stern, unyielding man who protects his family and demands respect and worship in return. It is clearly a daddy bear archetype, which can be mixed with other archetypes in the SM realm.

A fourth archetype is the image of the warrior. The hunter and the biker fall into this category, as do the rugby players I mentioned earlier (so do athletes in related sports–wrestlers, football players, etc.). A good example is the leather-clad, bearded group of warriors in the movie *Dune*. The beard is seen as a war ornament meant to intimidate, a part of the armor, a demonstration of strength and freedom, perhaps a trophy in the case of the hunter. It is the incarnation of pride. Fortunately warriors are nowhere to be seen in our Western societies (except on TV screens), but conquistadors and De

Niro in *The Deer Hunter* are on our minds, and bearded rugby players, wrestlers, and bikers are now fairly ubiquitous.

A fifth archetype is Santa Claus. While the patriarch image was the basic component of daddy bear fantasies, Santa seems to be associated with granddaddies. A man/child of advanced and indefinite age, Santa is a strong, jolly, good-natured, playful bear who likes to spoil us children, provided that we have been good (otherwise he could turn into an angry daddy). This is mostly a northern bear type (originally St. Nicholas), and therefore not very strong as a bear type in southern Europe.

The sixth type is the teddy bear. The bear cub falls into this category. It is not linked to any particular country, as most girls and boys get bears as toys. Its image is that of a sweet companion, always ready for a cuddle. It is the only unsexed type listed here. It is the "angel bear" type, a refuge for those seeking peace.

The seventh and last archetype I will examine is the mature male bear itself. It is the most complex type and the most neglected of all. I will not spend much time here on the animal itself, since what is important is the way its image mixes with our fantasies. The first characteristics that come to mind are the massive body and the thick fur, then the awkward, clumsy behavior. Its claws and teeth remind us that this is a ferocious, potent animal. You might get cuddled. You might get mauled. Of course everybody knows what a bear is, but bears are almost extinct in Europe, and the only places where live bears can be found are in zoos. Therefore this is mostly a North American type.

In summary, the North American idea of a bear will be made up of a rather rich spectrum of all the images above (and perhaps other images I have not mentioned), whereas southern Europeans will almost entirely miss images 1 (the woodsman), 5 (Santa Claus), and 7 (bears). Interestingly enough, what we seem to miss here is both nature and good nature, i.e., the seminal, moderating elements. Our bear archetypes seem to be rather different from the North American ones: more urban (2), and more aggressive (3, 4). Therefore southern European bear fantasies exist, but they stand closer to leather/SM archetypes than in North America.

Index